MELVILLE'S MISTAKE

Gideon Lincecum Nature and Environment Series

MELVILLE'S MISTAKE

Essays in Defense of the Natural World

Michael J. Bean

Texas A&M University Press
College Station

This paper meets the requirements of ANSI/NISO Z39.48–1992 (Permanence of Paper).
Binding materials have been chosen for durability.
Manufactured in the United States of America

Library of Congress Cataloging-in-Publication Data

Names: Bean, Michael J., 1949– author.
Title: Melville's mistake: essays in defense of the natural world /
    Michael J. Bean.
Other titles: Gideon Lincecum nature and environment series.
Description: First edition. I College Station: Texas A&M University Press,
    [2022] I Series: Gideon Lincecum nature and environment series I
    Includes index.
Identifiers: LCCN 2021043930 (print) I LCCN 2021043931 (ebook) I ISBN
    9781648430268 (cloth) I ISBN 9781648430275 (ebook)
Subjects: LCSH: United States. Endangered Species Act of 1973. I
    Biodiversity conservation—Government policy—United States. I Wildlife
    conservation—Law and legislation—United States. I Green movement. I
    BISAC: NATURE / Environmental Conservation & Protection I NATURE /
    Essays I LCGFT: Essays.
Classification: LCC QH76.B428 2022 (print) I LCC QH76 (ebook) I DDC
    333.720973—dc23
LC record available at https://lccn.loc.gov/2021043930
LC ebook record available at https://lccn.loc.gov/2021043931

For the ones I love:
My wife, Sandy, who urged, cajoled, and encouraged
me to complete this project
To my daughters, Amanda and Emily
And to my grandchildren, who give me such joy:
Elsa, Erik, and Ezra

Contents

A gallery of images follows page 97.

Foreword

You hold in your hands an illuminating book. You will see things you had not noticed or known. And the things you *had* seen, you will see better. That is what light does. Michael Bean is known as "the dean of wildlife law" for a very good reason: He is the lived experience of the whole sweep of modern wildlife law, its application, and the unforeseen problems and pitfalls of good intentions. Without that context, decisions cannot be their best, and old mistakes will be repeated. Context is what this book provides, and does so very well, with well-chosen examples and well-thought-out perspective-setting commentary. Bean is the living memory of the field. Students and younger professionals simply need this history of their own field if they are to have any hope of being not just busy—but being effective.

What makes Michael Bean's perspective unique is that he brings to this work a rare combination of legal expertise and his passion for natural history. On these pages, Bean shares with us his deeply personal early-life experiences that shaped his commitment to the natural world. His curiosity about, and fascination with, the wild creatures with which we share this world emerged in childhood and remained lifelong, never lost.

Michael Bean grew up in a small Mississippi River town in southeastern Iowa, some twenty miles downriver from Aldo Leopold's childhood home. There, as a youngster he explored the river's sloughs and backwaters and the creek that ran through the woods behind his home. Like the great conservation biologist Edward O. Wilson, Bean was intensely interested in snakes and insects. This passion for the creepy and the crawly beings led Bean to major in entomology in college. Eventually, however, he switched to political science and left Iowa to attend Yale Law School.

For the first couple of years after law school, Bean worked for a big corporate law firm in DC, an experience he described to me as "quite boring and unfulfilling." No surprise there. In 1976 Bean got a serendipitous opportunity to write a wildlife law book for the Council on Environmental Quality. That book, *The Evolution of National Wildlife*

Law, opened other doors. Among them, it introduced Michael Bean to the Environmental Defense Fund (EDF), whose founders were a group of Long Island scientists and educators who had launched a successful, epoch-making fight against DDT a decade earlier, helping usher in the modern environmental movement as an approach to conservation and the environment and whose tactics focused heavily on policy and law.

Bean led EDF's wildlife conservation efforts for three decades. Following that he was appointed counselor to the assistant secretary for fish and wildlife and parks at the Department of the Interior. When the Obama administration ended in January 2017, Michael Bean "retired." But he wasn't done, and he isn't, and this book is the physical manifestation of his ongoing work and commitment.

Touching history and natural history, this book traces the development of wildlife conservation laws and institutions—and the pioneering individuals who shaped them—from their modest beginnings to the present. This work reminds us, crucially, that the environmental movement must face, analyze, understand, and reverse our collective failure to successfully tackle pressing environmental problems in a timely manner.

Bean includes herein essays written in the 1980s warning of the hazards of plastic pollution and climate change—problems that have only grown much worse despite decades of knowledge about them and improving understanding. That these problems continue to worsen is a sobering reminder of the intractability of the politics around some environmental problems and the need for creativity in communicating and solving them.

Michael Bean is no mere technocrat of the law. He is a student of what has worked and what has not, someone willing to explore new approaches to solving conservation challenges. That stance has something fundamental to teach anyone aspiring to be a great and influential practitioner, or professor, or both.

—Carl Safina

Preface

April 22, 1970. Earth Day. The first Earth Day. I remember it as a day of celebration at the University of Iowa, where I was in my final semester of undergraduate studies. Festive crowds of students and townspeople enjoyed music, street theater, balloons, spring flowers, and each other on a warm and sunny day. I did not know it then, but protecting the environment by defending the natural world and the wild creatures that inhabit it would be the cause to which I would devote most of the rest of my life.

I was but twenty years old on that first Earth Day. The just-ended decade of the 1960s—a decade riven by political assassinations, antiwar protests, urban riots, and the civil rights struggle—had at that point occupied half my life. One last echo of that tumultuous decade was still to come, less than two weeks later, with the shooting of unarmed student anti–Vietnam War protesters by National Guard troops at Kent State University. There followed a final spasm of outrage, and then the decade was truly over.

Dramatic changes were in store for me in the decade of the 1970s: graduation from college; marriage to Sandy; moving away from the Midwest; attending Yale Law School; writing a book on wildlife law; launching an environmental law career at the Environmental Defense Fund; and preparing for fatherhood.

From the outset of my environmental law career my singular focus was on wildlife conservation and especially the challenge of averting the extinction of species. This book chronicles my thoughts—and presents a selection of my previous writings—on these topics. Some of those writings were published many years ago, likely before some of today's readers were even born. For that reason, these writings are preceded by new explanatory material to help the reader understand the background or broader context of the issue addressed. Where needed, I have also provided the reader with a brief synopsis of what happened thereafter.

I graduated from law school in 1973, the same year that Congress enacted the Endangered Species Act, a cornerstone environmental law that has the noble goal of preventing the extinction of wild plants and animals whenever possible. I would soon become committed to the effort to make this law as successful in achieving that goal as it could be. Over the course of time, my thoughts regarding how best to do that evolved, as the chapters that follow document. What has not wavered over that period is my conviction that defending the natural world and the wild creatures that inhabit it is one of the most important undertakings that anyone can pursue. I hope that is also clear from the chapters that follow.

Following an introductory essay on Herman Melville's thoughts on the extinction of whales, the book turns to the tales of two fish, the fates of which were in the hands of the United States Supreme Court. Then it takes a step back to explore the history of our federal wildlife conservation laws and the government agencies responsible for implementing them. Later chapters explore the importance of conserving biological diversity, the system of national wildlife refuges that has been established to help in that conservation effort, and some of the more consequential controversies and challenges that have arisen under the Endangered Species Act.

Along the way we encounter some of the leading figures in the history of wildlife conservation in this country. Among them are Rachel Carson, Aldo Leopold, and Theodore Roosevelt, as well as less well-known, but no less important, people such as John Lacey, Spencer Baird, and C. Hart Merriam.

The concluding chapters reflect the evolution of my thinking about the accomplishments and shortcomings of the Endangered Species Act. As is true of many regulatory statutes, the act has sometimes had unintended consequences that have undercut its goals—most especially with respect to how it has affected the actions of private landowners. Acknowledging that fact and working to address those unintended consequences occupied the later years of my career and are the subject of the final chapters of this book.

Many environmental injuries can, with time, be healed and reversed. Not so with extinction. It is one of the few truly irreversible environmental injuries. Once gone, a species will never return. That is why preventing the extinction of species, whenever it is in our power to do so, is the most urgent and most important wildlife conservation challenge. That is why I have tried, over the past four decades and more, to do what I could to defend the natural world and its endlessly fascinating creatures. That is why I have written this book, so that a new generation of conservationists and concerned citizens—armed with a clear-eyed understanding of the successes and failures of their predecessors—can better meet the challenge of preserving the earth's rich biological diversity.

Acknowledgments

Among the many who had a hand in helping with the completion of this book, one stands out. Whether the task at hand was editing, proof-reading, typing, constructively criticizing, or simply encouraging me to stick with it, Sandy Bean enthusiastically embraced it. She was, in short, the same helpful, devoted partner on this project that she has been on every (or nearly every) project I have undertaken during our fifty years of marriage.

Drafts of the manuscript were reviewed by American University professor Meg Weekes and by former Environmental Defense Fund colleague Amanda Phillips. Their thoughtful critiques and suggestions improved the organization and clarity of the final product, as did recommendations from Carl Safina and Georgetown University Law School professor Hope Babcock.

A special thanks is owed to Bob Irvin and to American Rivers, the conservation organization he skillfully leads as its president and chief executive officer. Bob generously offered me the use of an office at American Rivers while I worked on this project. Forty years ago, Bob served as an intern with me at the Environmental Defense Fund. We have been close friends and colleagues ever since.

Many of the essays, reviews, and articles included in this book grew out of work undertaken with a small group of extremely talented colleagues at the Environmental Defense Fund, especially David Wilcove, Robert Bonnie, Melinda Taylor, and Margaret McMillan. David has gone on to become a professor of ecology and evolutionary biology and public affairs at Princeton University. Robert went on to become a highly respected and successful undersecretary for natural resources and environment at the US Department of Agriculture during the Obama administration. Melinda became the executive director of the Kay Bailey Hutchison Center for Energy, Law, and Business at the University of Texas. On Margaret McMillan, I cannot heap enough praise. One could not ask for a more loyal and reliable colleague than Margaret was to me during nearly all of my time at the Environmental Defense Fund.

As I hope this book makes clear, I am indebted—all of us who care about wildlife conservation are indebted—to the many private landowners who share their lands with rare wildlife. As Aldo Leopold noted, they are the custodians of public trust. The conservation of many imperiled species will ultimately depend on how the nation's farms, ranches, and forestlands are managed by those who own them, yet their vital role is often not acknowledged. It was my privilege throughout my career to get to know many of them and through them to better understand how to make conservation succeed.

I had originally intended to stop there. But as fate would have it, I find myself writing this acknowledgment amid a novel coronavirus pandemic. Precisely how that pandemic began may never be known, but as of the time of this writing the most likely explanation is that it began at a live-animal market in the Chinese city of Wuhan. There a coronavirus that had never before been seen in humans was passed from its wild animal host—pangolins, bats, and even snakes have all been suggested as possible hosts—to a human working or shopping at the market. From there it spread throughout the city and from there to the rest of the world.

The human death toll from this disease has been staggering in the United States and elsewhere in the world. The economic impact has similarly been enormous. And all of this can be traced to a market where live wild animals were kept for sale in overcrowded, dirty, and inhumane conditions. This experience forces me to make a final acknowledgment, which is that when we treat nature and its wild creatures with callous indifference to their suffering, we can expect that nature may be callously indifferent to ours.

MELVILLE'S MISTAKE

Introduction

What Melville Got Wrong about Whales[*]

Herman Melville, it seemed, knew almost everything about whales. His tale of Captain Ahab's obsessive quest for the white Leviathan was woven around chapters that discuss whale anatomy, whales in mythology and the arts, whales in the fossil record, the whaling community of Nantucket, uses of whale oil, and so on. Melville's knowledge of whales was almost encyclopedic.

And yet, on the most important question that Melville asked about whales, he was dead wrong. In Melville's inimitable prose, the question was "whether Leviathan can long endure so wide a chase, and so remorseless a havoc; whether he must not at last be exterminated from the waters, and the last whale, like the last man, smoke his last pipe, and then himself evaporate in the last puff."[1] To this question, Melville emphatically answered in the negative. Whales, he believed, were simply too numerous, their human pursuers too few, and the vast expanses of the ocean too great for extinction to be a possibility.

Melville undoubtedly never heard the modern term "catch per unit effort," but he was aware that whalers in his day had to search longer and farther to bring back the same number of whales as in former days. He dismissed this fact, however, with the argument that whales, "influenced by some views to safety," had simply rearranged their groupings from many small pods to fewer but larger herds and had moved elsewhere: "If one coast is no longer enlivened with their jets, be sure, some other and remoter strand has been very recently startled by the unfamiliar spectacle."

Moreover, Melville argued, even if driven from waters everywhere else, whales could take final refuge in "two firm fortresses, which, in all human probability, will forever remain impregnable." Like the Swiss retreating from their valleys to the mountains in the face of invaders, whales pursued in the open sea "can at last resort to their Polar citadels, and diving under the ultimate glassy barriers and walls there, come up among icy fields and floes; and in a charmed

circle of everlasting December, bid defiance to all pursuit from man."
Clearly, Melville never foresaw the melting of the polar ice cap from
human-caused climate change that now seems likely.[2]

From the vantage point of a century and a half later, Melville's
steadfast refusal to regard the extinction of whales as thinkable seems
wholly irrational, a matter of blind faith masquerading behind a
facade of learned sophistry. At least Melville was able to acknowledge
that some whale fossils were of species no longer in existence. Thomas
Jefferson, on the other hand, had argued against the possibility that
any fossil creatures were of extinct species. In Jefferson's view, "such
is the economy of nature, that no instance can be produced of her
having permitted any one race of her animals to become extinct,
of her having formed any link in her great work so weak as to be
broken."[3]

And yet, even if Melville can be faulted for his steadfast refusal to
acknowledge the consequences of the industry he extolled, he should
not be judged too harshly. The belief that our means are too limited
and the resilience of our fellow creatures too great for our actions ever
to drive them to extinction—not just whales, but virtually any other
species—is with us still. Indeed, it is the reason that our acknowledgment of a species' endangerment often comes too late. It is, in short,
part of the explanation for the fact that meaningful legislation to
prevent the extinction of other species was so long in coming.

How that legislation—the Endangered Species Act of 1973—came
about, what its accomplishments and its shortcomings have been, and
some of the challenges it faces are among the many topics addressed in
the pages that follow. They are addressed through essays, op-eds, book
reviews, and other writings I produced over the course of a four-decade
career devoted to wildlife conservation. These writings include many
that were previously published and others that are published here for the
first time. Most of these earlier writings are preceded by new explanatory material to help the reader understand the background or broader
context of the issue addressed. Most are also accompanied by postscripts
that briefly explain what subsequently happened. In presenting these
materials, I hope that the reader will come to share my conviction that
the conservation of biodiversity, particularly of those species under
threat of extinction, is a goal both urgently important and within our

means to accomplish. It will also be apparent, however, that despite my conviction of the importance of conserving rare species, I am willing to frankly acknowledge the shortcomings in the manner in which the Endangered Species Act pursues that goal. The evolution of my thinking about how best to share our planet with its wild flora and fauna is reflected in the chapters that follow.

1

In the Beginning
Two Fish Tales

In June 1973, I graduated from Yale Law School, and a few days later the Committee on Commerce of the United States Senate reported its version of a bill that would shortly be enacted into law as the Endangered Species Act. The two events are unrelated. I note that fact because often in my career I have been either praised or blamed for having written the Endangered Species Act. Neither the praise nor the blame is deserved. In truth, I was blissfully unaware of the Endangered Species Act when Congress enacted it.

That I would soon become aware of it, however, was probably inevitable. In 1973, the practice of law was about to become my vocation, but the enjoyment of nature had been my lifelong avocation. My formative experiences as a boy were had in the sloughs and backwaters of the Mississippi River near my small hometown in Iowa. Less than twenty miles upriver, a few decades earlier, the young Aldo Leopold, who would become one of America's most influential conservationists, had similarly been shaped by his adventures in the Mississippi's sloughs and backwaters. I confess that at the time I was blissfully unaware of that too, as I did not even know who Aldo Leopold was until after I had left Iowa. The young Aldo, I expect, carried a shotgun on his adventures. I carried a net for catching insects and a bag for transporting snakes. It seems that the more obscure and reviled a creature was, the more it fascinated me. Little wonder then that I would ultimately be drawn to a law that had as its purpose the conservation of all creatures, regardless of how obscure or reviled.

My career in conservation came about somewhat serendipitously. In 1975, I was a young associate at a prominent corporate law firm in Washington. My small, bleak office was made even bleaker by the high wall of cardboard boxes towering over my desk. In each of them were copies of thousands of documents generated by our client in response to a subpoena in a mammoth antitrust case. Those were the same documents in the same boxes that I had been given the week I began the job some two years earlier. I hadn't recalled that my summer clerkship experiences had been like that. I was beginning to wonder what I had done to deserve such a fate and to think about how I could escape it. Somehow, I learned of an evening class being offered by the Smithsonian Institution on the topic of endangered species conservation. I needed a break, so I enrolled in it.

In that class, I learned about a case then pending on the docket of the United States Supreme Court. At issue was whether the federal government could order a private landowner to limit his pumping of groundwater to prevent the lowering of the water level in a Death Valley limestone pool to prevent the extinction of a fish that lived in that pool and nowhere else on earth. For someone long fascinated with obscure creatures, the Devil's Hole pupfish was about as fascinating as it gets, and I had never heard of it.

There wasn't much I could do about this matter, since the case was already before the Supreme Court. I certainly didn't have a client with an interest in the case, and it was too late to file a friend of the court brief anyway. So, instead, I persuaded myself that if I wrote an eloquent op-ed about the pupfish's plight for the *Washington Post*, perhaps one of the justices would read it and be influenced by it. That was the naïveté of youth for me to think that I would get my piece published, much less that a Supreme Court justice would read and be moved by it. After all, at that point I had never published anything other than a truly obscure student law review article, and it certainly had not influenced any Supreme Court justices.

So I wrote a lengthy op-ed, thinking that it might be appropriate for the Sunday "Outlook" section of the *Washington Post*, but I had no clear idea how to go about getting it published there or anywhere else. At the time, the *Post* had on its editorial staff Colman McCarthy. He didn't know me and I didn't know him, but I knew that he had often written about animal issues, so I decided to cold-call him and ask his advice. He generously offered to read my piece, and after he had done so, he encouraged me to submit it and advised me how best to do so.

To my astonishment, the *Post* quickly got back to me with the news that it would publish my piece on the first Sunday in October 1975. It didn't happen. Instead, on October 1, the pressmen at the *Post* went on a strike that lasted ten weeks. It was as bitter as it was long-lasting. Before it had ended, *Post* publisher Katherine Graham, who had won accolades for her courageous decision to publish the Pentagon Papers only four years earlier, was hanged in effigy by the strikers. The *Post* managed to put out a paper during most of the strike, but it was a slimmed-down version that had no room for extraneous material. My op-ed would have to wait.

I waited. As the weeks dragged on, I wondered if the *Post* would lose interest. I wondered if the strike would still be under way when the Supreme Court decided the case, thus rendering my op-ed no longer newsworthy. Ten weeks later, however, the strike ended and on December 21 the *Post* published my first op-ed, just three weeks before the Supreme Court heard oral argument in the case. The op-ed caught the attention of the magazine editor at Defenders of Wildlife, where it was reprinted in the April 1976 edition of *Defenders* magazine, two months before the Supreme Court would, for the first time in its history, decide the fate of an entire species. Here is what I had to say.

Desert-Dwelling Pupfish: Fate Is in Hands of Court
Washington Post, December 21, 1975

The desert is an unlikely place in which to find fish, though hardly as unlikely as in the United States Supreme Court. Yet the Court soon will decide a fascinating case involving a unique desert-dwelling fish.

While lawyers, legislators, and others anxiously await the Court's second decision on the death penalty question, few are aware that in this case, the Court will, for the first time in its history, decide the fate of an entire species.

The fish whose fate hangs in the balance is scarcely an inch long, and is known as the Devil's Hole pupfish, or *Cyprinodon diabolis*. How this fish, named for its puppylike manner of leaping and darting about, came to have its existence decided by the Court is itself interesting. How it may become extinct offers a lesson of extreme importance for citizens concerned for the survival of the world's wildlife and its people.

The story of the Devil's Hole pupfish begins more than 50,000 years ago, when the American Southwest was a vast system of rivers and lakes, including a lake more than 600 feet deep in what is now known as Death Valley. At some point more than 30,000 years ago, major climatological changes began. By the time of the last retreat of the glaciers, the complete desiccation of the area was well advanced. All that remained of the network of waters were a few creeks and marshes and an occasional spring. Underground, however, a 4,500-square-mile water system remained.

It was into the remaining surface waters that the ancestral stock of the modern pupfish retreated. Isolated in their separate microhabitats, they evolved into several distinct species.

One place where this evolution occurred is on the side of a mountain range east of Death Valley, where a deep limestone cavern holds a pool of water 10 by 65 feet. On one side, a rocky shelf 8 by 18 feet slopes gently beneath the surface of the water. Beyond its edge, the pool drops 200 feet into blackness below.

For a few hours during the day, however, the sun's rays strike the pool's surface above the rocky shelf, nurturing there the blue-green algae which start the food chain for the tiny pupfish. On that sloping rocky shelf, the total population of the Devil's Hole pupfish, fluctuating seasonally from 200 to 800, survives.

All evidence indicates that the pupfish has lived on that rocky shelf for at least 30,000 years. Until 1968, one might have thought it would last another 30,000 years. Then, however, a nearby landowner began drilling deep wells to pump water for his livestock. The impact upon the pupfish was immediate and drastic.

Since 1962, the water level in Devil's Hole has been monitored by a copper washer on the wall of the hole. Between 1962 and 1968, the average water level was 1.2 feet below the copper washer and it never dropped lower than minus 1.59 feet. In 1969, however, the pumping caused the water level to drop to 2.3 feet below the washer. If the water level were to fall to 3.0 feet below, the highest parts of the rocky shelf, essential to the feeding and breeding of the pupfish, would be above water. That first occurred in 1970, when the water dropped more than 10 inches to minus 3.17 feet.

The critical situation confronting the pupfish came to the attention of a small group of scientists who organized in 1970 into the Desert Fishes Council to coordinate efforts to save the fish. The pumping continued, however, and in 1971 the water level fell to minus 3.48 feet, exposing nearly 40 percent of the vital rocky shelf.

In 1972, the water dropped to minus 3.93 feet. More than 60 percent of the shelf was exposed, and the extinction of the Devil's Hole pupfish seemed imminent. The Interior Department took emergency rescue efforts, including placing a partially submerged artificial shelf in the pool with sunlamps suspended overhead. This effort, as well as other efforts to move some of the fish to other natural and artificial impoundments of water, including a concrete tank near Hoover Dam, was without success.

However, the government moved on another front. In August 1971, it brought suit in Nevada against Francis and Marilyn Cappaert, owners of the adjacent ranch, to enjoin them to limit their pumping of underground water from certain wells located near Devil's Hole. The government's legal theory is one of the more surprising aspects of the case.

Devil's Hole is located on land which was added to Death Valley National Monument by presidential proclamation in 1952. The proclamation was issued pursuant to the Act for the Preservation of the Antiquities, under which a President may declare objects of historic or scientific interest situated upon federal lands to be national monuments. Although the principal stated purpose of President Truman's action was to preserve the unique geological features of the area, its true impetus was the concern of a few scientists for the preservation of this only existing home of *Cyprinodon diabolis*.

The government argued in court that the express reservation from the public domain of Devil's Hole tract carried with it an implied reservation of enough groundwater to assure the preservation of the pupfish, a legal doctrine which has its origins in a 1908 decision of the Supreme Court.

The Cappaerts argued in reply that the doctrine on which the government relied applied only to surface waters, that the government had failed to follow proper procedures in bringing its suit and that, for various other technical reasons, their rights to the water were paramount to those of the government.

The district court and the court of appeals ruled in favor of the government and enjoined the Cappaerts to limit their pumping of underground water to the extent necessary to maintain a daily mean water level in Devil's Hole pool of minus 3.3 feet.

After the government filed its suit and before the district court's entry of an injunction in 1974, Congress enacted the Endangered Species Act of 1973, widely held then as signifying a dramatic and forceful national commitment to the preservation of an endangered species. The act boldly stated as its foremost purpose "to provide a means whereby the ecosystems upon which endangered species . . . depend may be conserved." Moreover, the act expressly incorporated the congressional finding that "various species . . . have been rendered extinct as a consequence of economic growth and development un- tempered by adequate concern and conservation."

One might have expected that the Endangered Species Act would have assured the preservation of the Devil's Hole pupfish. Not so. The Supreme Court's decision on the pupfish's fate will be based upon rather arcane principles of water rights developed nearly a century ago, and not upon the act which was proclaimed to be the bulwark of federal efforts to save endangered species.

The explanation is quite simple. Despite congressional recognition of the threat to wildlife posed by "economic growth untempered by adequate concern and conservation," the Endangered Species Act does nothing to prevent private landowners from doing anything they wish on their own land which results in the complete destruction of habitat essential to the existence of endangered species. Thus, it is only because the Devil's Hole pupfish lives on land set aside as a national monument that the government has any means of trying to save it.

The significance of what the Endangered Species Act does not do can only be appreciated when one realizes that habitat destruction is the principal threat to wildlife today. Most people think that extinc- tion is brought about by commercial slaughter or by sport hunting. Though there are some animals for which this has been a threat, virtually every endangered animal has been reduced in numbers principally as a result of human alteration and destruction of habitat.

In this respect, the apparently unique problem of the Devil's Hole pupfish typifies a more general problem. The Devil's Hole pupfish is one of nearly two dozen species of pupfish, of which at least five from the Death Valley area are thought to be extinct.

Some disappeared with the drying up of their water supplies; others succumbed to a more subtle form of habitat destruction, the introduction by man of predatory or competing non-native species. The few species that still survive face a new threat in the form of vastly expanded strip mining planned for Death Valley. Once again, despite the Endangered Species Act, the Interior Department claims it is powerless to block the mining.

Still other forms of habitat destruction, including physical alteration of land and waterways and chemical alteration by pesticides and pollutants, have brought many other species of wildlife to the brink of extinction.

Accordingly, if that which we denote as "progress" necessarily involves the destruction of much of the world's wildlife, one may ask, "So what?" Does it really matter if the bald eagle or the whooping crane disappears forever? Is it not more important that desert ranchers be able to raise their crops and livestock than that the pupfish survive? The answer to such questions may not be as obvious as those who ask them apparently think.

The Cappaerts' plans for a desert oasis may be short lived. Some biologists believe that irrigation there can only be temporarily successful because of the tendency of the soil to become excessively alkaline. Other experts believe that the underground water system can remain as a self-replenishing system only if limited amounts are extracted. Excessive pumping could overtax the replenishing ability, leading to its permanent collapse.

Against these more sober estimates of the value of continued pumping, one must weigh the considerations in favor of preserving endangered species. The foremost consideration is simply that nothing is quite so final as extinction. Once an animal becomes extinct, it is irretrievably lost; it cannot be reproduced, its mysteries cannot be revealed, its potential for advancing the lot of man cannot be restored.

This argument is amply borne out by the pupfish, which is known to exhibit several traits of extreme interest to scientific investigators, including an extraordinary tolerance of temperature extremes. The fact that the Devil's Hole pupfish retains this trait, essential to its survival many millennia ago but unneeded today, surprised evolutionary theorists and contributed to important rethinking in that field. The second remarkable trait of some species of pupfish is their ability to tolerate extremes of salinity. At least one species can tolerate water six times as saline as sea water. The means by which it maintains its osmotic balance is little understood, but it may eventually have important consequences for human kidney research.

A related argument for the preservation of endangered species is that no life form exists completely independently of the other life forms about it. This interdependence of all life forms is only barely understood at present, yet it is known that any human activity that so disrupts that fragile network as to remove altogether an entire link could well set off repercussions that will affect adversely every other link, including man himself. Those who profess indifference to the

extinction of species fail to recognize their own dependence upon the
whole fabric of existence about them.

Finally, a growing number of people attached substantial value
to the aesthetic and recreational opportunities afforded by the continued existence of a diversity of wildlife species. Disregard of the
environmental consequences of human activity strikes a blow to the
aesthetic and ethical sensibilities of a significant share of the populace.

How to balance each of these considerations against competing
interests is never easy, but it is nevertheless essential that serious
efforts to strike such a balance be made. It is therefore unfortunate
that when the Supreme Court decides the fate of the Devil's Hole
pupfish, it is unlikely that these considerations will be brought to the
Court's attention. Instead, the Court's efforts will be focused on the
complexities of ownership rights to subsurface waters and related
legal niceties.

While the Court deliberates, the pupfish will continue to leap about
in the warm waters of Devil's Hole pool just as it has done for 30,000
years, unmindful that just beyond the edge of the gently sloping rocky
shelf its final extinction awaits.

The Pupfish Prevails—for Now

A few months after the op-ed appeared in the *Post*, the Supreme Court
enjoined the pumping of groundwater to save the Devil's Hole pupfish
in the case *Cappaert v. United States*.[1] I wish I could tell you that the
court cited my op-ed in the course of its decision, but it didn't. Almost
certainly, the op-ed had absolutely no effect on the Court's decision, but
it had a major impact on the future course of my career. I was beginning
to see a way out of that otherwise endless antitrust case that had been
the nearly sole focus of my legal career up to that point. I was beginning
to think that I could accomplish that rarest of things in the law, marry
my vocation to my avocation.

For the pupfish, however, the result was more ambiguous. Chief Jus-
tice Warren Burger's opinion for a unanimous court held that in creating
Death Valley National Monument under the authority of the Antiquities
Act, the United States had, by implication, reserved sufficient water
to protect the unique species of fish that lived there. That meant the
United States could prohibit the Cappaerts, owners of a nearby twelve-

thousand-acre cattle and alfalfa ranching operation, from groundwater pumping that would lower the water level in Devil's Hole to a level that imperiled the pupfish. Earlier cases that had found an implied reservation of federal water rights had all involved surface waters. The novel legal holding in the *Cappaert* case was that "the United States can protect its water from subsequent diversion, whether the diversion is of surface or ground water."

For those who may have thought that the Supreme Court's decision represented a happy ending to the pupfish's story, the realization that it was just another chapter in an unfinished tale soon became apparent. The Cappaerts ceased their ranching operation and sold their land to a company that planned to develop it into thirty-four thousand residential lots, hotels, golf courses, and various other amenities. Instead of contending with just one landowner pumping groundwater, the United States now faced the prospect of having to contend with thousands. That threat was averted, however, when the Nature Conservancy purchased the land in 1984 and transferred it to the US Fish and Wildlife Service to establish the Ash Meadows National Wildlife Refuge.

Creation of the refuge seemed to finally secure the pupfish's positive future, and for the next two decades the population remained relatively stable at around three hundred fish. Then, for reasons unknown, it took a nose dive, sinking to only thirty-five fish in the spring of 2013. Since then, its numbers have climbed back up to around one hundred, a welcome improvement, but one that falls well short of past numbers.

In 2010, nearly thirty-five years after my op-ed, my first published article on any conservation topic, appeared in the *Washington Post*, my wife, Sandy, and I had the opportunity to visit Devil's Hole and see the pupfish. Even though I knew what to expect, I was still a bit taken aback by how isolated, remote, and unexpected Devil's Hole is. Sandy and I nervously climbed down a rickety metal ladder to descend from atop the sinkhole to the level of the pool some twenty feet or so below. We would spend less than half an hour watching these tiny bright blue fish dart about in a timeless ritual that likely began long before any human ever set foot nearby, and then we were gone.

Acknowledging an Error

Readers with knowledge of the Endangered Species Act will doubtless have noticed a glaring error in my account of the pupfish case. My statement that "the Endangered Species Act does nothing to prevent private landowners from doing anything they wish on their own land" is correct only with respect to plants. The act's prohibition against the taking of endangered wildlife, however, makes no distinction between private and other lands. In an admittedly weak defense of my erroneous assertion, I note that at the time I wrote (1975), the issue of the act's applicability to private land had not been tested. It has since been made clear, however, that the actions of private landowners affecting endangered animals fall within the scope of the act's broad prohibitions.

Perhaps my error regarding the reach of the act in 1975 foreshadowed my subsequent focus—some two decades later—on how best to achieve the act's lofty goals on the farms, ranches, and forestlands that make up the working landscape of privately owned land throughout much of the country. My belated recognition that stringent regulatory prohibitions could have unintended consequences with negative impacts on conservation underlay much of the work I did during the latter half of my career. That work, and the rationale behind it, is explored later in this book in chapters 10, 11, and 12. For now, I focus on what followed next in the wake of the pupfish.

Politics and Extinction

It took, I suppose, a bit of chutzpah for me—a total neophyte with respect to endangered species—to write a review of a book that had recently been written by one of the Smithsonian course instructors. But that is what I decided to do when I read Lewis Regenstein's *The Politics of Extinction* and concluded that its analysis of the species endangerment problem was wide of the mark. I submitted my review to *Natural History*, a magazine I had read enthusiastically since I was boy. The magazine accepted my review and published it in the January 1976 edition, about the same time that the pupfish article appeared in the *Washington Post*. These successes caused me to wonder: Could I make a career out of this?

The War against Wildlife, a Review of
The Politics of Extinction: The Shocking Story of the World's Endangered Wildlife,
by Lewis Regenstein
Natural History, January 1976[*]

The Environmental Protection Agency's prohibition of most domestic uses of DDT in 1972 and Congress's enactment of the Endangered Species Act of 1973 combined to raise public hopes that animals such as the brown pelican and others among the world's scarcest wildlife might yet be protected from extinction. The brown pelican and several other fish-eating birds (including the nation's symbol, the American bald eagle) suffered drastic decline in their numbers during the 1960s as a result of the gradual accumulation of DDT in the environment. Once ingested and metabolized, the chemical caused the eggs of the brown pelican to become extremely thin shelled or infertile. The obvious consequence was that more and more eggs were broken, fewer young were hatched, and total numbers dropped precipitously. In certain areas where the brown pelican had long flourished, such as coastal Louisiana, entire populations were completely eliminated.

The initial impact upon brown pelican populations of the ban on DDT seemed to indicate that public optimism had been justified. In many of those areas where the original populations had not been completely obliterated, remnant populations bounced back quickly. Their recovery was so good that state and federal wildlife authorities undertook to relocate some brown pelicans to the areas in which they had previously lived. Some of the relocation projects also showed signs of success. By April 1975, a relocated colony in Barataria Bay near Grand Isle, Louisiana, which had been started in 1968 with only 25 birds imported from Florida, had grown to more than 500 birds. Then in May the birds began to die, and in less than two months more than 80% of the restored colony was dead. The culprit this time, it is believed, was no longer DDT, but perhaps as many as eight other farm pesticides, including one known as endrin, which was found in all the dead birds that were examined. Apparently, spring flooding in the upper Mississippi Valley had washed so much of the chemicals downstream at one time that a mass poisoning of Louisiana's brown pelicans resulted.

The example of the brown pelican is instructive in several respects for those who are concerned with the problem of extinction. First, it illustrates the critical vulnerability of most species considered to be endangered today. Such species have become so reduced in their numbers, so restricted in their ranges, and perhaps so weakened by the stresses of rapid environmental change that a single occurrence—an accidental oil spill, the draining of a swamp, or the accidental introduction of competing or predatory species—could deliver the final coup de grace to entire local populations and perhaps the entire species. The second, and more troublesome lesson to be learned from the brown pelican experience applies not just to presently endangered species but also to those species that are relatively abundant today and not considered endangered. This lesson is simply that the environmental consequences of any human activity, and not just those that employ a relatively new and untested chemical technology, can never be foreseen with certainty and may, in retrospect, turn out to be immensely catastrophic. The final lesson, most ominous of all, is that the fight to save much of the world's vanishing wildlife may already be doomed by forces beyond any realistic prospect of short-term control, and that the most that its advocates can hope to gain is a few more years of survival before species after species disappear forever.

One who has not given up the fight on behalf of the world's wildlife is Lewis Regenstein, a young, articulate environmental activist, who serves as executive vice-president of the Fund for Animals. Regenstein's new book, *The Politics of Extinction*, is the latest, and potentially the most effective, weapon to be used by the Fund in its battle against governmental and political indifference to the plight of endangered wildlife.

In Regenstein's view, a substantial share of the blame for the desperate state of much wildlife today can be placed at the feet of politicians who are unable to enact effective protective legislation, bureaucrats who are too timid to enforce vigorously the legislation that has been passed, and the various vested interests, most especially the hunting and firearms lobbies, which have bought off the politicians, intimidated the bureaucrats, and misled the public. Regenstein's argument is made more effectively in those chapters devoted to single animal types such as the wolf, the grizzly bear, and the prairie dog.

The literal war that has been waged against these animals has been fought, Regenstein argues convincingly, at the behest and for the ex-clusive benefit of the "sport" hunting lobby, the cattleman's lobby, and the wool grower's lobby. Regenstein also explores the well-orchestrat-ed efforts of still other commercial interests: the tuna industry's effort to gut federal regulations designed to protect porpoises and dolphins, the fur industry's effort to weaken and circumvent restrictions on the killing of seals and spotted cats, and the failure of both national and international bodies to check the excesses of the whaling industry.

The above examples and others that Regenstein discusses in detail are comprehensively documented, generally convincingly, and always disturbing. In each instance, however, one can readily perceive that there is a clearly drawn conflict between a relatively specific commer-cial interest and an animal, the killing of which will either directly (as in the case of seals and spotted cats) or indirectly (as in the case of wolves and cougars) benefit that interest. The major shortcoming of Regenstein's book is that such clearly defined conflicts are probably atypical of the threats facing most endangered species, and Regen-stein's examples may therefore be of limited utility in formulating a more generalized assessment of the causes and consequences of ex-tinction. Similarly, his prescriptions may have little or no applicability to the difficult problem of preserving most endangered (and for that matter, nonendangered) species.

This is not to say that Regenstein has not written a very useful book. To the contrary, his principal examples, despite their selectivity, provide a sometimes shocking account of how the governmental apparatus can be manipulated by powerful commercial interests that do not have the slightest concern for ecological balance and seem incapable of comprehending the fundamental significance of extinc-tion. *The Politics of Extinction* could well stimulate a substantial public awareness of, and concern for, the problem of saving endangered wildlife. By alerting a few politicians to the existence of a genuine constituency, which has frequently been regarded as little more than a nuisance, it could make the bureaucrats more concerned that they may ultimately be called to account for their inaction.

The Politics of Extinction, despite its substantial potential to serve as a catalyst for both private and public action, is not without its flaws, some minor and others not so minor. One of Regenstein's irritating habits is to be rather flip and to intersperse his arguments with tidbits of irrelevant information by which he attempts to stain his adversary with guilt by association. For example, Regenstein amply documents the fact that a great many organizations that are regarded by the public as pro-wildlife conservation organizations are, in fact, strongly influenced and even financed by the National Rifle Association or others connected with the arms and munitions industry. These organizations, quite predictably, uniformly espoused the prohunting wildlife "management" philosophies of their benefactors. But having made this exposure quite effectively, Regenstein adds the wholly irrelevant and unnecessary barb that one such organization is represented by the same law firm that represented John Ehrlichman and H. R. Haldeman.

A more serious flaw is the inconsistent quality of Regenstein's documentation. Frequently his most dramatic claims are supported by no citation of authority whatsoever. Striking the balance between writing a book that is easy to read and one that is thoroughly documented with copious footnotes is never easy, but Regenstein can justly be criticized for opting too much for the former. His arguments depend too heavily upon the accuracy of the claims he makes to let them stand unsubstantiated.

In addition, there is the whole question of hunting. The Fund for Animals is one of the most openly anti-hunting organizations functioning today. Unfortunately, most of the debate in this country about hunting has taken place at the emotional rather than the rational level, and Regenstein never quite succeeds in elevating the argument. He dances around, but never quite attacks head on, the only rational argument that proponents of hunting have ever been able to offer in justification for their sport. That argument, quite simply, is that in the absence of natural predators, game animals would so quickly expand their numbers that starvation and disease would soon overcome them unless their numbers were kept in check by human hunting.

It has been rightly observed that the hunter's argument is more than a little self-serving, inasmuch as the essential premise is the absence of natural predators, and it is the hunters themselves who are principally responsible for the near obliteration of predatory animals such as the wolf, cougar, bear, and numerous others. Moreover, much as the hunter would like to cast himself in the role of nature's servant, performing the necessary task of natural selection, this sort of selection is unnatural and counter selective. The human hunter who passes up a big, strong buck for a sickly, infirm one is a most unusual hunter indeed.

Yet, valid as both these points are, they still do not constitute the principal argument that can be offered to rebut the hunter's favorite contention. That argument, put simply, is that the "starvation from overpopulation" thesis has been disingenuously applied across the board to all game species, whereas the only evidence that supports it is based upon a very few large animals, principally even-toed ungulates such as deer and caribou. There are convincing theoretical reasons why the larger animals in a given ecosystem, requiring the greatest area of supporting habitat, would be the first and perhaps the only animals to exhibit this sort of vulnerability to overpopulation. More-over, there is ample evidence that unlike deer, most animals are able to keep their own numbers in check through some natural mechanism by which the reproductive rate is affected by the availability of food.

Instead of addressing what really is the bottom line argument in the debate about hunting, Regenstein wastes his readers' time and jeopardizes his own credibility by suggesting that hunters suffer from a psychosexual imbalance and in all likelihood a latent homosexual tendency. Moreover, in his attempt to lay as much of the blame as he can at the feet of hunters, Regenstein leaves himself open to the charge that he accepts too uncritically one side of a hotly disputed debate among paleontologists about whether early man was the principal cause of the wave of extinction of giant mammals that occurred around the globe around 10,000 years ago at the end of the Pleistocene epoch. In fact, Regenstein at times seems willing to use either side of the debate depending on how it fits his purpose.

The final flaw in the *Politics of Extinction*, which has already been alluded to, is that it is essentially a book about politics and not about extinction. To understand the importance of this distinction, it is only necessary to recall the example of the brown pelican. It would be very difficult for Regenstein to point a finger of blame at any politicians or bureaucrats for the tragedy of the brown pelicans. Granted that for a long time the manufacturers of DDT fought their utmost to block EPA's prohibition and are now fighting to have it lifted. Nevertheless, if the initial reports are correct and DDT is only one of the nine pesti-cides that threatened the future of the brown pelican, we may yet have to face the prospect that either the brown pelican goes or we give up our pretension of feeding the world and become a nation of organic farmers. Even that solution, it should be pointed out, would not have saved the hair-lipped sucker, a rather bizarre fish of the Ohio River Valley that became extinct in the early part of this century when the clearing of land for the agricultural purposes in that area caused the

formerly clean waters in which the sucker lived to become so clouded
that it was no longer able to see the snails that made up its exclusive
diet.

The sad truth is that for every species like the grizzly bear there are
probably a dozen like the brown pelican and hair-lipped sucker. The
world's population explosion requires that more and more land each
year be cleared to house and feed it. Lewis Regenstein has studied the
problem of extinction long enough to know that the greatest single
threat to the future existence of most wildlife is the constantly accel-
erating pace of habitat destruction—both physical and chemical. He
admits as much at one point in his book but then devotes less than
five pages to the topic. The obvious reason is that the problem of
habitat destruction is infinitely harder to deal with than the types of
threats to wildlife that Regenstein treats. The villains are much more
difficult to single out; the solutions much harder to articulate and
to accept. We in the United States have often stated that we want to
maintain our standard of living, feed the world's billions, and at the
same time, protect our wildlife from extinction. One need not really
study the matter too long before concluding that a serious question
exists as to whether we can ever hope to accomplish all three. Yet if
the problem of saving wildlife is regarded as Regenstein describes it,
solely in terms of prodding a few politicians and bureaucrats into
action, we run the risk of blithely assuming that we have at last found
the key to the preservation of wildlife while the forces of extinction
roll inexorably on.

Beginning a Career in Conservation

The setback that the brown pelican experienced in Louisiana proved
to be only temporary. Since then, it has dramatically expanded both its
numbers and its geographic range. By 1985, it was no longer endangered
in the southeastern United States, and in 2009, its recovery complete, it
was taken off the endangered species list.

With the book review and the pupfish article under my belt, I began to
explore new job opportunities. By sheer coincidence and good fortune,
the Environmental Law Institute, a nonpartisan environmental policy
research organization, was at the same time looking for someone to write
a book on wildlife law. The institute had a contract with the President's

Council on Environmental Quality to produce such a book as part of the council's agenda for the nation's bicentennial year. Although my own credentials to undertake the project were remarkably thin, no one then on the institute staff had any more extensive credentials. So the institute hired me, and nine months later *The Evolution of National Wildlife Law* rolled off the Government Printing Office presses.

Publication of *The Evolution of National Wildlife Law* opened doors to new career opportunities, for it had made me not just an authority on wildlife law but a "leading authority." The door I chose to enter was that of the Environmental Defense Fund (EDF), the organization that had already waged a years-long and successful effort to achieve a ban on most uses of the pesticide DDT, which made possible the ultimate recovery of the brown pelican, peregrine falcon, and bald eagle. EDF had received a small grant from another conservation organization, the World Wildlife Fund, to hire a lawyer to focus exclusively on wildlife conservation. In December 1977, EDF hired me for that position, just as the Supreme Court was preparing to decide yet another case in which the fate of a fish hung in the balance.

Tellico Dam and the Little Fish That Nearly Halted Its Construction

Now back to 1973. A few months before the Endangered Species Act became law in December of that year, David Etnier, a University of Tennessee ichthyologist, discovered an altogether new species of fish, *Percina tanasi*, in the Little Tennessee River. Dubbed the "snail darter," the three-inch-long fish made its home in the swift-flowing shallows of the river. These same shallows would be inundated by the Tellico Dam, which the Tennessee Valley Authority (TVA) had begun constructing in 1967 and that was well on its way to completion by the time of Etnier's discovery.

Even before the snail darter's discovery, Tellico Dam was a controversial project. A cadre of local and national interests had long opposed it because it would eliminate one of the last free-flowing river segments in the region, flood ancient sites sacred to American Indians, displace local landowners of modest means, and—it then seemed certain—bring about the extinction of an endemic species. Despite these issues and the controversies they raised, Congress continued to appropriate funds for the dam's construction and TVA kept building.

When, in October 1975, the Fish and Wildlife Service listed the snail darter as an endangered species and designated the area to be inundated by the dam as its critical habitat, the stage was set for a new legal claim to be asserted. Four months later a group of plaintiffs that included Hiram Hill, a law student, filed a complaint in federal district court contending that the Endangered Species Act required TVA to halt construction of the dam because its completion would jeopardize the continued existence of the snail darter and destroy its critical habitat, a violation of requirements set forth in Section 7 of the act.

Although the district court rejected the plaintiffs' claims, the court of appeals reversed that decision and halted further construction unless Congress passed new legislation specifically exempting the project from the requirements of the Endangered Species Act. On November 14, 1977, the Supreme Court agreed to review the case. Six weeks later I began my new position at EDF, where one of my first assignments was to write a "friend of the court" brief in the case.

The halting of a massive project in which a federal agency had already invested around a hundred million dollars of taxpayer funds just to protect a tiny, largely unknown fish seemed to be sheer lunacy to most people outside environmental circles and to many newspaper editorial writers. I decided that the brief I would write would acknowledge that reaction but go on to argue that what might appear to be lunacy was in fact good sense and moreover an outcome that Congress intended. In short, my intention was to write an unusual sort of brief, one that minimized the dry legalese typical of most briefs in favor of something rather more stirring. Key excerpts from that brief follow.

**Excerpts from the Brief Amicus Curiae of Environmental
Defense Fund, National Audubon Society, National Wildlife
Federation, Natural Resources Defense Council, Sierra Club,
and Defenders of Wildlife in the case**
Tennessee Valley Authority v. Hill
March 1978[*]

In parts of the public press and elsewhere, the decision this Court is
called upon to review has been subjected to skepticism and doubt. To
halt completion of Tellico Dam at an advanced stage of its construction just to perpetuate a tiny species of fish which had not even been
known to exist when construction began has been seen by some as an
environmental folly. Petitioner's [TVA's] brief reflects this view when
it states that the "plain meaning" rule that guided the interpretation
of the Act by the court below should be rejected because "it is well
established that even the unambiguous meaning of statutory words
does not control when such a reading would be unreasonable in view
of the statute's purpose." In support of this proposition, petitioner
quotes the 1892 language of this Court in *Church of the Holy Trinity
v. United States* that . . . "frequently words of general meaning are used
in a statute, words broad enough to include an act in question, and
yet a consideration of the whole legislation, or of the circumstances
surrounding its enactment . . . makes it unreasonable to believe that
the legislator intended to include the particular act."

What then are the purposes of the Endangered Species Act, and
what does a "consideration of the whole legislation" reveal about the
meaning of the provision in question here? Had petitioner made
these inquiries, it would have discovered that the Act, in a multitude
of ways, represents a sweeping and uncompromising commitment
to the preservation of the earth's genetic diversity. The Act does this
first by boldly declaring a purpose of preserving "the ecosystems upon
which endangered species and threatened species depend." Neither
stuffed museum specimens nor caged zoo animals nor transplanted
populations in substitute ecosystems can satisfy this fundamental
goal. Instead, the Act demands and requires the preservation not only
of endangered species themselves but also of the habitats on which
they depend.

---

[*] Footnotes and internal citations omitted.

Why would Congress have made such a sweeping and uncompromising commitment to the preservation of the earth's genetic diversity by enacting a law which, on its face, appears to give paramount
importance to the interests of little known and apparently valueless
creatures? Because, despite those superficial appearances, Congress
was persuaded that the long-run interests of human welfare were best
served by preserving as much of the earth's flora and fauna as possible.
The legislative history is replete with examples, like that of the discovery of penicillin from a common mold, showing that even the most
obscure and apparently worthless life forms may someday prove to
be of incalculable benefit to man. . . . Congress was clearly aware that
extinction is an irreversible process and that its adverse consequences
may not be recognized for years, decades or even centuries. Because
of that awareness, Congress clearly regarded the preservation of the
earth's genetic diversity as a value of fundamental importance.

Since Congress saw the preservation of the earth's life forms as a
fundamental value, is it likely that it would have delegated to the various federal agencies the discretion to decide for themselves when that
fundamental value could be sacrificed in favor of other interests? If
Congress had meant for such agencies to have that discretion, would
it not have said so clearly and would not the legislative history have
demonstrated that intent? . . .

The result argued for here cannot fairly be characterized, as petitioner has suggested, as absurd or unreasonable. The Book of Genesis
records that God once destroyed all of man's works, but only after
first directing Noah to take with him into the ark his family "and
every beast after his kind, and all the cattle after their kind, and every
creeping thing that creepeth upon the earth after his kind, and every
fowl after his kind, every bird of every sort." The Endangered Species
Act represents a determined, perhaps even desperate, effort to keep
that biblical ark afloat. Along the way, it is true that a lot of species
have fallen off the ark, some have even been unknowingly crowded
off by man himself; never before, however, has any species been
intentionally thrown overboard.

But Is It Any Good to Eat? The Snail Darter's Subsequent Saga

The federal government's brief was even more unusual. In its main
body, it set forth the position of TVA that the dam should be completed

and, in a separate appendix, the diametrically opposite views of the Fish and Wildlife Service. With the Executive Branch thus divided, the government's position was argued before the court by no less than the attorney general himself, Griffin Bell. Bell brought with him a small vial in which a dead specimen of a snail darter had been preserved. He flashed it before the court to emphasize the fish's diminutive size and, implicitly, its unimportance.

Justice Lewis Powell, himself an enthusiastic bass fisherman, took the bait. When the lawyer for the dam's opponents came to the lectern, Justice Powell pressed him to explain "what purpose is served, if any, by these little darters? . . . Are they used for food? . . . Are they suitable for bait?"[2] There was irony in Justice Powell's query about whether one could eat them, but that would not become apparent until years later.

Notwithstanding the attorney general's efforts and Justice Powell's vigorous dissent, Chief Justice Warren Burger's six-member majority opinion held that the Endangered Species Act meant exactly what it appeared to say: TVA must halt construction of its nearly completed Tellico Dam to avoid jeopardizing the continued existence of the snail darter. His often quoted conclusion was that "it is clear from the Act's legislative history that Congress intended to halt and reverse the trend toward species extinction—whatever the cost."[3] Thus, the snail darter won, or so it seemed.

Many in Congress had second thoughts, however. Rather than exempt the dam outright from the requirements of the law, Congress instead created a special body of senior government officials and empowered it to grant an exemption to any project that met stringent criteria pertaining to national or regional significance, the absence of reasonable alternatives, and similar factors. Congress directed this body—informally called the "God Squad" because of its life-or-death power over species—to promptly consider Tellico Dam for an exemption. Most in Congress probably thought the God Squad would grant TVA an exemption. It didn't.

Confirming many of the very contentions about the dam that its opponents had made since before the Endangered Species Act was law, the God Squad unanimously concluded that the project had insufficient regional or national significance and that the benefits of completing it were less than those of the alternative of abandoning it. The celebrations of the dam's opponents were short-lived, however. Notwithstanding the Endangered Species Act and the conclusions of the God Squad, Congress, in the wee hours of the morning, slipped a provision—a so-called "rider"—into a must-sign appropriations bill directing the completion of the dam. After putting up a fight like that of a barracuda, the little darter was ordered by Congress to make way for the dam. Reluctantly, President Jimmy Carter signed the bill, effectively signing the snail darter's death warrant.

Or so one might have thought. Ironically, intensive searches turned up snail darter populations in several other areas. Indeed, it was found to be sufficiently widespread that in 1984 the Fish and Wildlife Service reclassified it from endangered to the less imperiled category "threatened." As for the God Squad, it has virtually never been needed since its creation in 1978, a reflection of the considerable effort federal agencies now make to avoid irreconcilable conflicts between federal projects and the needs of endangered species.

In sum, Congress left the Endangered Species Act substantially intact, the snail darter survived, and the TVA completed construction of Tellico Dam. That sounds like an ideal outcome, one that should have made everybody happy. It didn't. The fact that the snail darter survived came as a surprise, but it was not the only surprise in the wake of Tellico Dam.

Where the swift waters of the Little Tennessee River once flowed, the thirty-six-mile-long Tellico Reservoir now sits. Tellico Reservoir was to have been an angler's dream, with delectable large-mouth bass leaping from its surface and tasty catfish prowling on its bottom. It was to be the sort of place where even Justice Powell would have loved to cast a lure. The dream, however, turned out to be something quite different. The State of Tennessee soon cautioned against eating any of Tellico's catfish and urged that only limited quantities of other gamefish be consumed. Gourmands who sampled Tellico's offerings may perhaps have detected the delicate hint of polychlorinated biphenyls, better known as PCBs, the chemical compounds that made electrical transformers better and cancer more likely. Eat at your peril, the state advised.

Tellico's fate was especially ironic, not just because of Justice Powell's asking if snail darters were good as food but also because fishing was always one of Tellico's principal justifications. Tellico Dam produces no hydroelectric energy and only very minor flood-control benefits. "Flat-water recreation," including, most notably, fishing, was its reason for being.

The planners and engineers who looked out on the Little Tennessee River saw not a rare, free-flowing river, with sparkling clear water and an endangered species, but an opportunity to "improve" on nature with a dam. To them, the snail darter represented not the uniqueness of the place but an obstacle to be removed.

What a pity those planners and engineers never read the words of another Supreme Court justice, Oliver Wendell Holmes Jr., nearly a century ago. "A river," he wrote, "is more than an amenity, it is a treasure."[4] The treasure of the Little Tennessee River has been plundered, and the fish that swim in the artificial lake that replaced it may be hazardous to your health.

Holmes's observation holds true for many of our natural resources, including forests. The timber barons and land "stewards" who look at a mature forest teeming with a rich diversity of wild plants and animals see only board feet of lumber. They too can "improve" on nature by clear-cutting the forest and replacing it with a tree farm. Creatures that make particular forests unique, such as northern spotted owls in the Pacific Northwest or red-cockaded woodpeckers in the longleaf pine forests of the Southeast, are just obstacles in the path of progress. Why should anyone care? After all, are northern spotted owls and red-cockaded woodpeckers any good to eat?

2

A Brief History of Federal Wildlife Conservation Efforts

In 1841, John James Audubon, whose *Birds of America* had made him the most famous American naturalist of his day, wrote a letter to Secretary of State Daniel Webster. Webster, a prominent political figure of the time, had been appointed to that post by the ill-fated president William Henry Harrison. When Harrison died after only a month in office, however, Webster stayed on to serve his successor, John Tyler. Audubon's letter to Webster set forth a novel idea for the still young nation.

Audubon's letter actually had two purposes. Most immediately, he wanted the opportunity to illustrate the natural history specimens brought back from the four-year-long, government-funded US Exploring Expedition that had been led by the tyrannical Charles Wilkes (thought by some to have been the model for the megalomaniacal Captain Ahab in Melville's novel). More grandly, Audubon urged the creation of "a natural history institution to advance our knowledge of natural science."[1] Audubon even had a suggestion regarding who should head that institution—himself.

Five years earlier, in 1836, Congress had formally authorized the United States to accept a generous bequest by a British scientist, James Smithson, who, like Audubon, was the illegitimate son of a wealthy father. Smithson's bequest specified that it was to be used to create an institution in Washington, DC, "for the increase and diffusion of knowledge."[2] It would be a decade later, in 1846, before Congress would establish the Smithsonian Institution in fulfillment of Smithson's bequest. Although Audubon was not chosen to head it, the Smithsonian Institution was very much in alignment with Audubon's recommendation of an institution to "advance our knowledge of natural science."

Audubon's recommendation should be seen in a larger context as well. In emphasizing the advancement of knowledge about natural history—pure and simple—Audubon was giving voice to one of two competing strains of thought that would influence the history of wildlife conservation in America. We have already seen an example of the other in Justice Powell's questions about the snail darter: Do they serve any useful purpose; are they any good for food? If they serve no utilitarian purpose, the justice implied, they probably are not worth the conservationist's attention.

This chapter traces the history of federal wildlife conservation efforts—and of those two competing strains of thought within those efforts—over the past century and a half. In doing so, it also discusses the recurrent tensions between state and federal governments over the scope of their respective authorities, the early origins and later development of the federal agencies that are today responsible for conserving wildlife, and some of the prominent pioneers of the American conservation movement.

Robert Connery

In compiling this history I owe a debt of gratitude to the late Robert H. Connery and his perceptive 1935 book, *Governmental Problems in Wild Life Conservation*. It was a book I stumbled on quite by chance at a used-book sale of the Audubon Naturalist Society in suburban Washington, DC. Though I had by that time written a book of my own on wildlife law, a book for which I thought I had done exhaustive research, I had never before seen Connery's book or even a reference to it. Long out of print, it had escaped my notice and that of other students of conservation, which was a great misfortune.

Connery, who served for two decades as president of the Academy of Political Science, was a true polymath. He wrote books about urban riots, mental health, municipal taxation, energy policy, and a dazzling array of other topics. His book about governmental problems in wildlife conservation was his PhD dissertation and the only book he ever wrote on that subject. His *New York Times* obituary in 1998 noted that even that book "stirred considerable interest." And well it should have, for it was written at a time of great ferment and legislative activity in the history of American wildlife conservation, particularly concerning the respective roles and responsibilities of the states and the federal government. It was also a time of dramatic wildlife losses.

Only three years earlier, the heath hen had vanished from the face of the earth. Within Connery's lifetime—he was but twenty-seven at the time he wrote—the last surviving passenger pigeon, which had once been the most abundant species of bird in North America, had passed away at the Cincinnati Zoo. It is exceedingly rare to be able to date the extinction of any species with precision, but the death of Martha—the name her keepers had given her—made it possible for the passenger pigeon: September 1, 1914. Four years later, at the same zoo, the last captive Carolina parakeet expired. Its disappearance from the wild was likely complete by the time Connery wrote. Nearly gone was the whooping crane, of which there may once have been a population of more than ten thousand, but by the mid-1930s no more than a few dozen likely remained. Bold action was needed if the nation was to avert the further loss of its natural inheritance.

What is remarkable about reading Connery's book more than eighty years after its publication is how much today's governmental problems resemble those that he addressed in his time. In his introductory chapter, Connery frames the core problem confronting wildlife conservation in 1935 in the following terms: "Granted that in the future the government will control the taking of wild animals to an increasing degree, what are the most efficient methods for making its intervention effective within the limits of our constitutional system?"[3]

That question is one that we still struggle to answer today. As Connery correctly foresaw, the government (both state and federal) has controlled the taking of wild animals to an increasing degree. In doing so, however, it has sparked contentious and ongoing debate about the efficiency, effectiveness, fairness, and even the constitutionality of its means. The brief history presented here cannot resolve that debate, but perhaps it can help illuminate it.

The Scope of State Authority

Until early in the twentieth century, the taking of wildlife was regulated exclusively by the states under the authority of their general police powers. The most significant constitutional question concerned how far a state could go in exercising those powers. Specifically, could the state of Connecticut prohibit the transportation outside its borders of wildlife that had been lawfully taken within Connecticut? In 1896, that question was presented to the Supreme Court in the case of *Geer v. Connecticut.*[4]

The court, in an opinion by Justice Edward White, upheld Connecticut's authority to do so. In reaching its conclusion, the court used the
language of ownership to characterize a state's relationship to its wildlife.
As the owner in trust of its wildlife, a state could prohibit its taking
altogether or allow its taking subject to such qualifications as the state
may impose. The court reasoned that the prohibition against transport
out of the state qualified any right an individual might have to use lawfully taken wildlife. In a remarkable bit of logic that assumed its very
conclusion, the court found that the state's export prohibition imposed
no burden on interstate commerce because the wildlife in question could
never lawfully be an article of interstate commerce. Although it would
be decades before the actual holding of *Geer* would be overruled, that
decision's use of the language of ownership helped fuel a tug-of-war
between state and federal governments over the authority to regulate
wildlife that lasts to this very day, even as the court itself steadily moved
away from reliance on ownership as the basis for that authority.

The Fish Commission: First Step for a
Federal Role in Conserving Wildlife

Although regulating the taking of wildlife was done exclusively by the
states until early in the twentieth century, the federal government began
to play an ancillary conservation role not long after the Civil War ended.
It began with the creation in 1871 of the Fish Commission, to which
today's National Marine Fisheries Service traces its origins. The idea of
a fish commission was not entirely new. Massachusetts had established
the first formal fish commission in 1856, and by the time of the establishment of the federal commission fifteen years later, eleven states had
created them as well.

A joint resolution of Congress authorized the president to appoint a
commissioner of fish and fisheries whose duty was to oversee investigations into whether any "diminution in the number of the food fishes of
the coast and the lakes of the United States has taken place" and, if so, the
reasons for the decline. Most important, the commissioner was to report
to Congress on whether any "protective, prohibitory, or precautionary
measures should be adopted" to counter fish declines.[5]

Two aspects of the resolution establishing the commission are noteworthy. First, its focus was not on all fish (and certainly not on snail darters and pupfish) but rather on "food fish," reflecting the primary concern of the time with the potential loss of a source of food for a growing nation (a concern that animated Supreme Court Justice Lewis Powell a century later). Second, the scope of the resolution extended to fish of the "coast and lakes." In addressing fish of the coast, the resolution contemplated a federal role in which no single state could effectively conserve the fishery resource. In addressing fish of the nation's lakes, however, the resolution at least literally gave the federal government a role with respect to fisheries in water bodies confined within a single state, although the actual concern may have been with the Great Lakes and other multistate lakes that supported commercial fisheries. The resolution said nothing about riverine fisheries or fish propagation, although these omissions appear not to have limited the purposes for which Congress subsequently appropriated funds.

The first commissioner of fish and fisheries was one of the giants of nineteenth-century science, Spencer Baird, a self-trained naturalist who was instructed in the art of drawing birds by Audubon himself. Ironically, although Audubon's 1841 request to head a national natural history institution would go unfulfilled, it was his student Spencer Baird who, at the age of twenty-seven, became the first curator of the Smithsonian Institution, some four years after the creation of that institution in 1846. In the same year that he joined the Smithsonian, Baird also became permanent secretary for the recently established American Association for the Advancement of Science, the foremost scientific organization in the United States today.

At the time of his appointment as fish commissioner, Baird had already served as assistant secretary of the Smithsonian Institution for more than two decades, and in 1878 he would become its secretary. Spencer performed both roles at the Smithsonian and as fish commissioner simultaneously at no extra compensation. In recognition of his extraordinary service, Congress granted his widow a lump-sum payment of twenty-five thousand dollars shortly after his death in 1887. The auditorium in the Smithsonian's Museum of Natural History is named for him today.

Although Baird was preeminently qualified for the post, subsequent fish commissioners did not always achieve that position through merit.

Connery tells the story of the appointment of George Bowers of West Virginia to the post in 1897. To secure the nomination at the Republican National Convention of 1896, William McKinley needed the support of Senator Stephen B. Elkins of West Virginia. He won that support by promising to appoint Bowers—an Elkins ally—as fish commissioner. Years later, after Bowers had been elected to Congress, President Calvin Coolidge, who was apparently no fan of Commissioner Bowers, observed that "that was an awful price to pay for West Virginia."[6]

Almost from its beginning, the Fish Commission took on the task of artificially propagating and distributing food fish. Interestingly, the idea that the federal government should undertake this task was initially put forward by a representative of a state agency, M. C. Edmunds of the Vermont Fish Commission. His cousin, George Edmunds, was a senator from Vermont and had been the primary supporter of the resolution establishing the federal commission. Congress subsequently appropriated funds for an ever-growing list of fish-culture stations around the country and even for the maintenance of carp ponds in Washington, DC. The commission also oversaw many efforts to introduce various fish or shellfish to areas where they did not naturally occur, such as its efforts to introduce American lobsters to the Pacific Coast. It also undertook the propagation of goldfish and other ornamental species.

If the Fish Commission experienced mission creep, Congress could hardly complain because the commission for its first thirty-two years was an independent agency directly responsible to Congress and not part of the Executive Branch. That ended in 1903, when Congress terminated the commission and replaced it with the Bureau of Fisheries within the newly established Department of Commerce and Labor. When that department was split in 1912, the Bureau of Fisheries was kept in the Commerce Department, where its modern-day successor, the National Marine Fisheries Service, resides today. The National Marine Fisheries Service now shares the responsibility of administering the Endangered Species Act with the Interior Department's US Fish and Wildlife Service.

Origins of the US Fish and Wildlife Service

Today's US Fish and Wildlife Service can trace its origins nearly as far back as its Commerce Department counterpart. The first national

association of ornithologists, the American Ornithologists' Union, was
established in 1883. At its second annual congress the following year, the
union called on the national government to undertake the study and
dissemination of information about the nation's birds because of their
value to agriculture. Spencer Baird, already doing double duty as the
secretary of the Smithsonian Institution and commissioner of fish and
fisheries, lent his considerable influence to the effort. As a result, Congress appropriated funds to "investigate the food habits, distribution,
and migrations of North American birds and mammals in relation to
agriculture, horticulture, and forestry."[7] These investigations, initially
assigned to the Division of Entomology in the Department of Agriculture, were subsequently vested in a newly created Division of Economic
Ornithology and Mammalogy. As was clear from its name, and like
its fisheries counterpart, the division's focus was to be on economics,
particularly the impact of birds on the nation's food supply.

A somewhat broader mission was implied in later name changes, first
to the Division of Biological Survey in 1891 and then to the Bureau of
Biological Survey in 1906. As a bureau, it now functioned with greater
independence and importance within the Agriculture Department.
Throughout these various name changes, and for a quarter century, the
division and later the bureau were headed by another giant in the annals
of conservation, C. Hart Merriam. A physician by training and the son
of a congressman, Merriam was a protégé of Spencer Baird, who helped
secure his appointment as a naturalist on the Geological Survey's 1871
Yellowstone expedition led by Ferdinand Hayden. Hayden had been a
Civil War surgeon in the Union Army. Since childhood he had been
keenly interested in nature, an interest that had been stoked by his association with J. P. Kirtland, the first graduate of the Yale Medical School
and a naturalist for whom the now endangered Kirtland's warbler was
named.

Merriam, who was all of sixteen years old when he served in Hayden's
expedition, later spearheaded the American Ornithologists' Union's effort that led ultimately to the creation of the Bureau of Biological Survey.
Merriam was often referred to as the "father of mammalogy," the branch
of zoology devoted to the study of mammals. Among mammalogists,
Merriam was a "splitter" rather than a "lumper," meaning that he was
inclined to split recognized species into many different taxa based on

minor differences. For example, he recognized seven different species of coyotes and eight of grizzly bears. His penchant for recognizing different species on the basis of seemingly trivial differences was sharply criticized by his friend Theodore Roosevelt. However, when Merriam recognized a distinct species of elk in the Pacific Northwest and named it the Roosevelt elk, Roosevelt gushed with delight that "the noblest game animal of America" had been named for him.[8]

A final biographical detail is that Merriam was the grandfather of Lee M. Talbot, who served as chief scientist at the Council on Environmental Quality (CEQ) in the 1970s and as head of the International Union for the Conservation of Nature in the 1980s. Talbot was a critical behind-the-scenes player in the legislative negotiations that led to the Endangered Species Act. He remains active in conservation today at age eighty-nine, although he gave up his other passion of auto racing at age eighty-eight. While at CEQ, Talbot was instrumental in commissioning the preparation of a book on wildlife law, a book that I had the privilege to write, coincidentally at the age of twenty-seven.

As head of the Division (and later Bureau) of Biological Survey, Merriam had to contend with a Congress that was impatient with broad studies of the distribution and habits of wildlife and that favored more immediate practical actions of benefit to agriculture. Those pressures ultimately led the bureau to take on the control of animals considered by agricultural interests to be pests. In 1909, Congress began to provide funds for experiments in destroying undesirable rodents. Five years later it appropriated funds for experiments and demonstrations in methods of controlling wolves. Rodent and predator control was made a continuing part of the agency's mission with enactment of the Animal Damage Control Act in 1931. Robert Connery's book four years later made clear that such control efforts were not without controversy, concluding that "only time can determine the wisdom of the policy."[9] The passage of time and the evolution of social values did indeed lead to at least a partial reversal of policy. The federal government's predator-control efforts contributed to the near extirpation of wolves from the lower forty-eight states by the mid-twentieth century, followed decades later by their purposeful restoration under the Endangered Species Act.

In 1939, all these functions—those of the Commerce Department's Bureau of Fisheries and the Agriculture Department's Bureau of Biological

Survey—were moved to the Interior Department as a result of a government reorganization. The following year they were consolidated as the
US Fish and Wildlife Service. A later reorganization moved some of the
fishery responsibilities back to the Commerce Department, where they
rest today in the National Marine Fisheries Service.

The Lacey Act: Beginning of a Federal Regulatory Role

Amid these frequent reorganizations and renamings, the federal conservation agencies slowly began to be given regulatory authority in addition
to their long-standing research and experimentation responsibilities.
This process began in 1900 with enactment of the Lacey Act, which
made it a federal offense to transport across state lines wildlife taken in
violation of state law. The act was named for its chief sponsor, Iowa congressman John Lacey, a Civil War veteran who took a strong interest in
the conservation of not just wildlife but also of archaeological resources.
He was earlier responsible for legislation in 1894 penalizing wildlife
violations committed in Yellowstone National Park and, later, in 1906
he was a prime mover behind enactment of the Antiquities Act, the law
that had led to the designation of Devil's Hole as a national monument
and that is perhaps the most consequential conservation legislation
ever because it has been used by nearly every subsequent president to
secure the permanent protection of geologically, archaeologically, and
scientifically important lands.

   The congressional debate that produced the Lacey Act of 1900 reveals
widespread awareness of at least one catastrophic decline in a once-fa-
miliar species, the passenger pigeon. Within the lifetimes of those who
debated the Lacey Act, the passenger pigeon had been one of the most
abundant birds in the nation. Vast flocks were reported to have literally
blackened the skies for extended periods. Yet by the turn of the century,
this once-prolific bird had been reduced to a handful of survivors. Congressman Lacey apparently thought the bird had already gone extinct,
for he declared that "the wild pigeon, formerly in this country in flocks
of millions, has entirely disappeared from the face of the earth."[10]

   As noted previously, Lacey wrote the bird's obituary prematurely;
the last survivor, a female named Martha, would die September 1, 1914,
in a cage in the Cincinnati Zoo. Martha's death brings to mind the

words of one of Theodore Roosevelt's conservation allies, the scientist William Beebe, in 1906: "The beauty and genius of a work of art may be reconceived, though its first material expression be destroyed; a vanished harmony may yet again inspire the composer; but when the last individual of a race of living things breathes no more, another heaven and another earth must pass before such a one can be again."[11]

The collapse of the passenger pigeon had happened so quickly, and was so evident to so many, that Congress felt compelled to do what it never had done before—enact federal legislation for the conservation of wildlife. Before the Lacey Act, wildlife conservation had been the jealously guarded exclusive prerogative of the states. Indeed, the Supreme Court had intimated, only four years earlier, that the states were the owners of all wildlife within their borders. Nevertheless, prompted by the slaughter of birds for their meat and feathers, Congress enacted the Lacey Act. The first purpose of the bill, according to Congressman Lacey, was to authorize the secretary of agriculture (who then oversaw the Bureau of Biological Survey, predecessor to today's US Fish and Wildlife Service in the Interior Department) "to utilize his Department for the reintroduction of birds that have become locally extinct or are becoming so."[12] More broadly, the law made it a federal offense to ship unlawfully acquired wildlife—not only birds but other species as well—in interstate commerce. With enactment of the Lacey Act, federal wildlife conservation law was launched, and it was the endangerment and extinction of species that set it in motion.

As we have seen, the Lacey Act came too late to avert the extinction of the passenger pigeon. Nor did it rescue North America's only native parrot, the Carolina parakeet, the last captive individual of which also died in 1914. Next to vanish was the heath hen, a bird that was still somewhat common in Melville's New England but was completely gone by 1932. By 1941, the extinction of the whooping crane also appeared imminent. The crane had once occupied a breeding range over parts of Iowa, Illinois, Minnesota, North Dakota, and Canada, but by 1941 its entire population had been reduced to only twenty-one birds.

A principal purpose of the Lacey Act was to strengthen the enforcement of state wildlife laws by making it a federal offense to ship in interstate commerce wildlife taken in violation of state law. The impact of that was considerable, since, at the time, once wildlife that had been illegally taken left a state, that state had little practical ability to enforce its laws. Violation of the Lacey Act depended on an underlying violation of state law before the federal government could act. The Lacey Act was thus a very modest assertion of federal power, one that respected the prevailing notion at the time that the states owned the wildlife within their borders and thus had primacy with respect to its conservation.

Showdown over Migratory Birds

The assertion of a broader federal authority was soon to follow, however, in response to the growing recognition that the states alone could not effectively conserve migratory birds. In 1913, Congress enacted the Weeks-McLean Migratory Bird Act, which declared migratory birds to be within "the custody and protection of the United States"[13]—a direct poke in the eye of their purported owners, the states—and forbade their killing in violation of federal regulations. This bold assertion of federal authority was quickly challenged in the courts. The supreme courts of Maine and Kansas held it to be unconstitutional, as did two federal district courts. One of the federal cases made its way to the docket of the United States Supreme Court, where, after being argued twice, it was awaiting a decision when the State Department announced it had concluded a treaty with Great Britain, on behalf of Canada, to conserve migratory birds. The attorney general moved to dismiss the case, and the Supreme Court did so without ever ruling on the constitutionality of the 1913 legislation.

The negotiation of an international treaty was apparently at least in part a litigation tactic meant to shore up the constitutional basis for federal legislation protecting migratory birds. According to Connery's account, this tactic "was first suggested by a young solicitor in the State Department to a Justice of the Supreme Court who in turn discussed it with the President."[14] If that account is true, it reveals a relationship between the Executive Branch and the Supreme Court quite unlike what we regard as appropriate today.

Whether the underpinning of an international treaty would ensure the constitutionality of federal legislation was soon addressed. In 1918, Congress passed the Migratory Bird Treaty Act to implement the treaty.

That act prohibited the taking of migratory birds except in accordance with regulations of the secretary of agriculture (then) or the secretary of interior (now). Several challenges immediately followed, including one in which the state of Missouri sued a US game warden, Ray Holland, to restrain him from enforcing the new law.

Holland was no ordinary game warden. Even before the case that bears his name, he had been a prolific writer on conservation topics, often writing under the pen name "Bob White." He would go on to serve as editor of *Field & Stream* magazine in the 1920s and 1930s. Active in the nascent conservation movement in the early twentieth century, Holland had been vigilant in his enforcement of the new law. In fact, the case grew out of his arrest of several prominent citizens at a Missouri hunting club, among them Frank McAllister, the attorney general of the state of Missouri, and the Democratic committeeman from Missouri. No sooner had Holland arrested McAllister and taken his unlawfully killed ducks than McAllister had Holland arrested for possessing ducks without a state license. Those charges were not pursued, but the state did bring suit to enjoin Holland from enforcing the new law.

That case reached the Supreme Court and resulted in a decision that every law student reads in his or her constitutional law class for its holding that the Constitution's treaty-making power was itself a valid and independent basis for Congress to enact legislation that effectuated a treaty. Oliver Wendell Holmes, joined by six other justices, including Louis Brandeis and even Chief Justice Edward White, who had written the Court's *Geer* decision a quarter century earlier, upheld the law in the landmark decision *Missouri v. Holland*.[15] The state's argument, in essence, was that its ownership of wildlife within its borders and the Tenth Amendment to the Constitution gave it exclusive authority to regulate the taking of that wildlife. Holmes forcefully rejected that claim in the following way:

> To put the claim of the State upon title is to lean upon a slender reed. Wild birds are not in the possession of anyone, and possession is the beginning of ownership....
>
> ... But for the treaty and the statute there might soon be no birds for any powers to deal with. We see nothing in the Constitution that compels the Government to sit by while a food supply is cut off and the protectors of our forests and crops are destroyed. It is not sufficient to rely upon the states. The reliance is vain.[16]

Ironically, while the constitutionality of the Migratory Bird Treaty Act was upheld only two years after its enactment, the scope of that law remains uncertain a century later. Specifically, courts have split concerning whether it is a statute that narrowly regulates only hunting and similar activities that are purposefully intended to take migratory birds or that applies broadly to the taking of migratory birds by any means or in any manner, whether intended or not. Reversing decades of federal policy to interpret the law broadly, the Interior Department in the Donald Trump administration has embraced the narrow view that the Treaty Act applies only to hunting and similar activities purposely intended to take migratory birds.

Although the Migratory Bird Treaty Act vested the authority to regulate the taking of migratory birds in the federal government, for many years the states continued to hold considerable sway over setting bag limits. Efforts to persuade the Bureau of Biological Survey or the Congress through new legislation to reduce bag limits fractured the nascent conservation movement in the first decade after the act's passage. Surprising to today's reader is the fact that the National Association of Audubon Societies opposed early proposals to limit hunters to no more than fifteen ducks per day. The association issued a bulletin that concluded: "Each sportsman must decide this for himself. A majority in any state may, if they think it wise, attempt state regulation in this ethical field. THE FEDERAL GOVERNMENT, NEVER."[17]

This was too much for the determined conservationist William Hornaday, who as director of the Bronx Zoo had been instrumental in saving the American bison from extinction. With reference to the Association of Audubon Societies, he wrote of his desire to help "that unfortunate organization . . . march out of the pestilential swamp in which it had been floundering for seven years, put its past behind it, and once more stand on solid ground."[18] Hornaday's rhetorical excesses aside, the perception that the Bureau of Biological Survey had not been particularly ambitious in its conservation efforts was widely shared.

Connery, whose tone was as mild as Hornaday's was intemperate, put it this way: "One cannot but be impressed with the fact that during most of its history, the Survey has not been particularly aggressive in undertaking wild life conservation measures. The initiative for new developments seems to have come mainly from outside groups." Ever the optimist, however, Connery held out hope for a brighter future: "Fortunately, in recent years with the development of a consensus of opinion that the chief function of the Survey is to act as guardian of the wild-life resources of the nation, more progressive and forward-looking policies can be expected."[19] The reader can judge whether Connery's optimism has been borne out.

Conservation during the Great Depression

Although the nation was still recovering from the Great Depression, Connery wrote during a notably active period of wildlife legislative initiatives. These included the Fish and Wildlife Coordination Act of 1934, which was a response to the building of big dams that were having a devastating impact on anadromous fish and other wildlife. It heralded an effort to minimize and compensate for those impacts and required that wildlife be given equal consideration with economic and other considerations in the planning of major water resource developments. In that same year, Congress enacted the Migratory Bird Hunting and Conservation Stamp Act, also known as the Duck Stamp Act. Requiring waterfowl hunters to purchase a federal stamp annually authorizing them to hunt birds provided a reliable source of revenue to establish a system of national wildlife refuges that initially focused on the needs of waterfowl but that over time came to include refuges for many endangered species and other wildlife.

In 1935, the Lacey Act was broadened to include foreign commerce. The law now prohibited not only interstate but also international shipment of wildlife taken in violation of state law. In 1936, a migratory bird treaty was concluded with Mexico, patterned on the earlier treaty with Canada. Its ratification laid the foundation for effective bird conservation throughout North America. In 1937, Congress passed the Federal Aid in Wildlife Restoration Act. Known more commonly as the Pittman-Robertson Act, it dedicated the federal excise tax on arms and ammunition to the states in support of state wildlife conservation programs. It set the stage for the later Dingell-Johnson Act, which similarly dedicated the federal excise tax on fishing gear to the states in support of their fish conservation programs. Finally, the Bald Eagle Protection Act became law in 1940. It sought to protect the bald eagle, the symbol of the nation, and represented the first significant new federal wildlife regulatory law since the Migratory Bird Treaty Act more than two decades earlier.

Federal Wildlife Legislation amid an Environmental Awakening

The body of federal wildlife law remained relatively fixed for the next quarter century after enactment of the Bald Eagle Protection Act. Then, spurred on in part by publication in 1962 of Rachel Carson's influential book *Silent Spring*, there was a sudden burst of environmental legislation that stretched from the mid-1960s to the mid-1970s. These new environmental laws would include some that were focused specifically on wildlife and others that had broader purposes. They included three different endangered species laws in 1966, 1969, and 1973; the National Environmental Policy Act in 1969, which required all federal agencies to consider the environmental impacts of their major actions; and congressional approval in 1970—just months after celebration of the first Earth Day—of a Richard Nixon administration plan to reorganize the federal government and create the Environmental Protection Agency. The modern framework for controlling air and water pollution was established with enactment of the Clean Air Act in 1970 and the Federal Water Pollution Control Act Amendments (otherwise known as the Clean Water Act) in 1972.

The federal wildlife legislation enacted during this period also included the Wild Free-Roaming Horses and Burros Act of 1971 and the Marine Mammal Protection Act of 1972. The following year saw the completion of the negotiation in Washington of the Convention on International Trade in Endangered Species of Wild Fauna and Flora (CITES), which sought to regulate the international commerce in rare species of plants and animals. The Endangered Species Act of 1973 not only implemented CITES trade controls in the United States but also went several steps beyond by establishing a comprehensive program to conserve rare species and their habitats. In 1976, the Fisheries Conservation and Management Act capped a decade of legislative activism by ushering in a new era of federal management of marine resources in an extensive exclusive economic zone. Taken together, these several wildlife enactments represented a bold assertion of federal authority in an area that had traditionally been a responsibility of the states.

Recall that at this point *Missouri v. Holland* was more than a half century old and still stood as the Supreme Court's clearest endorsement of constitutional authority—in that case lodged in the treaty power—for federal legislation protecting wildlife. The even older decision of *Geer v. Connecticut*, premised on the proposition that the states owned the wildlife within their borders, had never been revisited and was thus still good law, although the court had increasingly distanced itself from that underlying proposition.

The doctrine of state ownership of wildlife and the federal government's extensive ownership of public lands were inevitably to collide. The first collision occurred in 1928, just eight years after *Missouri v. Holland*, in regard to the Kaibab National Forest in Arizona. In the view of the secretary of agriculture, there were too many deer in the forest, and their overabundance was damaging the trees and other forest resources. Accordingly, he ordered a thinning of the herd. The state responded by arresting those who were carrying out the secretary's order because they were acting in violation of state law. The United States sued to enjoin the state's enforcement efforts. The secretary's action, it argued, was grounded in the Constitution's property clause, which gives Congress "Power to dispose of and make all needful Rules and Regulations respecting the Territory or other Property belonging to the United States." The Supreme Court, in *Hunt v. United States*,[20] ruled that "the power of the United States to thus protect its lands and property does not admit of doubt . . . the game laws or any other statute of the state . . . notwithstanding." Although that reasoning seemed incompatible with the notion of state ownership of wildlife, the court never mentioned the *Geer* decision.

The statute that prompted the next collision was the Wild Free-Roaming Horses and Burros Act (Wild Horses and Burros Act). Shortly after its enactment, the Supreme Court had occasion once again to revisit the scope of federal authority under the property clause. The act proclaimed all unbranded and unclaimed horses and burros on the public lands of the United States to be "an integral part of the natural system of public lands" and directed the secretaries of agriculture and interior to protect and manage them "as components of the public lands."[21] To many of the western states, including New Mexico, they were essentially pests that consumed forage that was better put to use feeding livestock. Accordingly, when New Mexico captured and sold some of the federally protected burros and the federal government demanded their return, the stage was set for another constitutional battle between state and federal governments.

The state won the first round of that battle. It persuaded a three-judge district court that Congress had exceeded its authority under the property clause. The Supreme Court's 1928 decision in *Hunt v. United States* was distinguished on the basis that in that earlier case the secretary of agriculture had acted to protect against a threat to the land itself. Here, instead, the federal government was acting not to protect its land but the animals on that land. In doing so, it had exceeded its constitutional authority. The Supreme Court, in the 1976 case *Kleppe v. New Mexico,*[22] unanimously reversed. While declining to state the outer limits of the authority conferred by the property clause, the court held that it "necessarily includes the power to regulate and protect the wildlife living there."

At this point someone may be moved to object that wild horses and burros are not wildlife at all. They are instead feral animals, descended from domesticated stock and now living in the wild. While that is correct, the Supreme Court made no such distinction and couched its holding in terms of the federal government's authority over wildlife. Thus, the decision affirmed a second source of authority for federal wildlife legislation.

Endangered Species Legislation

As noted previously, Congress enacted three versions of endangered species legislation in 1966, 1969, and 1973. This section takes a closer look at how that came about. For many years before enactment of the first of these, and without much notice or fanfare, the Interior Department had been slowly but steadily building a portfolio of projects to address the growing risk of extinction for many species. Despite the lack of any specific statutory authority to seek to conserve endangered species, the Department of the Interior's Bureau of Sport Fisheries and Wildlife, which had been created by executive reorganization in 1939, began modest research and conservation projects directed at a few seriously imperiled species. Preventing the extinction of the whooping crane was one of the first projects. Another early object of concern was the nene, or Hawaiian goose, for which Congress passed a 1958 law authorizing the secretary of the interior to carry out a program of research, propagation, and management.

Eventually, these disparate projects coalesced around a more formal effort to understand the gravity of the extinction threat. In 1964, within the Bureau of Sport Fisheries and Wildlife, the Committee on Rare and Endangered Wildlife Species was established. One of its first products was a preliminary list of rare and endangered vertebrates, informally referred to as the "Redbook." The sixty-three species it identified represented the first unofficial list of endangered species in the United States.

Contemporaneous with these developments in the United States, a parallel effort was playing out in the international arena. The International Union for the Conservation of Nature, an amalgam of governmental and nongovernmental conservation entities, began to promote the idea of a global treaty to protect endangered species in the early 1960s. The impetus for its efforts was not unlike that which had spurred Congress to action in 1900. The extinction of many of the world's great whales, which Melville had thought inconceivable, was now perceived to be a real possibility. Similarly vulnerable were many of the world's spotted cats and other familiar species under siege from overexploitation and loss of habitat. The international effort would eventually bear fruit in 1973 with the negotiation of CITES, discussed in more detail later.

In the United States, Congress passed its seminal endangered species law in 1966. A catalyst for the law was the fact that Congress had balked at appropriating funds for the nascent endangered species effort initiated by Interior's Committee on Rare and Endangered Wildlife Species. Before it would appropriate significant funds, Congress wanted to make sure that the Interior Department had the necessary authority to initiate such a program. The 1966 Endangered Species Preservation Act was the result.

The 1966 act was a very modest first step into the endangered species arena. It directed the secretary of the interior to "carry out a program in the United States of conserving, protecting, restoring and propagating selected species of native fish and wildlife that are threatened with extinction,"[23] but the contents of that program were largely unspecified. The law authorized the secretary to utilize the then-new Land and Water

Conservation Fund to acquire land for the program and directed him to promulgate a list of native endangered species. Significantly, however, it imposed no prohibitions or restrictions with respect to the hunting or selling of such species or the destruction of their habitats. On March 11, 1967, the secretary published the first official list of endangered species. It totaled seventy-eight.

The 1966 act focused exclusively on species native to the United States and, implicitly at least, solely on vertebrates. The extinction threat, however, knew no national or taxonomic boundaries; for many of the world's most imperiled species, the American marketplace was the engine driving their overexploitation elsewhere. Recognizing these facts, Congress significantly expanded the federal endangered species program by enacting the Endangered Species Conservation Act of 1969. It authorized the secretary of the interior to promulgate a list of species—US or foreign—that were "threatened with worldwide extinction."[24] These species could include not only vertebrates but also mollusks and crustaceans. Importantly, for the first time ever, the 1969 law imposed a clear regulatory prohibition: no endangered species could be imported into the United States except for a limited set of special purposes. Among the first species added to the expanded list were eight of the great whales.

The 1969 law also directed the secretary to "seek the convening of an international ministerial meeting" to conclude "a binding international convention on the conservation of endangered species."[25] That meeting was hosted by the United States in early 1973. From it came a global treaty to regulate international trade in endangered species, including both plants and animals. In the United States, the treaty is known by its formal name, the Convention on International Trade in Endangered Species of Wild Fauna and Flora, or CITES. In much of the rest of the world, it is known simply as "the Washington Convention."

The international meeting that produced CITES gave added impetus to US efforts to revise the endangered species law that had been enacted only four years earlier. To conservationists and to the President's Council on Environmental Quality, which was a very influential voice in the Nixon administration, the 1969 law had a number of serious deficiencies. It encompassed neither plants nor most invertebrates. It did nothing to restrict the "taking" of endangered species. It imposed no real constraints on federal land managers or other federal agencies. It lacked the flexibility to distinguish among populations of a species, some of which might be in serious peril. Finally, beyond land acquisition authority, it had no mechanism to recognize or protect habitats of special significance to endangered species. Congressman John Dingell, a sportsman and wildlife enthusiast, used his subcommittee chairmanship in the House to push a bill remedying these shortcomings.

In hindsight, it is ironic that the provisions of the law enacted late in 1973 that have given rise to so much recent controversy sparked little debate at the time. Instead, one of the most contentious issues was the familiar debate over the relative roles to be given state and federal agencies. Among those who argued most steadfastly for state primacy was the National Wildlife Federation. At hearings it argued that states should "continue to exercise the prime responsibility for managing" endangered species and should "be given an appropriate opportunity to prepare and manage recovery plans, and retain jurisdiction over endangered species."[26] Congress instead chose to give the federal government primary responsibility for endangered species, while encouraging the states to develop parallel conservation programs of their own.

Both the House and Senate gave nearly unanimous approval to the Endangered Species Act of 1973. How much attention the Nixon White House, then engulfed in Watergate and other scandals, gave to the legislation can only be surmised. Just two months before the act reached the president's desk, Vice President Spiro Agnew had resigned, Nixon had prompted an uproar by firing Watergate special prosecutor Archibald Cox, and the House Judiciary Committee had begun impeachment hearings.

Despite those serious distractions, President Nixon offered a brief but eloquent statement when signing the bill into law. "Nothing is more priceless and more worthy of preservation," Nixon noted, "than the rich array of animal life with which our country has been blessed. It is a many-faceted treasure, of value to scholars, scientists, and nature lovers alike, and it forms a vital part of the heritage we all share as Americans." Referring to the "countless future generations" for which that heritage is held in trust, Nixon concluded that "their lives will be richer, and America will be more beautiful in the years ahead, thanks to the measure that I have the pleasure to sign into law today."[27]

Demise of the State Ownership Doctrine

We must return once more to the state ownership doctrine and the 1896 case that gave birth to it, *Geer v. Connecticut*. In a series of subsequent cases, the Supreme Court chipped away at the doctrine, most notably in the *Missouri v. Holland* and *Kleppe v. New Mexico* cases. Despite the steady erosion of the state ownership doctrine, *Geer* itself proved remarkably durable. In 1979, however, the Supreme Court was faced with a case, *Hughes v. Oklahoma*,[28] that presented facts quite similar to those that had been presented in *Geer*. At issue was an Oklahoma law prohibiting the shipment to other states, for purposes of sale, of minnows procured from the state's waters. The Supreme Court acknowledged "that time has revealed the error" of the *Geer* decision. Though states had a legitimate conservation interest in the wildlife within their borders, that interest was fundamentally no different from their interest in other natural resources, so a state could not further its interest by burdening interstate commerce to the degree that Oklahoma (and Connecticut) had done. Thus, the Supreme Court overruled *Geer* nearly a century later.

The demise of *Geer* and of the state ownership doctrine is of little practical consequence. For all the attention it got, the state ownership doctrine was never a serious legal impediment to the exercise of federal authority to conserve wildlife. But to acknowledge that the federal government has the legal authority to act to conserve wildlife is not to say that it should act, much less how it should act. In 1935, Robert Connery wrote that "conservation implies a balance between present use and future use" and that the "greatest problem" facing the conservation agencies of his day was "the adoption of such policies as will achieve this balance."[29] More than eighty years later, that remains the greatest challenge facing conservation program administrators. Many of the chapters that follow examine how well that challenge is being met, particularly with respect to endangered species.

3

Biodiversity and Why It Matters

On the first day of spring in 2019 I left home for an appointment in downtown Washington, DC. I said good-bye to Sandy, my wife of nearly fifty years, who was still in bed battling an apparent respiratory illness that had dogged her for more than a week. It would soon turn out to be something far worse. Returning home later that afternoon, I found the house ominously quiet and dark. She must be sleeping, I assumed. For a moment, I thought I would not disturb her but then decided to look in on her. When I did, I found her shaking uncontrollably, with a soaring fever and unresponsive to my questions. There followed a harrowing ambulance ride to the hospital and a week in the intensive-care unit during most of which she could breathe only with the aid of a ventilator.

Sandy had several pulmonary embolisms—blood clots in her lungs— as well as pneumonia and a life-threatening, out-of-control immune system response to infection known as sepsis. The blood clots were a particular mystery, since she had been on blood thinner medication for more than a year. Once her condition had been stabilized, it became vitally important to try to determine why she had continued to generate clots despite taking medication that almost always prevents them. To answer that question, and thus to reduce the risk of a recurrence of her illness, would require the help of a snake—a venomous snake.

Russell's viper is a highly poisonous snake native to the Indian subcontinent and Southeast Asia. Its venom affects the clotting ability of the blood of those who are bitten by it. Where it occurs, it is responsible for more deaths than virtually any other snake. Yet the very properties of its venom that make its bite so deadly can help save the lives of those, like Sandy, who experience blood clots.

To help diagnose Sandy's problem required a test called the "dilute Russell's viper venom time" test, or simply DRVVT. As its name suggests, it utilizes the venom of the Russell's viper to assess the clotting characteristics of a patient's blood. For decades, I had written about the value of the natural world as a source of medicines and potential new cures for all manner of diseases, a pharmacopeia of nearly limitless value. Yet, I must confess, that argument always seemed somewhat abstract and academic, a bit repetitive with the same examples offered in each retelling. It no longer does. Sandy's experience made that argument personal for me. That she is alive today, that we were able to celebrate our fiftieth wedding anniversary, is due—at least in part—to a venomous snake found only in southern Asia, due, that is, to the wonders of biodiversity.

The Tangled Bank and the Tapestry of Life

Russell's viper is part of what Charles Darwin called the "tangled bank" of life. In the final paragraph of his monumental work, *On the Origin of Species*, Darwin observed that "it is interesting to contemplate a tangled bank, clothed with many plants of many kinds, with birds singing on the bushes, with various insects flitting about, and with worms crawling through the damp earth, and to reflect that these elaborately constructed forms, so different from each other, and dependent upon each other in so complex a manner, have all been produced by laws acting around us."[1] The tangled bank of which Darwin wrote now goes by the name "biological diversity," or simply "biodiversity." Darwin's metaphor obliges us to focus simultaneously on both the individual components of the bank—the birds, the insects, the worms, and the plants—and their interdependencies. If we are to conserve the individual components, we must conserve the tangled bank itself.

I have always liked Darwin's metaphor of the tangled bank, but there is another that may be even better. An alternative metaphor with which to illustrate the interdependence—and the vulnerability—of life-forms might be an old tapestry, a prized family heirloom passed down from generation to generation. In the tapestry of life, each species is a thread. Each thread gives meaning to—and takes meaning from—the threads about it. The loss of any individual thread does not lead inexorably to the destruction of the entire tapestry. However, the fraying of individual threads diminishes the tapestry's luster and value. It puts added strain on other threads and increases the risk that they too will fray or snap. Unless we carefully maintain it, the tapestry that we pass on to the next generation will have degraded, diminishing both its utilitarian and its aesthetic value.

Darwin recognized, of course, that the existence of any given life-form was the result of a dynamic process. Over the long course of geologic history, many life-forms had disappeared and been replaced by others better suited to survive and reproduce in a changing environment. The extinction of species, therefore, was neither a new nor an unexpected result. If biodiversity is a tapestry, it is one in which the forces of natural selection are constantly at work, slowly removing weakened threads and replacing them with slightly different, but stronger threads.

The Novelty of Extinctions Today

If extinction is not new, what is new—at least in human history—is the pace at which it is now occurring. The best guess of scientists is that before 1600, on average, one species of bird or mammal became extinct every century. During the twentieth century approximately one species of bird or mammal became extinct every year. These known extinctions are dwarfed by the presumed loss of even more species—most of them invertebrates in the world's rapidly shrinking rain forests—that have not yet been named and described. In the United States alone there are nearly 450 vertebrates and more than 1,200 invertebrates and plants that are officially listed under the Endangered Species Act as endangered or threatened. Many more are likely to qualify for such listing.

There is something else new about the extinctions occurring today—their cause. In the earth's history there have been several spasms of widespread extinction, but each of these was the result of major geophysical or even extraterrestrial events, such as the collision with the earth of an asteroid that brought about the end of the age of dinosaurs. Never before has there been a worldwide spasm of extinctions caused by a single species—never, that is, until now, and the species that is causing those extinctions is our own.

As wetlands have been drained, grasslands plowed, rivers dammed, and forests felled, the countless plants and animals uniquely adapted to life in those habitats have been lost. The tapestry of life has been badly damaged by these losses, but still one may ask, So what? Those former wetlands, grasslands, and forests are now productive farms and thriving cities. The once free-flowing rivers have been transformed into avenues of commerce and sources of energy. Those too are part of the inheritance we bequeath to our descendants, and their value is readily recognized.

The value of biodiversity is harder to express and quantify. It is relatively easy to identify what has been gained by transforming natural habitats into farms and cities but much harder to determine what it has cost. The argument that any particular species may hold within it a cure for cancer seems abstract and speculative, notwithstanding the fact that many life-saving medicines have their origins in nature. So too the argument that the loss of any one species will set in motion a cascading series of ecological changes with negative consequences for human welfare. Is the world any worse off for the loss of the dodo some more than three centuries ago—the first documented extinction at the hands of humans? The surprising answer is that it may be.

Extinction of the Dodo: Did It Matter?

Some years ago Stanley Temple, an ornithologist who had for many years studied the birdlife of Mauritius, observed that one of the tree species on the island was nearly gone. There remained just a handful of living specimens of a once common, commercially valuable tree. Temple believed that those few remaining specimens were at least three hundred years old. He thought that was odd, given the timing of the disappearance of the dodo.

Temple attempted to germinate seeds of the tambalacoque tree (*Calvaria major*) and was unsuccessful until he tried the unlikely technique of force-feeding the seeds to turkeys. When the seeds were abraded by the stones in the turkey's gullet and excreted, they were able to germinate. Based on that evidence, he concluded that the dodo may have been essential for the tree's ability to reproduce. The dodo, he reasoned, ate the fruit and passed the seeds through its digestive system, thus preparing them for germination. It took more than three hundred years from the time of the dodo's extinction to make the connection with the subsequent near disappearance of a tree that had been a significant commercial resource. The disappearance of the forest in which the trees were once prevalent may have brought about still other ecological consequences. If Temple's hypothesis was correct, then the extinction of the dodo represented more than just the loss of a single thread from the tapestry of life. It led to the weakening or loss of other—possibly many other—threads as well.

The proposition that the extirpation of a species can have dramatic, cascading, and long-lasting ecological consequences seems certain to be true. That the disappearance of the dodo had such effects, however, is not so certain. Shortly after Stanley Temple published his paper linking the loss of the dodo to the decline of the island's calvaria forests, critics questioned both his methods and his conclusions. Temple eventually acknowledged that he had not proven the hypothesized relationship but maintained that it was still a plausible explanation for the island's ecological changes.

The Tropical Rain Forest: Crucible of Biodiversity

The crisis of biodiversity loss is most acute in the tropics, particularly in the remaining tropical rain forests, for it is there that most of the planet's biodiversity lives. When those forests are threatened, as by the fires that raged throughout the Amazon rain forest in Brazil in 2019, more is at stake than the fate of trees. The loss of tropical rain forests threatens not only to exacerbate the warming of the planet but also to diminish its biological riches. Those riches have been discussed by many authors, but seldom as convincingly or as entertainingly as by Adrian Forsyth and Ken Miyata in their 1985 book *Tropical Nature*. Here is my review of their exceptional work.

A Review of *Tropical Nature: Life and Death in the Rain Forests of Central and South America*, by Adrian Forsyth and Ken Miyata
Smithsonian, January 1985[*]

A few years ago, at a Congressional committee meeting, a Congressman from the Pacific Northwest scoffed at a witness's alarm over the deforestation of the tropics. Why isn't the solution, he asked, simply to replant the areas cut, just as the timber companies in his home state do? If Ken Miyata and Adrian Forsyth's book, *Tropical Nature*, had been available then, it surely would have been much easier to make the good Congressman appreciate the unique nature of tropical rain forests.

An informed appreciation of nature is a rare quality today. To some, nature, and especially nature in the lowland tropical forests of Central and South America that this book describes, is filled with unseen dangers and dark foreboding, or at best with vexatious and bothersome creatures better avoided. Others seem unable to see nature without imputing to it human qualities and judgments. Still others view nature as evidence of the miraculous hand of a supernatural Creator.

To these young authors, tropical nature is, indeed, nearly miraculous and sometimes dangerous, but above all else an endless source of fascination and intellectual challenge. Written by two biologists about the richest biological treasure on Earth, this book need not deter nonscientists, for it is to them that it is directed. Indeed, it invites an appreciation of biology as few other books do, and does so with extraordinary grace and humor.

The workings of a biological system as intricate and complex as a tropical rain forest can hardly be described in a book this brief, yet in a series of short chapters the authors capture the essence of many principles that govern life in the tropics. They start, literally, on the ground floor, explaining why rain forest soils, despite the extraordinary lush vegetation they seem to support, generally are unable to sustain silviculture or agriculture once the native forests are cut down. The reason, it seems, is that in the rain forest nutrients rarely accumulate in the soil, but instead are locked up in the living vegetation of the forest itself. When the vegetation is cleared, the soil that remains is nutrient poor, easily eroded, and often capable of "baking" hard like a clay pot.

From the forest floor we quickly climb to the canopy above, witnessing along the way one of the most extraordinary and, for this reviewer, least expected, struggles for survival. This struggle pits the forest's trees against the myriad of tropical vines and woody lianas that use the trees' structural support for access to that most precious rain forest commodity, sunlight. Each competitor utilizes a rich array of devices to reward itself and frustrate the other. For those accustomed to thinking of the struggle for survival as one principally pitting animal predators against their animal prey, this chapter will open a whole new world.

Animals get their share of attention. Not all are ones we think of as tropical. A chapter on migratory birds argues that many of "our" local songbirds are in fact tropical birds that migrate to take advantage of the bounteous insect food supply of temperate summers. When their winter habitats in the tropics have been felled, silence will mark our spring.

Other creatures may be less appealing. A chapter entitled "Jerry's Maggot" focuses on a large bot fly whose larval "maggot" stage develops within the flesh of Jerry, a remarkably tolerant graduate student. This large and noisy fly has devised a remarkable way of getting her offspring to their unsuspecting hosts by way of mosquitoes. How such a strategy for survival could have evolved through the pressures of natural selection is one of the mysteries this book seeks to unlock.

Two tragedies mark the book. The first is that one of its authors, Ken Miyata, drowned in the rapids of the Bighorn River before the book was published. The other is that the tropical forests about which he and Adrian Forsyth have written are themselves in mortal danger. The deforestation of the tropical rain forests has accelerated dramatically in the past two decades as new technology and expanding population press the forest frontier ever inward (Smithsonian Horizons, December 1984). Except in its final chapter, this book is not about the impending death of the rain forests. It is instead about their remarkable life. In telling that story so evocatively and entertainingly the authors are likely to enlist many in the effort to save this great resource.

International Cooperation for Biodiversity Conservation: The Decline of US Leadership

In 1972, the United States took the lead in hosting and promoting an international treaty to protect rare plants and animals from the effects of commercial trade. It was the first nation to ratify that treaty, known as CITES. Although unconstrained trade is a serious threat to many species, the biggest threat by far to biodiversity throughout the world is the destruction of habitat. Thus, it soon became apparent that CITES alone would do little to stem the loss of the world's biodiversity. More was needed.

The international community's response took the form of another treaty, the Convention on Biological Diversity, which was concluded in 1992. The ambition of this treaty was not only to stem the loss of habitat but also to secure a more equitable sharing among nations of the benefits of genetic resources, in the belief that nations in which biological resources such as the Russell's viper are found ought to share at least some of the financial benefit of the commercial uses of those resources. Unlike two decades earlier, however, when the United States led the world in embracing CITES, it hesitated to embrace the Convention on Biological Diversity.

The following op-ed urged that the United States resume its leadership on biodiversity conservation by ratifying the Biodiversity Convention. It was paired with an opposing opinion piece by the editorial board of *USA Today*. In the end, the opposing arguments prevailed. Today, 195 nations are parties to the convention. The United States is virtually alone in not having ratified this treaty.

USA Should Sign Treaty
USA Today, June 9, 1992*

Twenty years ago, the USA hosted the meeting that produced the Convention on International Trade in Endangered Species. We were first among 115 nations ratifying the treaty known here as CITES and elsewhere as "the Washington Convention" in recognition of its birthplace and America's leadership role in creating it.

CITES was the first global effort to protect shrinking biological diversity. Alone, however, CITES' trade controls do little to protect the planet's species. For most of the world's imperiled wildlife, the overwhelming threat is not trade but habitat loss. CITES can't halt the conversion of forest into pastures, wetlands into shopping centers or coastal dunes into resorts.

Recognition of the limitations of CITES prompted efforts at a broader agreement addressing the root causes of biodiversity loss. US leadership of two decades ago, however, has vanished. Our government won't join the new biodiversity treaty. It's too vague, the administration says, and objectionable because of how it seeks to share the economic benefits the developed world derives from exploiting biodiversity with the developing countries that harbor much of that diversity. The USA has advanced no alternative financing mechanism that it would support.

The retreat from world leadership in protecting biodiversity follows close on the heels of plans to weaken our own primary safety net for biodiversity, the Endangered Species Act. The USA should reconsider. Vanishing biodiversity is an urgent environmental problem because it is irreversible. Species lost today cannot be re-created tomorrow. With them disappear treasures of potential medicines, chemicals and knowledge to enrich human life in the future. On such vital matters, the USA should not be a nit-picking naysayer but a leader.

4

Rachel Carson, the Recognition of Pervasive Threats to Biodiversity, and the Birth of the Modern Environmental Movement

On a beautiful spring day in 1967, in a wooded area on the campus of Iowa State University, I was collecting insects for an introductory entomology course. I don't remember any of the insects I collected that day, but more than half a century later I can still vividly recall a bird I encountered on that outing. It was a robin, a common bird behaving in a most uncommon manner. Unable to fly, it struggled to retreat on foot as I approached. Like a person with a bad case of the chills, it trembled uncontrollably. I would have had no idea about the source of its affliction were it not for a book written five years earlier by a Fish and Wildlife Service biologist named Rachel Carson. Carson's book, *Silent Spring*, had sounded the alarm about the perils of many pesticides, especially a synthetic organic compound known as DDT. The robin before me, I thought, was likely experiencing the effects of pesticide poisoning. The experience of seeing this helpless bird left a lasting impression on me.

Although I was unaware of it at the time, halfway across the country, on New York's Long Island, a group of scientists and naturalists founded the Environmental Defense Fund (EDF) in that same year, 1967. Alarmed by the decline of ospreys and other birds, which they believed to be the consequence of DDT use, their purpose was to bring about an end to the widespread application of this ubiquitous pesticide. Against long odds, they succeeded five years later in persuading the Environmental Protection Agency to cancel most authorized uses of DDT. It was, and remains, one of the most important and consequential victories of the environmental movement, a victory that made possible the dramatic rebounding of ospreys, brown pelicans, peregrine falcons, and the nation's symbol, the bald eagle. It was, however, a victory that Rachel Carson did not live to see, for she had died in 1964, only two years after the clarion call of *Silent Spring*.

I spent thirty-one years of my career at EDF as the leader of its wildlife conservation efforts. In 1987, to celebrate the twenty-fifth anniversary of the publication of *Silent Spring*, EDF offered its members a special anniversary edition of the book, accompanied by an essay that Ellen Silbergeld and I jointly wrote. Ellen, whose research on lead poisoning in children would lead to her winning a MacArthur Foundation "genius" award, was then the head of EDF's Toxic Chemicals Program. She went on to become a distinguished professor at Johns Hopkins University, where she has focused much of her research on the public health impacts of industrial food-animal production, including studies of zoonotic pathogens such as Covid-19. Our essay follows.

Reflections on *Silent Spring*: An Anniversary Tribute to Rachel Carson and Her Work

–Michael J. Bean and Ellen K. Silbergeld[*]

In the still air above Washington a majestic bird wheels and glides, watching for a telltale flash of silver below. Hurtling downward, talons extended, an eagle plucks a struggling fish from the surface of the Potomac River. Within sight of the marble monument where the Great Emancipator sits, this minor drama of nature plays itself out daily, just as it did a century earlier and for millennia before that. Yet only a quarter of a century ago, the eagle's survival was very much in doubt. Ravaged by DDT, its nests were nearly empty and its numbers were falling dramatically.

Today the American bald eagle, symbol of the nation, has itself been emancipated from a tyranny. Its emancipator was not a president, like Lincoln, with a national army at his command. Instead, the unlikely hero was a shy female biologist, a civil servant in the bureaucracy of the Interior Department. Her emancipation proclamation was a book, *Silent Spring*; though it did not have the force of a national army behind it, it too revolutionized the world in which we live.

An emancipator without an army, Rachel Carson sounded a call to which an army of ordinary citizens responded. *Silent Spring* drove home the simple message that man does not exist apart from nature

[*] Reprinted with permission of Environmental Defense Fund.

around him, but is himself a part of it. In the poisoning of the world around them, an aroused public saw the poisoning of themselves. This recognition of the inexplicable link between human fate and the fate of other creatures represented the public's first real appreciation of the basic premises of ecology. From that fundamental insight has grown the modern environmental movement, which is now a familiar part of the social and political landscape.

If we were to judge Rachel Carson's achievement only by the wild creatures she helped keep from extinction, *Silent Spring* would be a book without parallel. Though still considered endangered in most of the United States, the bald eagle is clearly on the rebound. So is the peregrine falcon, once completely eliminated from the eastern half of the United States. Residual levels of DDT in the environment have gone down far enough so that reintroducing the peregrine in that part of the country has become possible. In the Southeast the brown pelican has recovered from its close brush with extinction and is steadily expanding its range northward again. The osprey has made a dramatic comeback and is now a familiar sight on Long Island, where it once nearly disappeared, in Chesapeake Bay, and even along the C & O Canal in the nation's capital.

But these are merely lists, and not true understanding. To comprehend the impact of this extraordinary book would require us to be able to stand back from the present, in 1987, and to try to understand what our environment would be like if there had not been the enormous changes in attitude and action that have occurred in the last twenty-five years. The difficulty in doing this is proof of the power of Rachel Carson's ideas, which have turned us so far in a different direction from the one in which we were headed. Perhaps another way to appreciate this anniversary is to count the victories that have been won in twenty-five years. We could count the pesticides and chemicals banned and restricted, or list the statutes and regulations passed and enforced, or even count the citations to Carson's writings in our literature, to try to demonstrate how deeply embedded in our culture her ideas have become. But, in fact, it is practically impossible to think of the world in any other way than the way Rachel Carson taught us: as a unified system of biological interdependence in which we humans have no overriding right of exploitation and no freedom to ignore the duty of respectful stewardship.

One hundred years ago—taking the first synthesis of benzenoid chemicals as a convenient benchmark—we naively thought we were entering a brave, new, man-made world, armed with newly synthesized chemical tools and ready to extract the world's vast supplies of natural resources in order to house, feed, clothe, heal, and entertain ourselves for the millennia to come. In that century, as a species, we grew and expanded over the earth. From petrochemicals we invented new substances for housing, clothing, transport, and food; we cured diseases; we fed millions. The potential of nature as a source of exploitation seemed limitless and costless.

But by 1962, the bills were coming due. The century of exploitation had permanently transformed the world and had shown how fragile are the networks of coexistence between us and the rest of the planet. The new world, with all its wonders, was bought at the price of a chemical dependence whose extent is still largely unknown. Change, particularly at the extraordinary pace of the last century, has had a price. It was Rachel Carson's genius to begin the process of accurate accounting: she presented the bills on behalf of the natural world. Clearly she warned that one of the unavoidable costs was likely to be irreversible change in the very structure of the world we were trying to possess.

The modern environmental movement that *Silent Spring* spawned has helped to create a large and uniquely American body of law and regulation, as well as a major new federal agency charged with environmental protection. Putting those laws into action, using Carson's tools of science and advocacy, those of us who follow in her footsteps have been able to create a series of truly appropriate monuments to her work. The history of the Environmental Defense Fund is deeply entwined with the sustained and powerful public response to *Silent Spring*. In 1967, three scientists living on Long Island and a fourth in Michigan, who were as alarmed as Carson by the effects of DDT on the osprey, invented a new way to put science together with law in order to protect endangered creatures. They formed the Environmental Defense Fund and by 1972 its efforts had led to the nationwide banning of DDT: a fitting tribute on the tenth anniversary of *Silent Spring* (though, sadly, one that Rachel Carson did not live to see). By the end of the decade, several other "hard" pesticides—chlordane, dieldrin, aldrin, and heptachlor—were severely restricted in their uses. In 1977, PCBs were banned at the source, no longer allowed to be made anywhere in the United States.

And the natural world has responded. The bald eagle, peregrine falcon, brown pelican, and osprey are still continuing to recover.

These are victories that would have seemed impossible to hope for twenty-five years ago, and they are real. Accomplishing them has taken exactly the kind of effort that Rachel Carson foretold: a concerned and vigilant campaign, sustained over years, to overcome the entrenched opposition of vested interests and inertia of a complaisant bureaucracy, and persuade both of their obligation to act. Carson knew that it would always take a creative collaboration between science and law, and the strength of the people, to protect those without a voice or a vote. It is still a constant struggle, even with the body of environmental law that has been nurtured by the maturing environmental movement over the intervening twenty-five years. But Rachel Carson gave us the most critical ingredients for environmental protection: an informed and passionate public, committed to protection and stewardship of the environment. The instilling of a basic understanding of our place in, and dependence upon, nature is the fundamental legacy of *Silent Spring*. The modern environmental movement, with its network of professional advocates and stewards and its organized groups of citizens, is just one of the tangible products of that legacy.

Like all great works, *Silent Spring* has been misread, abused, and, of course, denounced by those whose particular interests have been most threatened by the growth of an ecological conscience in America. It has not been a happy twenty-five years for those who would keep exploiting the natural world without balancing profit against reason. It has not been an easy time for those who want to ignore the ecological consequences of their actions, to believe that humans should be allowed to alter the ecosystem without limit, and can do so without repercussions on human well-being. So *Silent Spring* has had its detractors and Rachel Carson, posthumously, her enemies. Some attacks were remarkably vitriolic. One singled out Carson as the intellectual source of a "conspiracy" of misguided scientists and social experimentalists, who were plotting to strip humanity of its wondrous chemical weapons in the war to seize wealth and comfort from a hostile nature. These attacks do no more than acknowledge Rachel Carson's importance. They reflect grudging tribute to the success of her ideas, not only in the interior world of people's minds and hearts but in the exterior world of buildings and bulldozers and spray planes as well.

But most of the criticism of *Silent Spring* fundamentally misses the point. Rachel Carson was certainly a scientist, and her scientific works are another substantial legacy. But *Silent Spring* was never meant to be a scientific monograph. Though Rachel Carson spoke from her experience as a scientist, in *Silent Spring* she spoke to all of us, warning us of the consequences of our failure to understand that we live in a series of natural niches that we occupy with the other species of the earth, and that the niches have varying sensitivities to chemical and physical modifications.

She has been accused of "unscientific" exaggeration, of "overstating" the dangers of chemicals such as DDT without admitting their benefits. DDT didn't actually harm birds that much, it is argued, and even if it did, birds have quickly and completely recovered since DDT was banned. Leaving aside its obvious self-contradictions, this argument misses a much more important question: what cost did we bear in learning the lessons of DDT? There is a world of nature that has been lost through our century of chemical and physical atavism; there are complex natural communities that we will never know again. With infinite care and large amounts of money, we substitute elaborate artificial wetlands for the natural ecosystem that development has destroyed. But we must not be misled into thinking that these provisional attempts at restoration and remediation are a return to the world that once was. We are in danger of replacing the natural world with simulacra, theme parks dedicated to the memory of what we have lost. We cannot recover the world before DDT, dieldrin, aldrin, chlordane, heptachlor, and PCBs. Every organism on the planet, even the penguin in the Antarctic wilderness, now comes into the world laden with these chemicals. Every mammal's baby nurses on milk contaminated with them. Indeed, every human egg cell, even before ovulation and fertilization, is bathed in these chemicals because they have penetrated even to the follicular fluid of the human ovary.

Carson's insights into the biological continuum that links us to the rest of the biosphere have been born out more and more strongly over time. Her original warning about the effects of DDT on birds was related to the potential of DDT to damage reproduction. Recent advances in molecular biology have shown us to be bound ever closer to the other organisms on the planet. It is therefore not surprising (and certainly would not have surprised Rachel Carson) to learn that DDT also affects human reproduction, acting like a synthetic estrogen to disrupt normal processes of reproductive physiology. Most recently, DDT has been suspected as a cause of an outbreak of abnormal sexual development in children in Puerto Rico. Thus, although there are fresh problems and fresh environmental controversies that have arisen long after 1962—such as biotechnology, ozone depletion, acid precipitation, carcinogen risk assessment, and hazardous waste—none of them exceeds the scope of concern first delineated in *Silent Spring*.

Where do we now go? To count our victories is to realize how much remains to be done. DDT may be gone from the shelves, but it is still in our bodies. Kelthane, a pesticide contaminated with up to 2 percent DDT, remains for sale. Chlordane is still registered for termite control, even though many thousands of American homes have been contaminated by it. The United States' food supply is still tainted with residues of carcinogenic and toxic pesticides, and imported food brings a "circle of poison" back to us as foreign countries spray their crops with pesticides we sell to them, long after those pesticides have been banned for use in this country. Even with new and more rigorous criteria for evaluating new pesticides, dangerous agents still regularly slip through the net. Although they are less likely to be persistent, and less likely to be nonspecific "wide spectrum" pest killers, they are more likely to be acutely toxic to humans and others. Last year, the EPA allowed the registration of a new herbicide, fluridone, without realizing that its environmental breakdown product was a well-established cause of birth defects. Even more seriously, for most pesticides and chemicals already on the market, there is a staggering void of fundamental information, which makes it impossible for scientists to give any meaningful evaluation of their true impacts on humans and the environment. The chemical treadmill is still turning, and most of American agriculture still trudges upon it, even though biological controls and other nonchemical means of reducing pest damage have been well demonstrated and hold a secure niche in today's battle against pests.

Silent Spring taught us all to look for the connection between our actions and the environmental destruction that can occur as a consequence, often a consequence far removed from the original action. The spirit of scientific inquiry into those connections, fostered by *Silent Spring*, lies at the root of the recent discovery that the way we produce electricity (and other forms of energy) is destroying our lakes and forests through the phenomenon of acid rain just as surely as our former dependence upon DDT and its toxic kin once threatened to hush the songbirds in the springtime. The same spirit of inquiry is today revealing that our dependence on chlorofluorocarbon gases in refrigerators, air conditioners, and even fast-food containers is destroying the protective layer of ozone in the earth's upper atmosphere, and exposing all life on our planet's surface to a dangerous increase in ultraviolet radiation. Those same manmade gases, together with the ever-increasing release of carbon dioxide from the burning of fossil fuels, now threaten radical changes in climate, increasing the temperature of the earth's atmosphere. When the Amazonian rainforest is ravaged for short-term agricultural development, the surface soil, once stripped of vegetation, loses its thin reserves of nutrients, and agriculture quickly fails. In *Silent Spring* Rachel Carson questioned the wisdom of some of the basic premises underlying the methods by which we produce our food. Today, her scientific and spiritual heirs have extended those same questions into other, equally basic aspects of how we live and work.

Much remains to be done. But no longer is it a choice as to whether we should try, or a struggle to find supporters. No one thinks that environmental protection should not be a cornerstone of our actions on the planet; no one can now claim, as a matter of supposed scientific fact, that chemicals are magic bullets or that unwanted species can be killed at will. A coalition of common interests, nowadays even uniting environmentalists and industry in some conspicuous cases, now joins to negotiate the much smaller distance between the different sides, working on how to achieve both the goods necessary for social progress and the protection of the natural world. Recent attempts to overturn the great environmental consensus of the past quarter century, despite the partisan political power behind them, have been abjectly unsuccessful, met by national outrage over the assault on our shared national assumptions.

Today we all take the basic message of *Silent Spring* for granted, because we must. We cannot save ourselves, or better ourselves, apart from saving and bettering the world. Before Rachel Carson wrote this book, society's path was a temptingly downhill road of heedless dominion. She showed us what was over the horizon on that path, and pointed to another: a more daunting uphill path of living with nature in interdependence and responsibility. Science, ethics, and values all direct us to the uphill path. It is impossible to conceive of what our world would look like without *Silent Spring's* influence, and impossible to have done what all of us have done in the last twenty-five years without the spirit of Rachel Carson.

5

Wildlife Refuges

A Legacy of Theodore Roosevelt

Rachel Carson spent many summers on the picturesque rocky coast of Maine. There she found joy and inspiration in the diverse living creatures of the region's tidal pools, salt marshes, and sand dunes. In 1969, five years after her death, the US Fish and Wildlife Service, the agency for which she had worked most of her life, honored her by naming a recently established refuge on that coast for her: the Rachel Carson National Wildlife Refuge. That refuge is part of a nationwide system of lands where the conservation of wildlife is paramount, a system that began more than six decades earlier when another giant figure in conservation history, Theodore Roosevelt, established the nation's first wildlife refuge.

The organization with which I spent more than three decades of my career, the Environmental Defense Fund, has its headquarters in New York City, just a few blocks away from Roosevelt's boyhood home. The home is now managed by the National Park Service as the Theodore Roosevelt Birthplace National Historic Site. Visitors to it, a five-story brownstone, will note that the future president's bedroom faces an urban back alley looking much the same as what the young Teddy awoke to every day.

His window leads to a makeshift gymnasium extending over the alley. His father built the gymnasium so the young TR could overcome his asthma, training like an Olympian to strengthen his chest and lungs. The concrete floor, wire-mesh fence, and dark confines of his gym make an unlikely setting for a boy who would become the greatest appreciator and student of nature to lead the country since Thomas Jefferson.

But when TR's uncle, Robert Roosevelt, took him out of the city and into the duck marshes of nearby Long Island at sunrise or deep into what would become the Adirondack Forest Preserve, an indelible connection was made between a youth and the tapestry of life around him. Young

TR saw that the smallest and the largest things in nature were connected and that he was part of it.

He saw and felt this most clearly in the mammals, birds, and fish living freely in wilderness areas far removed from the sound and hubbub of his Manhattan home. On outings with Uncle Robert he watched in amazement as wildlife followed the ancient rituals of migration and reproduction, and he marveled at nature's grand design, at once so complex and diversified and finely tuned that words can hardly describe it—but he tried, by keeping voluminous journals and collecting specimens of all that he experienced.

As TR matured into a young man, he learned again and again that his appreciation of nature was not universally shared and that many of his contemporaries underestimated how vulnerable and perishable these wild places and creatures were. Perhaps no other individual has grasped the enduring importance of wildlife and wilderness to the American character with more certainty and imagination than Theodore Roosevelt. On March 14, 1903, the president declared a small, unassuming island full of pelicans in Florida's Indian River our first national wildlife refuge.

How did it happen? Because of the Roosevelt family's prominence and TR's extraordinary interest in wildlife and natural history, his social circle included many of the scientists at the American Museum of Natural History in New York City. Among them was Frank Chapman, the museum's curator of birds. When Chapman learned that there was only one significant breeding site for brown pelicans on the East Coast, he asked his friend the president to protect it. Legend has it that Roosevelt asked one of his legal advisers, "Is there any law that will prevent me from declaring Pelican Island a Federal Bird Reservation?" When told there was not, Roosevelt responded, "Very well, then, I so declare it."[1] The legend is probably true, since it is fully consistent with TR's character. Later in his presidency, when Congress passed a law stripping the president of authority to establish forest preserves, TR responded by reserving another sixteen million acres before the law took effect. Eventually, Roosevelt was responsible for establishing not just the first national wildlife refuge but also the first fifty-one national wildlife refuges, as well as five national parks and numerous national forests.

Altogether, Roosevelt was responsible for publicly protecting a total of 232 million acres.

Roosevelt's action in establishing the Pelican Island refuge spawned an idea, unique in the world, that a network of federally protected lands could and should be permanently set aside for wildlife. It was a proclamation on behalf of a nation with an emerging consciousness about the value of things wild and free. And it was a promise to preserve wildlife and habitat both for its own sake and for the benefit of the American people. From its humble start at Pelican Island the National Wildlife Refuge System has emerged.

A Nationwide System of Refuges

Today, the refuge system has grown to more than ninety-three million acres, an area about the size of Montana. It now includes more than five hundred refuges and more than three thousand waterfowl-production areas spread across the fifty states and several US territories, a network so vast and sprawling that the sun, as it makes its daily trek across the North American continent, always seems to be shining on some part of it. And the marvels it holds are truly inspiring to contemplate.

A mother brown bear wades into a fast-running river teeming with Chinook salmon on Alaska's Kodiak Island and, with one deft stroke of her paw, swats a fish onto the bank to feed her cubs. Millions of horseshoe crabs swarm in the moonlight on the tidal shores in Delaware and are followed by another spectacle as tens of thousands of migrating shorebirds stop to refuel on billions of eggs left by the crabs. A diminutive Florida Key deer, now part of a growing herd of four hundred, nudges its tiny spotted fawn into the tepid Gulf waters for its first swimming lesson. These delicate creatures' ability to swim between the islands of the Keys saved them from almost certain extinction during the 1950s after habitat destruction and poachers had reduced their total number to fewer than fifty.

Several million ducks and geese—an astonishing concentration of waterfowl—rise en masse to darken the sky above Klamath Basin on the border of California and Oregon. They share the same airspace with more than five hundred bald eagles and majestic Mount Shasta. A Comanche skimmer dragonfly darts from its perch on a shoreline reed across the still waters to snatch a flying insect on the wing, then returns to the very same spot, the sun glistening off its bicolored stigmas in the midday heat at New Mexico's Bitter Lake National Wildlife Refuge.

The network of strategically located lands that makes up the National Wildlife Refuge System protects nearly three hundred endangered species, safeguards breeding and resting places for millions of migratory birds, and conserves premier fisheries and coastal refuges for marine mammals. Many of the refuges are being used effectively to rescue and recover species from extinction. River otters, whooping cranes, elk, wild turkeys, alligators, wood ducks, and pronghorn antelope—all once much reduced in numbers—are thriving today thanks in part to the refuge system, the Fish and Wildlife Service employees who manage it, and the system's energetic support structure of two hundred community partnerships and more than thirty thousand volunteers. And it is a system that perpetuates a stunning array of the nation's ecosystems: tundra, desert, forest, great rivers, marshes, mountains, prairies, estuaries, and coral reefs are all represented under its canopy of protection.

More than thirty million people visit our national wildlife refuges every year. Nature lovers, birders, hikers, photographers, hunters, and fishermen: they come for many reasons and are often politically active, first in line to defend and protect our refuges and endangered species. Their passion for the great outdoors is contagious. "For us in the minority," American conservationist Aldo Leopold wrote, "the opportunity to see geese is more important than television, and the chance to find a pasque-flower is a right as inalienable as free speech."[2]

But what of the great many Americans who rarely if ever set foot in a wildlife refuge? Too many of us live our lives at a frantic pace, shopping in malls, talking on cell phones, eating fast foods, and driving in rush-hour traffic. As a people, we are overworked, overweight, and often overwhelmed. It is easy to forget about the simple pleasures of slowing down and getting out into nature. Yet, as the American poet Carl Sandburg observed, "One of the greatest necessities in America is to discover creative solitude."[3] There is no better place to do that and to "renew contacts with wild things,"[4] as Leopold urged, than in a national wildlife refuge. Awaiting discovery there are the sense of connection to primal forces that shaped our continent and ancestors; the adventure of exploring new country; and the feelings of renewal, inspiration, and awe.

Refuges are living, breathing places where the ancient rhythms of life can still be heard, where nature's colors are most vibrant, and where time is measured in seasons. They are gifts to ourselves and to generations unborn—simple gifts unwrapped each time a birder lifts binoculars, a child overturns a rock, a hunter sets a decoy, or an angler casts a line. As we enjoy these gifts, we should also heed Theodore Roosevelt's vision and warning: "Wild beasts and birds are by right not the property merely of the people who are alive today," he said, "but the property of the un-known generations, whose belongings we have no right to squander."[5] For all who care about the future of wildlife in America, those words remain as much a call to action today as they were a century ago.

Expanding the Purposes That Refuges Serve

Throughout its history, a major purpose of the National Wildlife Refuge System has been to provide the habitats needed to sustain huntable pop-ulations of migratory waterfowl. In achieving that purpose, the refuge system has been remarkably successful. Increasingly, other conservation objectives have been pursued through the refuge system, including endangered species conservation and more general biodiversity goals. In 1992, at the North American Wildlife and Natural Resources Confer-ence, the annual national conference of wildlife professionals, I took part in a discussion of biological diversity and the refuge system. I began my presentation with the intentionally provocative idea of a refuge devoted primarily to butterflies.

It was an idea that was not embraced, at least not by the Fish and Wildlife Service. The following year, however, an enterprising butterfly enthusiast named Jeffrey Glassberg founded a new organization, the North American Butterfly Association. One of its most inspired and in-spiring accomplishments was the creation of a National Butterfly Center in Mission, Texas. The center's one hundred acres of both natural and human-created habitats attract a host of butterflies and human visitors. Though the product of a private conservation organization, the center looks very much like the butterfly refuge I envisioned in the following paper.

Biological Diversity and the Refuge System: Beyond the Endangered Species Act in Fish and Wildlife Management
Transactions of the 57th North American Wildlife and Natural Resources Conference, 1992[*]

Imagine, for a moment, a national wildlife refuge, a substantial part of which is devoted to a huge planted flower garden designed to attract and show off a great diversity and profusion of butterflies. Well-stocked with ornamental flowers selected for their ability to entice lepidopteran visitors, such a "garden-refuge" would surely attract many human visitors as well. Properly planned, it could offer genuine education and conservation benefits, particularly inasmuch as many of our native butterflies are declining in range or numbers. Somehow, nevertheless, such a "garden-refuge" goes against deeply embedded notions of what a national wildlife refuge should be.

Why is that? Is it because such a garden-refuge is so patently an artificial environment, a construct not of nature, but of man? Is it because such a refuge, to meet its wildlife (i.e., butterfly) objectives, must rely heavily upon cultivated, non-native plants? Is it because such a refuge fails to preserve a natural diversity and abundance of flora and fauna upon it, but instead must be intensively manipulated and managed through human endeavor to produce an unnatural abundance of a narrow range of animal species? Is it because butterflies aren't important enough to devote a national wildlife refuge to them? Or is it simply because no one ever thought about having a refuge of this character before?

Rather than try to answer these questions now, I simply want to use them to explore the broader issue of what we should want from our National Wildlife Refuge System and, in particular, how the growing concern with the conservation of biological diversity—broadly conceived—might be more effectively integrated into refuge objectives and management. To begin that inquiry, I want to focus for a while on the Fish and Wildlife Service's "Refuge Manual," the compilation of official policies that guide management of our refuges.

The Refuge Manual suffers at times from a pronounced case of schizophrenia. It tries to have its cake and eat it too on a whole lot of issues. Start with the very goals for the Refuge System. Four broad goals are set out in the Manual to guide Refuge management. They

[*] Permission granted by the Wildlife Management Institute, Inc.

include preserving and restoring threatened and endangered species, perpetuating the migratory bird resource, providing an understanding and appreciation of fish and wildlife ecology, and "preserv[ing] a natural diversity and abundance of fauna and flora on refuge lands" (2 RM 1.4).[6]

The last goal, preserving a natural diversity and abundance of flora and fauna, might well rule out our hypothetical butterfly refuge, since its very object is to achieve an unnatural abundance of a particular type of fauna. It might, but it doesn't because the Refuge Manual has more to say on this subject. Although set forth as one of the basic goals of the Refuge System, preserving a natural diversity and abundance of flora and fauna turns out not to be an absolute goal after all. It is immediately qualified in a general policy statement regarding "population management." There the Manual declares that "[t]he attainment of natural diversity is not an over-riding objective of refuge management, but it should be an underlying consideration for all habitat and population management activities" (7 RM 1.4A). Put differently, our hypothetical butterfly refuge is back in the game, since achieving natural diversity and abundance turns out to be only an "underlying consideration" in carrying out other management objectives (which might be maximizing butterfly viewing opportunities), and not a prescription for what those objectives should be.

This fundamental tension between the goal of preserving natural diversity and the fact that most refuges are actively managed and manipulated to achieve other pre-established objectives shows up repeatedly in the Refuge Manual, including in the section devoted to "exotic species introductions and management." There, a clear policy that "[t]he National Wildlife Refuge system exists for the protection and management of plants and animals native to the United States" is set forth (7 RM 8.1). Consistent with that policy, the introduction of exotic species is to be permitted only for biological control reasons. These policies are harmonious with the 1977 Presidential Executive Order directing the Fish and Wildlife Service and other federal agencies to restrict the introduction of exotic species into natural ecosystems under their jurisdiction (*see* Executive Order 11987 [1977]). They also would seem to spell the end for any plans for a butterfly refuge that relies upon ornamental flowers and other exotics to increase butterfly production.

But wait, there is more. Like the goal of achieving a natural diversity and abundance of flora and fauna, the Manual's stated commitment to native species and antipathy to exotic species weakens when one moves from the general to the particular. In particular, the Manual's more specific guidance on the subject of waterfowl management encourages the planting of native grasses whenever possible, but expressly permits the use of non-native grasses "when native grassland management will not achieve the refuge waterfowl production objective" (7 RM 3.5B). In other words, when refuge waterfowl production objectives exceed what would result from the natural diversity and abundance of fauna and flora on a refuge, the natural diversity of the fauna can be altered so as to achieve an unnatural abundance of waterfowl. Indeed, the Manual's recommended "standard mixture" of planted grasses consists of wheatgrass, alfalfa, and sweet clover, all exotic species, which, under the Manual's exotic species policy, are not to be introduced on refuge lands except for biological control purposes. Compare 7 RM 3.5(B)(2)(a) with 7 RM 8.1. In short, one part of the manual authorizes the use of exotics for a purpose that another part prohibits.

The point of this discussion is not to suggest that our refuge management policies pertaining to waterfowl are misguided. Rather, it is simply to suggest that the Refuge Manual itself, the basic guiding document for the management of the National Wildlife Refuge System, is so riddled with exceptions and contradictory policies that almost anything—even a refuge for butterflies—can be squared with it. And that fact, coupled with the further fact that the very concept of biodiversity conservation is itself rather open-ended and imprecise, means that almost any set of refuge management actions can be justified, post hoc, on the basis of their contribution to biological diversity.

That result is not particularly satisfactory. My purpose in the remainder of this paper, therefore, is to suggest a direction in which the Fish and Wildlife Service should try to move in order to make biological diversity less an "underlying consideration" and more an affirmative objective of refuge management.

In the history of the development of the National Wildlife Refuge System, two themes have been paramount. The original, and still very vital, role that the System was to play was in the conservation of migratory waterfowl. A more recent emphasis stems from the Endangered Species Act. In the past decade or so, most of the expenditures for refuge acquisition have been for endangered species purposes.

These two objectives, waterfowl conservation and endangered species preservation, have been the driving forces behind the expansion of the Refuge System (outside of Alaska, at least). But between waterfowl conservation and endangered species preservation lies a huge universe of potential conservation concern, from nongame conservation, generally, to watchable wildlife, declining songbirds, disappearing amphibians, centers of species richness, centers of endemism, and the like. Does the Refuge System try to address these new concerns merely as peripheral considerations in the pursuit of its very limited primary goals, or does it expand those primary goals to encompass these concerns as genuine objectives in their own right?

Although it may seem elementary, it is important to acknowledge at the outset that scale is extremely important in assessing actions to benefit the conservation of biological diversity. To illustrate, consider a tract of land on which a long-leaf pine and wiregrass community exists. This tract of land may well offer less diversity, in terms of number of species supported, than a similarly-sized tract of hardwood forest. The diversity of the first tract could be increased by managing it so as to bring about its conversion to hardwood forest. But if that first tract is the only pine-wiregrass tract remaining in a region dominated by hardwood forest, the conversion of that tract to hardwood, enhancing diversity at the local scale, will diminish diversity at the larger, regional scale.

This recognition of the critical importance of scale is quite important for the National Wildlife Refuge System. That system is intended to serve national purposes. Its potential contribution to enhancing the conservation of biological diversity necessitates, therefore, that the scale of reference informing decisions about actions to advance biodiversity be regional or national, and not parochial.

Another, perhaps elementary, point is that the first step in assessing the potential for the Refuge System to contribute more effectively to the conservation of biological diversity is through a systematic inventory of the living resources, and potential resources, of the System. Without a comprehensive baseline of what we already have within our System, in terms of both species and natural communities, it will not be possible to offer a meaningful evaluation of whether we are progressing toward, or slipping away from, the goal of enhanced conservation of biological diversity.

Knowing what is on our National Wildlife Refuges, however, is only part of what is needed. It is also critically important to know what is going on outside of those refuges. If natural community types that are or could be represented within the Refuge System are disappearing outside the System, that fact is a very persuasive reason to try to keep them represented within the System. Here again, it may be much more important for refuge managers to manage for relatively low diversity community types that are under heavy pressure outside the System than for higher diversity community types already abundant elsewhere.

To serve the goal of conserving biological diversity, our National Wildlife Refuges ought to function as sentinels, capable of detecting trends in species abundance or distribution that portend potentially grave consequences for the future well-being of wildlife. When two years ago, the news broke that many different species of amphibians appeared to be declining precipitously, and for unknown reasons, across much of North America, it ought to have concerned all of us that the source of this news was not the Fish and Wildlife Service. Although it has millions of acres of refuge lands scattered across all regions of the country, the Service didn't have the data collecting capability to detect (or refute) this alarming conservation development. Perhaps more disturbing, however, is the fact that since the news broke, the Refuge System has not been catalyzed into action to follow up those initial reports with some serious, long-range studies to monitor amphibian populations for the purpose of determining whether the apparent decline is real and, if so, what its causes are. The long-term declines of migratory songbirds, amphibians, saturnid moths, and other wildlife are all examples of declining biological diversity that has not yet reached the point of triggering the Endangered Species Act. A National Wildlife Refuge System that was attentive to these trends could contribute enormously to the timely identification of conservation solutions that avoid the controversy and disruption that accompany last-ditch efforts to avert imminent extinction.

Climate change is another example of how our Refuge System could function as a sentinel. Species at the periphery of their historic range are likely to be among the most sensitive indicators of subtle climate changes. A Refuge System that sought to monitor such populations closely could serve as a bellwether of impending threat to biological diversity beyond those to which we have been long accustomed.

These are all new roles for our National Wildlife Refuge System.

They are roles, however, that are suited to the dramatically changing circumstances in which we live. Biological diversity, a catchword, perhaps for the simple proposition that our attention must be focused on more than just the ducks and whooping cranes that have occupied it for so long, needs to be not just an underlying consideration in managing our refuges. It needs to be in the forefront of our thinking about what the National Wildlife Refuge System can and should do for our future.

Antioch Dunes: A Wildlife Refuge for an Insect

Though my 1992 paper made no mention of it, there was in fact one national wildlife refuge that had been established, at least in part, for butterflies—or at least for one particular species of butterfly, the Lange's metalmark. To the casual observer it looks rather like most of its metalmark cousins, but to the trained eye it is unique. Its uniqueness stems from its isolation in California's biologically rich Antioch Dunes. The Antioch Dunes were once part of an expansive system of rolling sand dunes on the San Joaquin River's southern banks near San Francisco. Strong winds sculpted the landscape into a shifting mosaic of sandy hills. The rapidly changing environment of the dunes rewarded those creatures that could quickly adapt to such challenging circumstances. Quite a few did: indeed, the Antioch Dunes have long been noted for their unusual concentration of "endemic" species, those that occur nowhere else in the world.

By the 1970s, not much of the Antioch Dunes remained. Hemmed in by residential subdivisions, railroad tracks, and an industrial facility and scarred by years of sand mining that left huge, empty pits, the dunes in places resembled more a moonscape than a landscape. Once biologically rich areas had been rendered virtually barren of life or overtaken by nonnative invasive plants. Still, some of the creatures that called this their last home remained. Among these was the Lange's metalmark butterfly. It and two rare plant species that also occur there are protected as endangered species.

Despite the problems afflicting the dunes, the Fish and Wildlife Service decided in 1980 that the dunes and their vanishing denizens might yet be saved. In that year the service purchased two discontinuous land parcels to establish the Antioch Dunes National Wildlife Refuge. Never before had a national wildlife refuge been created for a rare insect and rare plants, and it remains today the only refuge created for that purpose. In a December 1983 press release commemorating the tenth anniversary of the Endangered Species Act, the Fish and Wildlife Service cited the establishment of the refuge as an example of the many important achievements in its program to save endangered species. Yet the Lange's metalmark is closer to extinction—much closer—today than it was then.

Key to the metalmark's recovery, according to the Fish and Wildlife Service, is restoration of its natural habitat to increase its food supply. When it comes to food, there are few pickier eaters than the Lange's metalmark. In its caterpillar stage, it will eat only one type of plant, false buckwheat. The adult butterfly's habits are nearly as fussy. Extensive efforts to restore the habitat of the dunes have been undertaken, even bringing in dredged sands from the nearby port of Stockton. Planting the larval host plant has had some temporary success, but invasive grasses and weeds have been a nearly insurmountable problem. As a result, the population of the butterfly initially climbed but has since plummeted. Its peak abundance was in 1999, when the high daily count for the year was 2,342 adults. In every year since 2009, however, the high daily count has been fewer than 50.

The sands of time are running out on the Lange's metalmark. Each year, eggs laid the previous autumn will hatch and the tiny caterpillars will crawl off to feed on their host plant. By summer the survivors will be ready to burst out of their pupal cases as winged butterflies. For a brief time, they will dance like fairies amid the flowers of the ancient Antioch Dunes. Then they will be gone for the summer, perhaps forever. If they survive, it will be thanks to the creation of a wildlife refuge for them four decades ago.

An Unusual Wildlife Refuge in Canada

In his book *Biophilia*, E. O. Wilson wrote that "human beings have an innate fear of snakes or, more precisely, they have an innate propensity to learn such fear quickly and easily past the age of five."[7] I am apparently a slow learner, for I am still waiting to learn that fear. Rather than a fear of snakes, I have had the great good fortune of a lifelong fascination with them. Thus it was that shortly after my retirement from the Interior Department in 2017 I traveled to Canada to visit a most unusual wildlife refuge, one devoted to the conservation of snakes.

In the Province of Manitoba, near the tiny town of Narcisse, a little more than an hour's drive from Winnipeg, is the Narcisse Wildlife Management Area. In the United States, wildlife management areas are state-owned sites acquired with funds derived from the sale of hunting and fishing licenses and from the federal excise taxes imposed on the sale of hunting and fishing equipment. They are managed primarily for recreational use by hunters and anglers. The Narcisse Wildlife Management Area is something quite different. It is owned and managed by the Province of Manitoba, but its purpose is to protect—and to promote the public enjoyment of—what is perhaps the greatest concentration of snakes of any place in the world.

My fascination with snakes began, as best I can recall, with a gift from my childhood friend Mickey. I no longer remember Mickey's last name, or nearly anything else about him, but I clearly remember the gift he gave me when we were only six or seven years old. It was a gift of three recently born DeKay's snakes, a diminutive species named for James Ellsworth DeKay, a nineteenth-century zoologist who was the first to collect a specimen of this species on New York's Long Island. A contemporary of John James Audubon and Jared Kirtland, DeKay studied at Yale for a time, but his studies there were cut short by his expulsion for threatening a college tutor with a club. That blemish on his character did not keep him from becoming a physician and the author of a multivolume work on the vertebrate wildlife of New York.

Mickey's gift to me sparked a childhood filled with snake-collecting adventures, most of them with my neighbor-friend Larry Krueger. At one time or another he and I had a menagerie that included garter snakes, ribbon snakes, ringneck snakes, hognose snakes, milk snakes, black rat snakes, water snakes, and other nonpoisonous snakes. We kept them in a shed to which we attached a sign that read "B & K Snakehouse . . . See Baby Rattlers and Moccasins . . . 10 cents." Only a few of our customers asked for their money back when the "baby rattlers" turned out to be the rattle toys with which infants play and the "moccasins" were of the sort worn on one's feet.

I regard my lifelong fascination with snakes as one of my life's great good fortunes. There is one other, and that is my good fortune to have married a wife who has tolerated my fascination with snakes. I think she could not have been entirely surprised when I told her that at the top of my list of places I wanted to visit in retirement were the world-famous snake dens of Narcisse. With a roll of her eyes, she consented. The snakes of Narcisse are red-sided garter snakes, a species that is small, harmless, and about as cute as a snake can possibly be. As cold weather approaches in the autumn, about 150,000 of them make their way from miles around to five subterranean dens near the small town of Narcisse. There they spend the winter in limestone sinkholes and associated fissures, keeping far enough below the surface to avoid freezing but not so deep as to be imperiled by groundwater. In these dens they endure the long, bitter winter of the Canadian prairie, awaiting the return of spring.

When spring arrives and temperatures rise into the sixties, the snakes begin to stir. Since the snakes have not eaten for months, you might think that finding a meal would be the first thing on their minds after exiting the dens. It isn't. The first thing on their minds is mating. The males emerge first from the dens and patiently wait for the females, which are generally larger, to follow. What happens when a female finally emerges has to be described somewhat delicately. The female is mobbed by a dozen, or sometimes several dozen, males, each trying to win her favor. The result is a writhing, almost spherical ball of serpents that moves across the land as if it were itself a living organism. A brochure for the site likens it to a "tangled mat of spaghetti," although one that is in constant motion. I wonder whether a sight such as this might have inspired the myth of Medusa's coiffure. Somehow, amid this frenzy of activity, the female makes union with one of the males and the cycle of life continues. Almost instantly the unsuccessful suitors disentangle and head off in search of another female. No reptile dysfunction there.

Visitors to the site can observe all this up close from a well-kept loop trail that connects the dens. The trail is flat, with a smooth surface of crushed limestone, making it easy to navigate with strollers. Each of the dens is protected by a wire barrier that keeps overly enthusiastic visitors from getting too close to the mating frenzies. A ranger or do-cent is stationed at each den to answer questions and to point out to a mesmerized visitor that a snake is about to crawl across his or her foot (yes, that happens).

When planning this visit, I anticipated that we might have the place pretty much to ourselves, given the general lack of enthusiasm for all things snake. It quickly became apparent to us, however, that we could be in for a surprise. The customs official at the Winnipeg airport, the agent at the car rental office, the receptionist at the hotel registration desk, the servers at the restaurants, the shopkeepers in the stores, and virtually every other Canadian we encountered on the trip asked us what brought us to Manitoba. We decided to answer with candid honesty: "We're here to see the snakes of Narcisse." Almost to a person, the response to this bold declaration was some variation of "Fantastic! I love going to that place." Only one person we encountered responded with the "Ewww, I hate snakes" reaction I had anticipated. More than one commented that they planned to take their mothers there on Mother's Day. That seemed bizarre until I learned that Mother's Day often coincides with the peak emergence of snakes from their dens, so if you want to be a dutiful son or daughter and spend the day with Mom but not miss the snakes, you will need to bring her along.

For visitors coming from afar, like ourselves, timing a visit is a bit tricky. When the snakes emerge depends on the weather. If warm spring weather arrives early, the snakes may come out in late April. If it is late, peak emergence may be delayed until mid-May or later. The Wildlife Branch of the Manitoba Department of Sustainable Development provides periodic updates on the status of emergence at http://www.gov.mb.ca/fish-wildlife/snakes_narcisse/index.html, but unless you are prepared to revise your travel plans at the eleventh hour, that information is of limited utility. We were lucky. We planned for a three-day window in the first week of May. The first of those days was auspicious, with a forecast for lots of sun and temperatures in the upper seventies. We were rewarded with lots of snakes, at least a thousand by my estimation.

Getting to the dens is quite easy. They are about an hour and a half's drive north of Winnipeg on well-maintained, lightly traveled roads. The landscape is flat; the vegetation is prairie grassland, interspersed with stands of birch trees. The birch trees near Narcisse gave the first clue about why this area is so hospitable to overwintering garter snakes. The trees were short and stunted, the result of growing in a thin layer of nutrient-poor soil atop limestone. The sinkholes and fissures that fracture that limestone provide just what the snakes need to survive the winter. We had expected to find perhaps another car or two parked in a roadside pull-off at the site but were instead startled to find dozens of cars in a parking lot capable of holding many more. Adjacent to the parking lot were serviceable bathrooms and an extensive picnic area with nearly every table occupied. There were lots of young families with kids and retiree couples as well.

The first in a series of informative kiosks gave an overview of the area and its natural history, together with a map of the trail to the dens. Towering above all this was an enormous entrance sign announcing that this was the location of the Narcisse Snake Dens. One of the kiosks included a statement that I had to read twice to believe. It said that visitors were allowed to pick up and handle the snakes, at least the ones not engaged in amorous activity at the dens. In sharp contrast to the strict hands-off rule that applies to parks and wildlife refuges in the United States, the managers at Narcisse seem to understand that holding these creatures is a key part of replacing fear with fascination.

It seems to work. I watched as one young family with two sons encountered a snake along the trail. The older boy, perhaps eight, had no fear of holding it, but his brother, who was a couple of years younger, was initially hesitant even to touch it, much less hold it. Something about the older boy's gentle exuberance and obvious delight must have persuaded the younger sibling to extend his hand. Eventually, the little guy was just as delighted as his brother to hold this no longer fearsome creature. As I watched him, I could not help seeing myself more than six decades earlier holding the precious gift that my friend Mickey had given me.

6

Three Threats to Biodiversity in the Modern Age
Climate Change, Plastics, and Commerce

In 2008, the US Fish and Wildlife Service designated the polar bear as a threatened species. It was the first species to be given the protection of the Endangered Species Act because of the threat posed to its survival by climate change. The threat is simple and direct: global warming is melting the Arctic Sea ice on which the bear depends. A century and a half earlier, Melville had staked his belief that humans could never drive whales to extinction on the confidence that whales could, if necessary, take refuge under their "Polar citadels," protected there by "the ultimate glassy barriers and walls." In 1851, however, Melville could not have imagined that those ultimate glassy barriers might someday no longer exist. Neither could Congress when it enacted the Endangered Species Act in 1973.

A thorough search of the legislative history of the Endangered Species Act for any mention of climate change, the greenhouse effect, or global warming will turn up nothing. The hearing transcripts, committee reports, and floor debates never mention these topics. Overexploitation, pollution, and habitat loss were believed to be the major drivers of species endangerment and extinction then. Climate change could not be a driver of endangerment and extinction for the simple reason that the climate did not change, at least not within a time frame that mattered for purposes of the Endangered Species Act. The climate, in short, was implicitly presumed to be stable. Thirty-five years later, with the designation of the polar bear as a threatened species, it became clear that the presumption of climate stability was no longer tenable. Climate change was real and, most important, it was happening at a surprisingly rapid pace.

Climate change is one of three threats to biodiversity that were either unknown or greatly underappreciated when Congress enacted the

Endangered Species Act. Another is the proliferation of plastics, particularly in marine environments. The third is the threat from invasive exotic species that accompany the movement of goods in interstate and international commerce. Each of these threats to biodiversity in the modern age is discussed in turn.

Climate Change

The year 1988 was once the hottest year on record. It is nowhere near the hottest now. According to a National Aeronautics and Space Administration (NASA) report issued in January 2021, that title is now shared by 2020 and 2016. Indeed, the seven hottest years since reliable measurements began in the late nineteenth century have been the past seven years. The year 1988 is no longer even in the top ten. In early 1989, I wrote that the year that had just ended "will no longer be considered unusual by the middle of the twenty-first century." I was wrong. It is already unusual, not for being so hot but rather for being so cool. Such has been the pace of climate change that a prediction that may have appeared to be unduly alarmist when made in 1989 turned out to have been hopelessly optimistic.

The article that follows was published only months after presidential candidate George H. W. Bush had pledged to fight the greenhouse effect with the "White House effect," and three years before the 1992 United Nations Framework Convention on Climate Change, the first of several international agreements intended to reduce the emissions of carbon dioxide and other greenhouse gases that contribute to global warming. Despite that pledge and those agreements, however, the earth's atmosphere continues inexorably to warm and its oceans to rise.

The United States, once a world leader in the effort to galvanize action against climate change, has abandoned that role. One of President Donald Trump's first acts in office was to announce his intent to withdraw the United States from a voluntary international agreement made at the 2015 UN Climate Change Conference in Paris, the first nation to do so. An aggressive campaign to sow doubt about the science behind climate change—dismissing it as a hoax—and our collective ability to do anything about it succeeded in its goal of producing political gridlock.

Meanwhile, emissions of carbon dioxide continue to increase, in the

United States and throughout most of the rest of the world. Indeed, in late 2018, researchers at the international scientific group the Global Carbon Project concluded in a series of studies that global emissions of carbon dioxide would reach their highest levels ever, increasing over the prior year by 2.7 percent. Total carbon dioxide emissions in 2018 were anticipated to be roughly 75 percent higher than they were in 1989 when the following article was published.

Although climate change will likely affect a broad array of species, the article that follows focuses narrowly on migratory waterfowl and shorebirds in North America. For the most part, waterfowl populations—aided by aggressive efforts to secure their wetland habitats—have remained relatively stable despite increasing evidence of climate change. Shorebirds have not fared nearly as well, although assessing the relative contributions of climate change and other factors causing their decline—for example, coastal development and intensive recreational use of nesting beaches—is difficult. Thus, the concerns expressed in the article remain as timely today as they were when written thirty years ago.

Waterfowl and Climate Change: A Glimpse into the Twenty-First Century
Orion, Spring 1989*

The summer of 1988 was a fitting time to reflect on what the future holds for wildlife, particularly waterfowl, in the twenty-first century. Intense heat seared the North American continent virtually all summer long, while drought parched the wheat and corn belts. Pothole wetlands in the northern prairie and Canadian parkland regions, traditionally the most productive breeding areas for the continent's ducks, went dry. Even Saskatchewan's Old Wives Lake dried up for the first time since 1937. Ducks in search of a place to raise the next generation were forced to fly farther north, where they crowded into less hospitable areas. The autumn duck population fell to 66 million, a more than 10 percent decline from the previous year and the second lowest level ever recorded.

Government officials responsible for managing waterfowl responded to the decline by restricting duck hunting. The new restrictions, they said, were necessary until the current crisis was over, until things

* Reprinted with permission of The Orion Society.

returned to "normal." A US Fish and Wildlife Service press release captured the prevailing outlook when it quoted one of its officials opening his remarks with "When the water comes back—and it *will* come back. . . ."

There will doubtless be some cooler and wetter years ahead, but it now seems equally certain that the unusual weather events of 1988 will no longer be considered unusual by the middle of the twenty-first century. In short, returning to "normal" is a fanciful idea, for profound changes in the earth's climate seem inevitable over the next half century. These changes are likely to have substantial impacts on North America's wildlife, as becomes evident if one examines the effects upon waterfowl—one of our most abundant, most economically valuable, and longest-managed wildlife resources.

The cause of the major climate changes ahead is what has become popularly known as the greenhouse effect. Its most immediate consequence is a warming of the earth's atmosphere. By the middle of the next century, average global temperatures are expected to be three to nine degrees Fahrenheit warmer than at present, a change larger than any that has occurred since the Ice Age. A focus on average temperatures may be misleading, however, for the models from which these predications are made show above-average warming in the higher latitudes, and much less change near the equator. These temperature changes, in turn, may contribute to significantly altered precipitation patterns. Reduced precipitation and much drier summers are anticipated in continental interior areas. Extreme weather events, such as intense heat and prolonged drought, could become more frequent. Thus the prairie pothole region of the north-central United States and the Canadian parkland region above it may be both hotter and drier than in the past, far more like 1988 than the "normal" conditions that preceded it. These areas, among the most important breeding grounds for many of our most abundant ducks—mallards, pintails, blue-winged teals—are likely to produce many fewer birds.

Ducks will discover that not just their breeding grounds will have changed because of the greenhouse effect, but other habitat as well. Increased global temperatures are expected to bring about a dramatic rise in sea levels throughout the world. This will occur as a result of the melting of polar ice caps and the thermal expansion of warmer sea water. Rising seas will inundate many coastal marshes now protected as waterfowl refuges in the National Wildlife Refuge System. Other marsh areas will be dramatically transformed by the intrusion of salt water into fresh or brackish water systems. Evidence that this is already occurring can be seen at Blackwater National Wildlife Refuge on Chesapeake Bay, where rising water levels have eliminated about a third of the refuge's marshland over the past forty years. Some marshes will be able to shift inland in the face of rising seas; others will be blocked by cities and other human constructions. Even those able to retreat inland will probably no longer be within the boundaries of protected refuges.

These are just some of the direct effects of climate change on our waterfowl. Significant as these changes are apt to be, they may be dwarfed by other, indirect effects stemming from human response to a changing climate. The area of human activity that has generally had the greatest impact on waterfowl is agriculture, particularly through the conversion of potholes and other wetland habitats into dry fields for the growing of crops. How is agriculture going to react to the changes in climate now being forecast, and how will that reaction affect waterfowl?

In general, agricultural regions, like natural vegetational communities, can be expected to shift northward in response to a warming climate. A crude effort at quantifying that shift can be made through the use of economic models that link information on rainfall and other climatic variables with crop production. Those models suggest that in many areas of the country, including the prairie pothole region, foreseeable climate changes will mean more land brought under production as growing seasons lengthen, and more irrigation water used to grow crops on those lands to compensate for less dependable rainfall. In short, prime waterfowl breeding areas will be stressed not just by heat and drought, but by increasing pressure for agricultural conversion and by increasing competition for scarce water supplies. In places where ponds remain, the economic incentives to plow or graze right down to the water's edge, thus destroying potential nesting areas and needed cover, will magnify the adverse impact of loss of surface water.

Other consequences will follow from the above changes. More acreage devoted to agricultural production will mean more pesticides used. More irrigation demand will mean not just less water available for ducks, but also potentially more leaching of salts and dangerous trace elements like selenium in irrigation return flows. As a result, incidents of waterfowl poisoning like that which occurred at Kesterson National Wildlife Refuge in California a few years ago may be more frequent. There, so many dead and deformed ducks, coots, and other water birds were found that Interior Secretary Donald Hodel ordered the refuge closed. Recent surveys of western National Wildlife Refuges indicate that the toxic contamination problem is becoming widespread.

Climate change could disrupt waterfowl habits in yet another way. Ducks and other migratory birds apparently time their migratory cycles according to the length of daylight. At present, this means that ducks arrive on their breeding grounds and begin rearing their young when the insects and plant shoots upon which they typically feed are readily available. In a world transformed by climate change, however, the timing of plant growth and insect emergence in relation to length of daylight may be greatly altered. As a result, the synchrony of brood-rearing with food abundance may be broken.

Even without climate change, prospects for waterfowl in the next century are clouded at best. The 99 million acres of wetlands that remain in the continental United States today represent less than half the total that existed when the country was founded. The rest have already been drained, filled, or otherwise lost, and the process continues. Each year, another half million acres or so of wetlands are destroyed. Many of these losses are in areas especially valuable for waterfowl, such as the bottomland hardwood swamps of the lower Mississippi valley, a prime wintering area for wood ducks. Louisiana, where more ducks are thought to overwinter than in any other state, loses some fifty square miles of coastal marsh each year, due to the combined effects of coastal subsidence, rising sea levels, the proliferation of canals in the marshes to service the oil industry, and flood-control measures that have diminished the river's ability to replenish its deltaic marshes. If these trends continue, and there is no evidence as yet that they will not, the toll on waterfowl will be enormous.

Wetland losses affect waterfowl in a myriad of ways. On the breeding grounds, nesting productivity declines when highly territorial species compete for less and less space. The crowding of waterfowl into fewer and fewer ponds also increases the risk of epizootic diseases and serves as a magnet for predators. Whether to control those predators in order to protect waterfowl is a question that is beginning to stir controversy. Each of these problems, already growing acute, will be compounded in the century ahead if the predictions of climate change prove right. Waterfowl will not be the only wildlife significantly affected by climate change. Sandpipers, plovers, and other migratory species that depend upon a network of prairie wetlands will also suffer. The arctic-nesting sanderling, which has declined dramatically over the last decade and a half, may see that decline magnified by climate change. Perhaps hardest hit will be non-migratory species or those with restricted distributions and relatively narrow ecological requirements, birds like the Everglades snail kite, Kirtland's warbler, and the Mississippi sandhill crane.

The survival of these, including many now protected in parks or refuges as threatened or endangered species, will depend on their ability and that of the vegetational communities with which they are associated to shift northward in response to changing climatic conditions. Such major shifts in species and plant communities have often occurred before in history. Now, however, human barriers in the form of metropolitan areas and vast agricultural landscapes may prevent many species from moving. Instead, they will be effectively trapped within the boundaries of the parks or refuges they now occupy, while the habitats within these boundaries are markedly transformed. Even without human barriers, climate change is apt to be so rapid as to outstrip the ability of some vegetational communities to adjust spatially.

There is very near consensus that some amount of climate change is inevitable; past and ongoing emissions of greenhouse gases have already committed us to some degree of warming for at least the next several decades. The only options we have now are to slow the rate of warming and to anticipate and plan for the changes that will result. Slowing the rate of warming will require more efficient utilization of energy, a transition to forms of energy other than fossil fuels, and stemming the loss of forests throughout the world. These are critical global and societal steps, though not ones that persons concerned about waterfowl have heretofore regarded with much interest.

The dry, parched landscape of Winnemucca Lake National Wildlife Refuge in Nevada is a silent reminder of the pitfalls of failing to perceive and respond to future waterfowl needs. Once a lush wetland complex in the middle of the Nevada desert, Winnemucca Lake Refuge supported abundant waterfowl and other wildlife. But when the refuge was established, no legally protected water rights were acquired. As a result, the waters that fed its wetlands were diverted by irrigators and other upstream water users. Eventually, no water at all reached the refuge; its wetlands disappeared and so too the waterfowl that once used them. Winnemucca Lake's legal designation as a National Wildlife Refuge was eventually revoked in 1962; its practical value as a refuge for wildlife had ended years earlier.

Few National Wildlife Refuges in the western United States have legally protected water rights. Yet climate change will probably bring both reduced rainfall and increased demand for irrigation water. At least in the West, the emphasis in waterfowl conservation strategy must shift toward the acquisition of water rights. Elsewhere, the emerging picture of our future climate and its consequences suggests still other redirections of effort. To increase the likelihood that coastal refuges will persist after a climate-change-induced rise in sea level, waterfowl managers ought to be acquiring undeveloped upland areas adjacent to refuges so that the marsh habitats can move inland with the rising seas. In the breeding areas, land acquisition efforts may need to focus on the more northerly, traditionally less productive areas into which ducks were displaced during the drought of 1988. In many instances, the areas acquired with climate change considerations in mind may not be particularly valuable for waterfowl today. But if waterfowl is to continue to be one of our most abundant and valuable wildlife resources, today's conservation efforts must anticipate dramatic changes in the needs of these birds in the twenty-first century. People concerned about the status of waterfowl need to recognize their stake in the problem of climate change and take an active part in helping to solve it.

As the foregoing suggests, climate change may adversely affect wildlife in a variety of ways. For example, likely to be even more important for wildlife than changes in temperature are the effects of global warming on the availability of water. A striking illustration of that phenomenon was provided by a 2020 study that appeared in *Science*, which concluded that the average annual flow of the Colorado River had declined by 20 percent, due primarily to increased evapotranspiration, which itself was the result of decreased snowpack caused by global warming.

The Colorado River hosts several endangered species of fish. Their survival and ability to reproduce depend on having adequate flows of water at critical times of the year. A decades-long effort to assure those adequate flows while simultaneously allowing diversions for municipal, industrial, and agricultural uses will be made even more challenging if the annual flows of the river continue to decline. Although the polar bear may be unusual in that climate change is the single, overriding threat to its survival, the Colorado River fishes are probably more typical in how climate change affects them. For them, and for most endangered species, there are already a host of threats that have caused their endangerment. Climate change represents one more threat, one more challenge to be faced in the effort to prevent their extinction.

Plastics: A Costly Convenience

"Plastics." That single word was perhaps the most memorable line in *The Graduate*, the 1967 breakout film for acclaimed actor Dustin Hoffman. Hoffman played the role of Ben Braddock, whose parents were hosting a party to celebrate his recent graduation from college. A family friend, Mr. McGuire, took the young Ben aside with the explanation that he wanted "to say one word to you, just one word." Ben looked on expectantly as Mr. McGuire solemnly uttered that one word—"plastics." Expressionless, Ben asks, "Exactly how do you mean?" to which Mr. McGuire answers, "There is a great future in plastics. Think about it."

A half century later, the world's oceans are awash in plastic. Oceanic currents and gyres concentrate floating plastic debris in enormous patches. In subtropical waters of the eastern Pacific Ocean, one such patch has been dubbed the Great Pacific Garbage Patch. According to a 2018 study published in the journal *Nature*, an estimated 1.8 trillion pieces of plastic are afloat in it, amounting to at least seventy-nine thousand tons of plastic debris.[1] A 2016 study by the World Economic Forum projected that at current rates, there will be more tons of plastic in the world's oceans than tons of fish.

In oceanic environments, plastic debris is more than just an eyesore. It is also a threat to many imperiled marine animals. To a green sea turtle, a plastic bag in the water column apparently looks like a jellyfish, a meal for the turtle. Unable to digest or pass the bag, the turtle can become emaciated or die. Albatrosses are also put at risk by oceanic plastic debris. These pelagic birds forage widely at sea, consuming fish that they then bring back to their nests and regurgitate into the beaks of their young. Much of this regurgitated material turns out not to be food at all but plastic debris that the parent bird mistook for fish, resulting in starvation and death for many of the young. Lost or abandoned plastic fishing nets, some enormous in size, can continue ensnaring marine life for years or even decades. Endangered whales, other marine mammals, and imperiled sea turtles are often the victims of such "ghost fishing."

The threat of plastics to imperiled marine life was not foreseen when Mr. McGuire gave his famous one word of advice to Ben Braddock. Nor was it foreseen when Congress enacted the Endangered Species Act six years later. None of the provisions of that law seem well suited to addressing a threat of this nature, despite its ubiquity. Other strategies are needed, in particular, strategies to reduce the use and encourage the reuse and recycling of plastics. Some of those were suggested in my op-ed that appeared in the *Denver Post* in 1988. Though progress has been made in the subsequent decades, the Great Pacific Garbage Patch is a reminder of how much remains to be done.

When Convenience Becomes Costly Public Burden
Denver Post, January 4, 1988

Communities from coast to coast are seriously considering ordinances to restrict certain plastic products.

One of modern society's seeming conveniences is increasingly being viewed askance because communities are discovering convenience has its cost. In particular, the environmental costs of our proliferating use of plastic are mounting.

In coastal communities, one of the adverse effects of our dependence on plastics is particularly conspicuous. Earlier this year, more than 300 tons of debris were removed from 154 miles of Texas beaches in a single day, most of it plastic.

But pollution of the oceans with plastic debris is not just an aesthetic problem; scientists have recently discovered that it is also a major ecological one. Many sea animals, including birds, turtles, and mammals, eat floating plastic debris, apparently mistaking it for their normal food. It is not just indigestible, but sometimes deadly.

A recent study of a seabird colony in Hawaii found that 90 percent of the chicks had bits of plastic in their gullets, fed to them by parent birds who scooped it up at sea. Entanglement of marine wildlife in plastic debris adds to the toll—more than 50,000 fur seals off Alaska are thought to perish this way each year.

A less visible consequence of our plastic use occurs in many communities searching for a solution to the mounting trash problem.

As landfills near their capacity, a great many communities are turning to incinerators to get rid of their trash.

At the same time, as plastics replace other materials in the marketplace, plastic represents a larger and larger fraction of the municipal solid waste stream. Representatives of the plastics industry try to point out that plastics in the waste system helped fuel the incineration process. But they also have other, undesirable consequences.

The ash residue from municipal incinerators often contains heavy metals and other chemicals dangerous to human health. Plastic products are an important source of these harmful heavy metals, especially cadmium. The concentration of cadmium in ash from many municipal incinerators exceeds the levels that the Environmental Protection Agency regards as hazardous. The same is true for lead, which, according to a recent New York study, is a common component of many plastic bags.

To dispose of hazardous waste properly is a very expensive proposition, one that few communities expected to face when they opted to build their incinerators. Yet, as plastic products constitute a greater and greater share of the waste stream entering incinerators, heavy metal–loaded hazardous ash will be the increasingly likely output of those same incinerators.

The high cost of building incinerators and disposing properly of the huge quantities of ash they produce have made recycling programs look more and more appealing to many communities. Here again, plastic products present an obstacle.

In general, the rate of recycling for metal, paper and glass is much higher than for plastic. Thus, as plastic increasingly replaces metal, paper and glass in the marketplace, we are shifting from readily recycled materials to materials that are not readily recycled and that must—without major new research and development initiatives—be burned or buried in landfills. What had seemed a simple convenience is becoming a costly burden.

The plastics industry is fighting restrictions on plastic products tooth and nail. Some years ago, it fought a Minnesota law restricting plastic milk bottles all the way to the Supreme Court, and lost.

One might hope that it would fight with equal vigor the problems that are making so many local communities turn to restrictive legislation against plastic.

In the thirty-two years since this op-ed was published, the nation has made great strides in some respects. Recycling has been widely embraced and is now second nature for most Americans, a change in behavior comparable to the decline in smoking. Plastic products, however, remain a problem. Made from petroleum, plastics contribute to the emission of greenhouse gases. Plastic bags, by clogging waste-sorting machines, complicate the task of recycling other materials.

Because of these and other problems, in early 2020 the states of New York and Oregon banned the distribution of most single-use plastic bags. California had done so earlier, and Hawaii has effectively done so through ordinances adopted by each of its counties. Thus, four states now outlaw most plastic bags, and others may follow. These measures, even if only partially effective, can have significant consequences, for New Yorkers use an estimated twenty-three billion plastic bags annually. In California, plastic bag use has declined by 72 percent since its ban took effect. In California and elsewhere throughout the country, consumers are growing accustomed to bringing their own reusable bags with them when they shop, another behavioral change that reduces the still significant threat of plastics to biodiversity.

Snakes on a Plane: Commerce and Invasive Species

In the summer of 2006, a movie that was part action flick, part comedy, part horror movie, and mostly preposterous farce hit the silver screen. It bore the unforgettable title *Snakes on a Plane*, and it offered up a plot that was guaranteed to frighten the wits out of anyone with even the slightest hint of ophidiophobia. A passenger plane bound from Hawaii to Los Angeles carried, unbeknown to those on board, a cargo of hundreds of poisonous snakes. Of course, the snakes escaped, and havoc at thirty-five thousand feet ensued.

The plot of *Snakes on a Plane* was frankly ridiculous, yet a real-world snakes-on-a-plane threat has long worried conservationists. That threat, like those of climate change and plastic pollution, was barely recognized, if at all, when Congress passed the Endangered Species Act in 1973. Because Congress recognized that commercial trade in elephant ivory, rhino horn, the fur of spotted cats, and similar things was a grave threat to those species, it provided the regulatory tools to address that threat.

What it did not fully recognize was the potential for commerce in all sorts of other products—lumber, nursery stock, and so on—to carry with it hitchhiking plants and animals that, if brought into new environments, were capable of severely disrupting natural communities and native species through predation, competition, and spread of disease.

That invasive, nonnative species are one of the most widespread and significant threats to endangered and threatened species in the United States was documented in a study by my former colleague David Wilcove and others in 1998. Their study found that exotic species were a contributing factor to the imperilment of nearly half (49 percent) of all the species protected by the Endangered Species Act.[2] Only habitat destruction and loss contributed to the imperilment of more species. Yet it is often difficult for many people to appreciate the gravity of this threat, even an environmental advocate such as former vice president Al Gore.

Less than six weeks after taking office, President Bill Clinton initiated the "National Performance Review" and put Vice President Gore in charge of it. The purpose of the review was nothing less than "reinventing government" so that it "works better, costs less, and gets results Americans care about."[3] The vice president undertook his charge with gusto, even appearing on *The David Letterman Show* to mock government regulations setting standards for ashtrays used by government agencies. (Yes, people could smoke indoors then, and government offices were equipped with ashtrays for the convenience of those who did.) The report that eventually emanated from the review mocked a host of other regulations and allegedly wasteful government expenditures.

The report singled out two examples of allegedly foolish federal expenditures. One of them was a one-hundred-thousand-dollar earmark for an Interior Department program to train dogs to sniff out brown tree snakes on airplanes flying from Guam to Hawaii. As the following previously unpublished essay argues, however, it was a poorly chosen example, one that showed that even an environmental champion such as Al Gore can sometimes fail to understand and appreciate the gravity of the threat to native wildlife posed by the unwitting introduction of nonnative species.

Of Snakes and Reinventing Government
1993 (previously unpublished)

Vice President Gore's recent ashtray-smashing appearance on late-night TV gave a big boost to his "Reinventing Government" report and its proposals to overhaul the way the federal government works. Unfortunately, one of the government actions the report singles out for ridicule may be Hawaii's last best hope to avert an ecological and economic travesty of staggering proportions.

In a section criticizing Congress for the practice of "earmarking" how money it appropriates must be spent, the Gore report gives two examples of what it clearly regards as congressional silliness. One of these is a directive to the Interior Department to spend one hundred thousand dollars training beagles to sniff out brown tree snakes. A lead editorial in the *Washington Post* and a news story in *US News & World Report* embraced the tree-snake example in concluding that the report is right on track. It isn't.

Around the time of World War II, brown tree snakes were accidentally introduced to Guam from the Philippines, where they naturally occur. The snakes probably arrived in Guam aboard a military cargo plane, but that is not known for certain. What is known is that, once there, the snakes became an ineradicable menace, increasing in number and spreading throughout the island.

The steady advance of the snakes across the island of Guam can be charted by the history of local power outages. These mostly arboreal snakes will climb practically anything, including utility poles, where they seek to hide in electrical transformers. In 1990, they caused at least seventy power outages on the island, inflicting literally millions of dollars of repair costs on the island's inhabitants.

By the time the snakes had completed their occupation of the island, they had turned every native bird species of Guam into an endangered species. "Occupation" is hardly too strong a term; in places, the snakes have achieved densities of fifteen thousand per square mile. Several native bird species were driven to extinction; others, nearly so. The last few surviving Guam rails and Guam kingfishers were rescued and taken into captivity. Whether their progeny will ever be able to return to Guam depends on finding a way to eliminate or control the snakes. Although much money has been spent trying control ideas, none has yet worked. Meanwhile, the forests of Guam are nearly empty of birds, and the snakes are invading homes and yards.

As most Hawaiians know, no snakes naturally occur anywhere in their state, nor are Hawaii's native animals capable of defending against or controlling snakes. In these respects, Hawaii is just like the island of Guam. If brown tree snakes make their way to Hawaii, the results are entirely predictable. Power-supply disruption and the extinction of many of Hawaii's already endangered birds will certainly follow. The enormous public investment already made in conserving Hawaii's unique natural heritage will be for naught.

Once established, the snakes will almost certainly prove impossible to eliminate, as the experience in Guam demonstrates. The only workable strategy is prevention—hence the idea of snake-sniffing beagles. At least six brown tree snakes have already been found at Hawaiian airports, stowaways in the wheel wells or cargo holds of planes arriving from Guam. None has yet made it off airport property, at least as far as anyone knows.

Rather than eliminate funding intended to prevent the tree snake's introduction to Hawaii, Congress ought to step up funding for this and other programs to prevent potentially harmful species from being accidentally introduced into new environments. If we had effective governmental programs to prevent threats such as this, rather than ineffective programs to limit the damage after it has been done, we would truly have accomplished a useful reinvention of government.

The ecological and environmental havoc introduced species can cause in new environments is abundantly clear in Hawaii. The problem, however, is by no means uniquely Hawaiian. Eastern and Great Lakes states are reeling from the effects of the introduced zebra mussel, a clam that clogs intake pipes of factories, water-treatment plants, and other facilities. Federal, state, and local governments are spending millions to remedy the damage caused by that accidental introduction. If introduced, the brown tree snake will be Hawaii's zebra mussel—but with fangs.

Detector Dogs: A Postscript to the Snakes-on-a-Plane Story

The effort to keep brown tree snakes from becoming established in Hawaii and decimating its native birdlife, as they have done to the birdlife of Guam, has succeeded so far, but it has required constant vigilance.

The use of snake-detecting dogs is a critical component of that effort. A comprehensive study of brown tree snake control efforts found that "around 99% of Guam's outgoing cargo is inspected by [US Department of Agriculture Wildlife Services] detector dog teams."[4] Detector dogs are also used as a last line of defense against the unwitting import of snakes at high-risk destinations such as Hawaii and the Commonwealth of the Northern Mariana Islands. So, far from being an example of foolish government waste, the investment in training dogs to sniff out snakes has been a vital part of the effort to protect endangered birdlife in Hawaii and elsewhere.

An interest in wildlife acquired in childhood is never lost. The author, shown here at age thirteen, examines a young eastern hognose snake.

John James Audubon, famous for his paintings in *The Birds of America*, wrote to Secretary of State Daniel Webster in 1841 to propose the creation of a natural history institution for the nation. Audubon even had a suggestion for who should head it—himself.

Spencer Baird, who once studied under Audubon, was the nation's first commissioner of fish and fisheries, the first curator for the Smithsonian Institution, and head of the American Association for the Advancement of Science.

Herman Melville believed the relentless pursuit of whales could never bring about their extinction. If necessary, he thought whales could take refuge under the "ultimate glassy barriers" of polar ice. He clearly foresaw neither the advances in whaling technology nor the effects of climate change on Arctic ice.

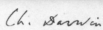

Charles Darwin referred to the diversity of living organisms and their interrelations as a "tangled bank." Today we call that concept "biodiversity."

The first significant federal wildlife law, the Lacey Act of 1900, was named for its author, Congressman John Lacey of Iowa. He is also credited with writing the Antiquities Act of 1906, the law under which Devil's Hole and the Devil's Hole pupfish were preserved.

Theodore Roosevelt, shown here with Sierra Club founder John Muir at Glacier Point in Yosemite National Park, established the first national wildlife refuge in 1903. Allegedly, when told that no law prevented him from establishing the refuge, he replied, "Very well, then, I so declare it."

Rachel Carson, shown here with Fish and Wildlife Service illustrator Robert Hines, warned of the dangers of DDT and other pesticides in her 1962 book, *Silent Spring*. Five years later the Environmental Defense Fund was formed and began a legal battle against DDT. The author later joined EDF and served there for more than three decades.

Aldo Leopold's insights into conservation have influenced generations of wildlife conservationists, including the author, who found that Leopold offered many useful lessons into the effective implementation of the Endangered Species Act.

Tom Eisner was a pioneer in the field of chemical ecology, a champion of invertebrate conservation, and a highly effective advocate of the Endangered Species Act. Photograph by Susan Middleton and David Liittschwager.

The dodo, a flightless bird from the island of Mauritius, was easy prey for early European sailors. Its extinction in the seventeenth century may have caused a cascade of ecological changes there.

In the nineteenth century the passenger pigeon was likely the most abundant bird on earth. By 1914, it was extinct, an example of how swiftly a species can collapse.

The Carolina parakeet, a denizen of the southeastern United States, was the only parakeet native to North America. It became extinct in the early twentieth century.

The Supreme Court's decision halting construction of TVA's Tellico Dam to avoid jeopardizing the survival of the snail darter was the first of several high-visibility conflicts under the Endangered Species Act.

The discovery in 1981 of a small surviving population of black-footed ferrets, once thought extinct, in Wyoming made possible an ambitious captive breeding and reintroduction effort.

Regulations to reduce the drowning of green sea turtles and other sea turtle species in shrimp nets sparked enormous controversy in the 1980s. The use of turtle excluder devices in such nets has greatly reduced sea turtle drownings.

The reintroduction of gray wolves in the Yellowstone ecosystem has been one of the most dramatic successes of the Endangered Species Act. Ironically, a lawsuit brought by environmental organizations nearly halted the effort.

The red-cockaded woodpecker was the first species for which safe harbor agreements were used to enlist private landowners in its conservation efforts. The agreements proved popular and they worked.

Nonnative species are a major threat to native biodiversity. Shown here is the author at a research facility in Everglades National Park, where Burmese pythons—a popular pet—have had a major detrimental impact on park wildlife. Photograph by Sandy Bean.

7

In Praise of Spineless Creatures

No, this chapter is not about Congress. Rather, the spineless creatures that are its subject are what the distinguished biologist E. O. Wilson once called "the little things that run the world"[1]—the insects, arachnids, crustaceans, mollusks, worms, and other creatures that together make up a group of organisms called invertebrates. If human beings were to disappear, life for earth's other creatures would change very little. Were invertebrates to vanish, however, ecological collapse would quickly result from the loss of pollinators and decomposers and from the disruption of the food chains that ultimately sustain us. Our demise would soon follow.

Although invertebrates are vitally important, they, like the comedian Rodney Dangerfield, "can't get no respect." To the extent that they pay them any attention at all, most people find most invertebrates either repellent or frightening. A lucky few, however, find them endlessly fascinating. I have been among that fortunate few from early childhood. My grandmother Bean deserves some of the credit for that, since she regularly supplied me with praying mantises, walking sticks, and other small creatures she found in her prized flower garden in Iowa. Another source of serendipitous good fortune was that the home in which I grew up backed onto woods through which flowed an ephemeral stream, a very minor tributary of the Mississippi River called Dry Creek. In those woods and that creek, I spent the best days of my youth, reveling in the company of snakes, frogs, turtles, and crayfish. Growing up in a small Iowa town, I was the only one I knew who had a butterfly net and collected insects. I was careful not to be seen by my peers with my net lest they label me an oddball or worse. An intense interest in insects and a constant dread of being ridiculed were I to be seen with a net likely contributed to my long-standing like of solitude. Although I often was without human companions, I always had plenty of company. They just had six or more legs rather than two. They were also more interesting to me than most of the human companions I might have had.

As I prepared to go off to college, my high school classmates were surprised to learn that I intended to study entomology. Once in college, however, my aspiration to become an entomologist proved short-lived. Amid the social turmoil of the late 1960s, I convinced myself that I ought to study something more "socially relevant" than entomology. My college faculty adviser—Jean Laffoon, a courtly gentleman with an unusual combination of interests in the order of insects known as Diptera (flies and their relatives) and the songs of Bertolt Brecht plays—sought to convince me to stick with my entomological studies, encouraging me to fulfill my desire for social relevance by reading the works of E. O. Wilson on the lives of social insects. I thought he just didn't understand. The irony, as it turned out, was that I ended up on a career path in environmental law, one of the true rewards of which has been the opportunity to meet and occasionally work with Wilson.

Although the vast majority of plants and animals on earth are invertebrates, they compose only about one-sixth of the US species on the endangered and threatened species list. Their underrepresentation on that list probably reflects little more than that our knowledge of the status of most invertebrates lags well behind our knowledge of most vertebrates. Rarely noticed by the average citizen unless they constitute an annoyance, and seriously studied by a relative handful of scientists, most invertebrates live lives of relative obscurity and anonymity.

There are exceptions, of course. Towns with names such as Oyster and Bivalve in New Jersey, Shelltown in Maryland, and Oyster Bay in New York (where Theodore Roosevelt spent childhood summers and later purchased Sagamore Hill, an estate that served as his summer White House and is now protected as a National Historic Site) are testimony to the important role that at least some invertebrates once played in the lives of various human communities. Even Muscle Shoals, Alabama, may have taken its name (misspelled) from the abundance of freshwater mussels that thrived in the shallows of the Tennessee River there (an alternative explanation has it that the town took its name from the muscle required to pull the boats of early settlers across the shoals). Unfortunately, the mussel shoals of Muscle Shoals are now largely gone and so too are most of the native oysters that lent their names to many once-thriving towns along the mid-Atlantic seaboard. The names persist, rather like the enormous shell middens left behind by Native Americans, as reminders of a now-vanished abundance.

The decline of these economically valued mollusks overshadows the no-less-dramatic decline of a myriad of other "less important" invertebrates. It is mostly these latter species that fill the ever-expanding list of endangered invertebrates, a list that as of early 2020 included ninety-one insects, ninety-three mollusks, seventeen arachnids, fifty-three snails, twenty-eight crustaceans, and twenty-five corals (note how different these numbers are from 1993 discussed in the following article). Sadly, despite protection as endangered or threatened species, few of these have yet to show any discernible improvement in status, and only one has yet recovered and been taken off the list.

Following are two essays about invertebrate conservation that originally appeared in *Wings*, the handsome little publication of the Xerces Society, a nonprofit organization devoted exclusively to that subject. I served for a time as a member of the Xerces board of directors, as did E. O. Wilson and the late Thomas Eisner, another giant among entomologists and invertebrate conservationists.

Invertebrates and the Endangered Species Act
Wings, Summer 1993[*]

Four years before Congress enacted the Endangered Species Act of 1973, it authorized the protection of at least some invertebrates faced with the threat of extinction. In the Endangered Species Act of 1969, Congress empowered the Secretary of the Interior to identify and protect wildlife species threatened with worldwide extinction, including mollusks and crustaceans. Previous similar authority had been limited to vertebrates.

Notwithstanding this grant of authority, only one invertebrate—the Manus Island tree snail—was ever listed as endangered pursuant to the 1969 law, which was replaced by the modern Endangered Species Act in 1973. Among its sweeping changes, the 1973 law authorized the listing and protection of any species of plant or animal, including invertebrates, as an endangered or threatened species.

In 1976, the first insects, the Bahama and Schaus' swallowtail butterflies, were officially designated as endangered species. Today, they

[*] Reprinted with permission from the Xerces Society for Invertebrate Conservation.

are joined by over 100 others: 26 additional insects, 11 crustaceans, three arachnids, and 68 gastropods and other mollusks. All but seven of these occur in the United States or its possessions. Collectively, invertebrates comprised some 13 percent of all listed US species and 26 percent of all listed US animal species. Invertebrates are likely to comprise an ever-larger fraction of the listed wildlife species in the future. Nearly 1,200 invertebrates have been identified as candidates for possible future listing, versus only about 570 vertebrates.

To date, no invertebrate has recovered sufficiently to be taken off the endangered or threatened list. Only two of the 81 then-listed invertebrates were regarded by the US Fish and Wildlife Service as improving in status as of 1990: the Socorro isopod and the fat pocketbook pearlymussel. Some 33 of these were considered to be still declining or possibly extinct. Among the latter, the Palos Verdes blue butterfly likely became extinct in the early 1980s, notwithstanding the Endangered Species Act, when its last known habitat was destroyed in the course of creating a local park. The city of Rancho Palos Verdes, California, was prosecuted for this action but successfully defended on the theory that the law did not apply to local units of government. The law has since been amended to make clear its application in such situations.

The above statistics regarding the status of listed invertebrates compare unfavorably with listed species overall. Some 11 percent of listed species are thought to be improving, compared to only 2.5 percent of invertebrates. For freshwater clams, the situation is particularly disturbing. Of the 48 species listed as of 1990, 93 percent were thought to be declining or possibly extinct, compared to only 35 percent of listed species overall.

A more striking contrast can be drawn by comparing the expenditures for invertebrates with those for vertebrates. In fiscal year 1991 (the most recent year for which data are available), state and federal agencies combined spent an average of $1.1 million for each listed bird species, $684,000 for each listed mammal species, and only $44,000 for each listed invertebrate species. The average spending for invertebrates is strongly skewed by an expenditure of $1 million each for the valley elderberry longhorn beetle and the Schaus' swallowtail butterfly; eliminate the spending for these two species and the average expenditure for listed invertebrates drops to $17,500. In 1991 federal agencies spent less than $5,000 each for more than half the listed invertebrates.

The relative paucity of resources being devoted to endangered invertebrate conservation is not simply a matter of their being smaller creatures occupying smaller ranges than most endangered vertebrates. Indeed, many of the endangered mussels occupy multi-state ranges. A contributing factor is the lack of official interest in, and occasional antipathy to, invertebrates in general. Invertebrates are featured much more prominently in the anti-Endangered Species Act propaganda being circulated by the Act's adversaries than they are in the implementation of the Act itself. A recent pop-up card circulated by opponents of the Act featured the fat pocketbook pearlymussel and the tuna cave cockroach (a candidate for future listing) as examples of expensive environmental frivolity. The National Wilderness Institute, which, despite its benign sounding name, is a caustic critic of endangered species protection, regularly charges that money raised on the appeal of eagles and panthers is being spent for rodents and insects. If the public only knew, they imply, it would be less supportive of the Endangered Species Act.

Though invertebrates are a favorite target of the Act's opponents, they have actually featured in very few significant controversies. Probably the most prominent such controversy involved the Tennessee Valley Authority's proposed Columbia Dam on the Duck River in Tennessee. In the late 1970s, the dam was stymied due to the presence of the birdwing and Cumberland monkey-faced pearlymussels, both endangered. The Mission blue butterfly briefly held up development on San Bruno Mountain south of San Francisco in the early 1980s. That controversy was eventually resolved with the Endangered Species Act's first "habitat conservation plan," a mechanism that Interior Secretary Bruce Babbitt hails as a creative means of resolving development and species conservation controversies. For most invertebrates, however, conservation efforts have gone forward in relative obscurity, generating little controversy. Whereas the proposed reintroduction of species like the gray wolf in Yellowstone National Park has been intensely controversial, the American burying beetle and other invertebrates have been reintroduced without contention.

Congress is likely to consider significant amendments to the Endangered Species Act later this year or next. Many of those, like H.R. 1490, recently introduced by Congressman Billy Tauzin (D-LA), would dramatically reduce protection for endangered species across the board. His proposed changes in the listing process would greatly delay future listings. This would particularly affect invertebrates, which comprise a large fraction of the candidate species awaiting future listing. His proposal to require greater "balancing" of economic and conservation considerations in decisions made under the Act would likewise probably redound to the particular detriment of invertebrates.

Later amendments may focus specifically on invertebrates. The Act already treats invertebrates less generously than it does vertebrates in two respects. First, insects are singled out as the only group of organisms that cannot be protected if a particular species is determined by the Secretary of Agriculture to be an agricultural pest. Not surprisingly, this provision has never been used, since a species on the brink of extinction is hardly likely to be a serious pest. Second, whereas the Act authorizes the protection of species, subspecies and "distinct population segments" of vertebrates, only species and subspecies of invertebrates may be protected. This provision was a compromise between the House and Senate in 1978; the House had voted to eliminate protection for invertebrates altogether.

The record of accomplishment of the Endangered Species Act for invertebrates is modest, but significant. Perhaps most important, it has drawn attention to the fact that the crisis of extinction confronts not just birds and mammals, but a myriad of less well-known, less conspicuous, but no less important, creatures. That attention has helped mobilize significant resources to focus on the conservation of species about which few were aware or concerned until quite recently. Continuing a strong Endangered Species Act, now under attack from a host of business and ideological interests, should be a high priority for all who are concerned about the conservation of creatures both big and small.

Just as Mark Twain once quipped that rumors of his death had been greatly exaggerated, so too did my preceding article exaggerate the demise of the Palos Verdes blue butterfly. In 1993, when the article was written, the butterfly had not been seen for a decade, hence the conclusion that it was likely extinct. Sure enough, however, the year after the article appeared, so too did the butterfly. Still another small population was discovered in 2001, and at least one other has been established through reintroductions. Authors are seldom happy to be wrong, but in this case I am happy to have to correct the record. The Palos Verdes blue butterfly still clings tenaciously, but tenuously, to life.

There is other good news. In 2013, the first imperiled invertebrate to have recovered and been taken off the list of endangered and threatened species was announced. Known as the Magazine Mountain shagreen, it is a tiny snail found only on the talus slopes of Magazine Mountain in the Ozark–St. Francis National Forest in Arkansas. To say that it is obscure hardly does justice to the word. Indeed, there are probably more words on this page than there are people who have heard of the Magazine Mountain shagreen and far fewer still who have ever seen one. Nevertheless, its very obscurity is reason for hope: the Endangered Species Act was never intended to focus only on the charismatic and familiar. Rather, its goal is to keep every cog and wheel in the machinery of life that we possibly can, and the recovery of the Magazine Mountain shagreen shows that this goal is being taken seriously.

The Magazine Mountain shagreen may soon have company on the list of formerly endangered invertebrates. As of this writing in late 2020, another invertebrate has been proposed for removal from the endangered and threatened list because of its apparent recovery: the Nashville crayfish from the Mill Creek watershed in Tennessee. Siltation and water-quality decline led to its listing in 1986, but measures taken to address these threats and the resilience of the crayfish to them may mean that the protection of the Endangered Species Act is no longer needed. Still, these are atypical examples in the effort to conserve invertebrates, as the following article suggests.

Lessons from Two Endangered Invertebrates
Wings, Fall 2001[*]

In 1980, the federal government, largely to publicize the problem of endangered species, issued a list of the "ten most endangered" species. On it were two invertebrates, the birdwing pearlymussel (*Conradilla caelata*) and the lotis blue butterfly (*Lycaedes idas lotis*). Invertebrates then comprised less than a fifth of the more than 200 recognized endangered animal species in the United States; now, they comprise more than a third of the nearly 500 endangered animal species.

Today, the birdwing pearlymussel, while still imperiled, faces a brighter future. The lotis blue butterfly, on the other hand, has likely gone extinct; it was last seen in 1983. In the differing stories of these

[*] Reprinted with permission from the Xerces Society for Invertebrate Conservation.

two species, perhaps a few lessons useful to the conservation of both vertebrates and invertebrates can be discerned.

As a group, freshwater mussels are the most imperiled of organisms in the United States. According to the standardized rankings of The Nature Conservancy, more than two-thirds of them are considered possibly extinct, critically imperiled, imperiled, or vulnerable. More distressful still is the fact that, despite years of protection under the Endangered Species Act, nearly all of the sixty-nine officially listed species are still declining, according to the assessment of the US Fish and Wildlife Service.

The birdwing pearlymussel, however, may beat the odds. Ironically, its improved chances for survival are due to actions taken in anticipation of damming its last significant habitat. In the late 1970s, a huge controversy swirled around the efforts of the Tennessee Valley Authority (TVA) to complete Tellico Dam on the Little Tennessee River, a dam that threatened the survival of the endangered snail darter. Notwithstanding a Supreme Court ruling in favor of the tiny fish, Congress eventually directed the completion of the dam.

While the Tellico Dam controversy raged on, another TVA dam project was underway. This was the Columbia Dam on central Tennessee's Duck River, home to the birdwing pearlymussel. In anticipation of creating a fifty-four-mile-long reservoir behind the proposed dam, the TVA bought up some sixteen thousand acres of farms and other land. However, the dam was never completed, due in part to changes in TVA leadership and philosophy, and at least in part to the requirements of the Endangered Species Act. Meanwhile, by idling much of the land along the river, the TVA had launched an unexpected restoration in the quality of the Duck River's water. Buffered from heavy pollutant loadings of nutrients, pesticides, and silt, the mussels of the Duck River flourished. Overall mussel density increased nearly threefold in a decade; density of birdwing pearlymussels doubled; and yet another species that had been thought to have been extirpated there, the tan riffleshell (*Epioblasma florentina walkeri*), was found to be not only present, but reproducing.

The birdwing pearlymussel's lease on life is now reasonably secure. Plans for completing the Columbia Dam have been scrapped. Most of the land that the TVA acquired for the reservoir will now be protected as parkland. Though an unintended consequence of the TVA's land acquisition efforts, the ongoing recovery of the mussel is a powerful testament to the value of buffering river corridors from the effects of development, intensive agriculture, and other practices. Not only imperiled mussels, but crayfish, stoneflies, and other aquatic organisms can benefit from that simple lesson.

The lotis blue butterfly's story has a less happy ending. It was added to the endangered species list in June 1976, the same month that the birdwing pearlymussel was added. The factors that led to its endangerment were never known with certainty. They likely included loss of its sphagnum bog habitat to development, and vegetational succession that eliminated its larval host plant. Indicative of how little is truly known about the natural history of the lotis blue butterfly, the identity of its larval host plant was never established with certainty, although it is thought to have been a legume known commonly as seaside birdsfoot trefoil (*Lotus formosissimus*). A prolonged drought in the late 1970s, which desiccated the principal bog from which the lotis blue butterfly was known, may have delivered the coup de grace.

The effort to save the lotis blue butterfly clearly got started too late. By the time of its listing in 1976, its population was already dangerously small, making it vulnerable to weather extremes that it had doubtless survived many times before in its history. Even had its loss been forestalled then, however, a vigilant effort to fight back the tide of invasive plant species disrupting habitats throughout California would have been essential. The enormity of this threat to many imperiled species, including the endangered Bay checkerspot butterfly (*Euphydryas editha bayensis*) of the San Francisco Bay area, is only now beginning to be appreciated.

The lotis blue butterfly also apparently had its last place of refuge on land that was in private ownership. In that respect as well, it is typical, for many other imperiled species survive primarily or exclusively on privately owned land. As the noted conservationist Aldo Leopold observed more than sixty years ago, "conservation will ultimately boil down to rewarding the private landowner who conserves the public interest." For the lotis blue butterfly it is apparently too late, but for the many other imperiled invertebrates of this country, there is no more urgent task than creating positive incentive for the owners of the land on which they live to manage that land so as to perpetuate and improve the habitat those species need. The fortuitous happenstance that resulted in habitat improvements benefiting the birdwing pearlymussel is no substitute for a concerted effort to work with both private and public land owners to restore and enhance endangered species habitat.

Regrettably, I cannot report that my obituary for the lotis blue butterfly—unlike that for the Palos Verdes blue butterfly—was premature.
When the foregoing two articles were written, in 1993 and 2001, both of
these butterflies had not been seen since 1983. The lotis blue butterfly has
still not been seen and must, after some thirty-seven years, be presumed
to be almost certainly extinct.

The Cumberland monkeyface pearlymussel continues to thrive, at
least in the Duck River, where it has expanded its range and increased
its numbers. Other endangered mussels in other rivers of the Southeast
have recently experienced inexplicable die-offs, but the Duck River
has thus far been spared. The protection of much of the land within
its watershed and the TVA's cooperation in improving the oxygenation
of waters released from the Normandy Dam upstream have produced
the still all-too-rare phenomenon of success in the conservation of an
invertebrate.

That the Duck River still flows freely over its mussel-rich shoals is
thanks in large part to the tenacity of a local lawyer named Frank Fly.
Frank was raised on a family farm on the river, secured a law degree from
the University of Tennessee College of Law, opened up a law practice in
the small town of Murfreesboro, and spent the better part of his for-
ty-seven-year legal career fighting to keep the Tennessee Valley Authority
from despoiling that river with Columbia Dam. Sadly, as this book was
being written, Frank died after a long battle with Lou Gehrig's disease.

Thomas Eisner, a Champion of Invertebrate Conservation

In the summer of 1952, two aspiring young biologists set out from Cambridge, Massachusetts, on a meandering road trip that would take them
to the West Coast and back again. Having armed themselves with nets,
collecting jars, forceps, and other tools of the entomologist's trade, their
goal was to explore and better understand the insect life of the diverse
ecosystems that make up the American landscape. Born some two weeks
apart in June 1929, they were just twenty-two years old when they hit
the road, the same age as Darwin had been when he set sail aboard the
HMS *Beagle*. Their counterpart to the *Beagle* was a 1942 Chevrolet that
seemed to consume as much oil as it did gasoline. They called it the
Charrúa II in honor of a seasonally nomadic and nearly extinct group of

indigenous people in South America. Summer is the season for insects, so, like those Amerindian nomads, the two biologists were on the move.

These two adventurers had much in common besides their age. Both were Harvard University graduate students. Both had been avid collectors of insects since early childhood. Both had an innate curiosity about the natural world around them and an exceptional talent for divining its mysterious workings. Both would eventually be recipients of the National Medal of Science, the most prestigious award given to American scientists. Both would become passionate advocates for conserving the natural world and its living creatures.

In other ways, these two could not have been more different. One was born in Birmingham, Alabama, the only child in a fractured family that soon split apart. The other was born in Berlin, Germany, part of a family that would go to extraordinary lengths to stay together in the maelstrom of prewar Europe. One was Edward O. Wilson. The other was Thomas Eisner.

Hans Eisner, Tom's father, was born in Silesia in 1892. At age nineteen he became a pharmacist's apprentice, a career that was cut short by the outbreak of World War I. Drafted into the German army in 1916, he served in both the artillery and the infantry. Following the end of the war, he studied chemistry at the University of Berlin's Kaiser Wilhelm Institute for Physical Chemistry and Electrochemistry, headed by the famous, and infamous, German chemist Fritz Haber.

Haber was famous for having been the first to synthesize ammonia, an accomplishment for which he was awarded the 1918 Nobel Prize in Chemistry. He was infamous for having played a key role in developing chemical weapons that Germany used against the Allies in World War I (a form of warfare that both sides employed). Following the end of the war, Haber began to explore the feasibility of extracting gold from seawater. Although it proved impractical to do so, Eisner's contributions to the effort earned him a PhD in 1923.

Finding employment in postwar Germany proved to be nearly as difficult as finding gold in seawater. He initially tried launching a line of cosmetics, but that plan was derailed amid the political turbulence of the Weimar Republic. In March 1933, when Adolf Hitler gained total control of the German state, it was finally clear to Hans, a Jew, that he and his young family would need to pursue their future elsewhere.

The following month, Hans and his artist wife took their six-year-old daughter and three-year-old son, Thomas, and left Germany for what they thought would be the security of Spain.

Speaking no Spanish, Hans knew that life would be challenging in Spain. What he did not know was that only three years after arriving, his hope of security there would be shattered by the outbreak of the Spanish civil war. When a gun battle erupted on the very street where the Eisner family lived in Barcelona, Hans knew that he had to pack up his family and leave once again, this time to France. The Eisner family's stay in France would be brief, but long enough for the young Thomas to add French to his growing repertoire of languages. Tom later proudly remembered that while still a child he was able to curse Hitler in three languages.

With the menace of Hitler hanging over all of Europe, Hans decided to leave the continent altogether and move his family to South America, where the pharmaceutical company for which he worked in Spain had branches in Argentina, Brazil, and Uruguay. Unable to get a visa to Argentina, and unwilling to learn yet another new language in Brazil, Hans and family departed for Uruguay, where they would spend the next decade. There Tom enrolled in an English school and developed a passion for collecting butterflies, aided by the gift from his parents of a butterfly guide for his twelfth birthday. From his father he acquired two other interests, music and photography, that—like the butterfly guide—would stay with him for the rest of his life.

The Eisner family would make one final move, this time to the United States. Hans was determined that his two children be given the best possible education and convinced that they could do so only in America. In March 1947, they boarded an American freighter in Montevideo harbor and twelve days later disembarked in Boston. The goal of getting the best possible education for Tom was more difficult than expected. In the wake of World War II, many American colleges were filled with former servicemen taking advantage of the benefits of the GI Bill. Tom applied to Harvard, Amherst, Rochester, and Cornell. All turned him down. Scaling back his aspirations, Tom first enrolled in a secretarial school and then in the now-defunct Champlain College in Plattsburgh, New York. Champlain College consisted of a former army barracks repurposed after the war into a two-year school primarily serving veterans. It would last only until the outbreak of the next war, in Korea, when it reverted to military use. It was in business long enough for Tom to complete two years of study in which he did sufficiently well to gain admission to Harvard as a transfer student.

It was at Harvard that Tom befriended and became roommates with Edward O. Wilson, a friendship that would last for the rest of their lives. After completing their PhDs, Wilson stayed on as part of the Harvard faculty, while Eisner accepted an offer to join the faculty at Cornell University. It was the same school that, a decade earlier, had rejected his application for admission. Eisner had that rejection letter framed and proudly hung on his office wall.

When Tom began his career at Cornell, the popular image of evolution at work emphasized tooth and claw as the strong overpowered the weak and the swift overcame the slow. Tom's work opened up a new dimension in the evolutionary struggle, one that revealed the role of chemistry in the struggle to survive and reproduce. Invisible to the human eye was an entire arsenal of chemical weapons that insects employed to deter predators, disable prey, attract mates, and gain a competitive advantage. Plants, too, utilized an array of chemicals to fend off insect herbivores. Tom's genius was in bringing these unseen battles into view and in explaining them in ways understandable to a popular audience.

It was that genius that made Tom such a perfect witness in congressional hearings on the Endangered Species Act. Tom testified in several of those hearings in the 1980s and 1990s. He often brought with him a prop in the form of a small vial containing a specimen of some obscure species he had studied. Once it was a bryozoan with chemical properties of potential medical application. Another time it was an endangered species of mint found only in Florida and having extraordinary insecticidal properties. His props never included familiar, charismatic species. And that, after all, was the point.

When in 1978 the former attorney general Griffin Bell had held aloft a similar vial containing a small snail darter, his evident purpose was to impress on the Supreme Court the smallness—and thus the unimportance—of that species. When Tom Eisner passed around his small vials to the members of a congressional committee, it was to illustrate his point that even the smallest, most unfamiliar, and uncharismatic of species had potentially great value and importance. Tom, as best I can recall, never declined a request to come to Washington to testify at a congressional hearing on the Endangered Species Act. Participating in those hearings entailed no small commitment of his time, for Tom had a lifelong aversion to flying. Instead, he would drive the roughly 250 miles from Cornell to Washington, a trip that took some five and a half hours each way.

Though Tom was passionate about biology and about the conservation of nature, he was no less committed to the cause of human rights. In the 1970s, the American Association for the Advancement of Science formed a Committee on Scientific Freedom and Responsibility, on which Tom served for many years. Its purpose was not only to speak out for foreign scientists who were victims of governmental persecution but also to draw attention to American scientists in governmental agencies who suffered reprisals for exposing agency misconduct. It was a cause that Tom readily embraced.

Tom had two other lifelong passions, music and photography. With his camera he could capture the essence of the biological stories he sought to tell. Over the course of his career, more than a dozen of his photos graced the cover of *Science* magazine, which was more than any other photographer's at the time (and may be still). He was also an accomplished pianist who enjoyed recounting how on one of his transatlantic voyages his daily practicing on the ship's piano caught the attention of another passenger. She asked him if he would play while she practiced her singing. Tom happily agreed. The other passenger, it turned out, was Lena Horne, the famous singer, stage and screen actress, and civil rights activist.

I once accompanied Tom and E. O. Wilson in a cab ride from the Environmental Defense Fund office in Washington to a meeting on Capitol Hill. They sat in the rear seat and I sat up front, in the shotgun seat. I was eager to hear what these two most extraordinary ecologists who had been friends since graduate school would say to each other. Would they reminisce about the summer they spent exploring together in Eisner's jalopy, the *Charrúa II*? Would they discuss their latest natural history discoveries or their next planned science projects? I wish I could say that yes, these were the things they discussed, but candor compels me to admit that what they actually talked about were their shared ailments of advancing age. It was a reminder that even one's heroes are ordinary human beings with ordinary human concerns.

The Pulitzer Prize–winning writer Natalie Angier once wrote that Tom Eisner's enthusiasm for insects was so great that one nearly expected "a pair of antennae to sprout from his forehead."[2] There were never any antennae on Tom's head, but inside his head was an exceptional mind, one that virtually created the entirely new discipline of chemical ecology. Near the end of his career, Tom completed a book that was part autobiography, part retelling of some of his more fascinating discoveries, and part portfolio of many of the best of his remarkable photographs. He gave that book a title that summed up the passion that had inspired and motivated him from earliest childhood. He called it simply *For Love of Insects.*

8

An Endangered Act?

Remember the snail darter in Tennessee? The uproar over that tiny fish and Tellico Dam was just the first in a series of high-visibility controversies sparked by the Endangered Species Act. Others followed quickly in its wake. These controversies have shaken the once-solid foundation of support for the act, but, remarkably, the law has thus far weathered each new storm. Many of those storms pitted politically powerful interests against the act and the species it protected, repeatedly raising the question, Is the act itself endangered?

In the 1980s, for example, thousands of shrimp fishermen along the South Atlantic and Gulf Coasts furiously resisted the imposition of gear requirements to reduce the drowning of endangered sea turtles in their trawls. They engaged in massive civil disobedience, including by blockading the Houston Ship Channel with some two hundred of their boats. Members of Congress from the region largely sided with the shrimpers in calling for changes to the act.

Not long after that battle reached its peak in the Southeast, another erupted in the Pacific Northwest with the listing in 1992 of the northern spotted owl as a threatened species and the subsequent dramatic reduction of timber harvest on federal forestland in the region. Like their southeastern counterparts in the shrimp fleet, loggers in the Pacific Northwest clamored for Congress to rein in a law that they regarded as having put the interests of wildlife ahead of their own economic well-being.

In the mid-1990s yet another major regional conflict erupted. The subject this time was a federal plan to release wolves in Yellowstone National Park and in the wilderness areas of central Idaho. A half century earlier, wolves had been purposely eradicated from these areas—indeed, from virtually all of the continental United States—to accommodate the interests of ranchers and their livestock. Now the federal government wanted to bring them back, an idea that struck many ranchers as evidence that government officials in Washington cared little for their plight.

Other conflicts broke out in other places. As real estate development gobbled up coastal sage scrub habitat in southern California and scenic ranchland in the Texas Hill Country, a clash with the Endangered Species Act seemed all but inevitable. It came when the California gnatcatcher and two Texas songbirds were added to the list of threatened and endangered species. Suddenly the shrimpers, loggers, and ranchers in the nation's hinterlands found themselves in common cause with deep-pocketed development interests in some of the most rapidly urbanizing areas of the country.

There was still more to come. In the second decade of the twenty-first century, farmers in California's Central Valley, an area with some of the nation's most productive agricultural land—and some of the nation's most politically powerful agriculturalists—found themselves in the middle of a drought and in the middle of a powder keg of conflict over what should be given priority in the allocation of available water: their farms or the several endangered fishes of the state's bay-delta ecosystem.

As these controversies piled up, one after the other, support for the Endangered Species Act in Congress wavered. Although it had been enacted with near-unanimous support in 1973, the act faces an increasingly uncertain future. In theory, Congress is supposed to review periodically the implementation of laws like the Endangered Species Act and revise them in light of that experience through a process known as "reauthorization." Technically, what Congress reauthorizes is the appropriation of taxpayer funds to implement the revised law for a period of years. Amid increasingly acrimonious and partisan debate, Congress did reauthorize the act in 1978, 1982, and 1988. The 1988 reauthorization was for a period of four years. Since that reauthorization lapsed in 1992, Congress has repeatedly tried and failed to reauthorize the act. Funds have been appropriated, but almost annually since 1992 the law's opponents and defenders have mobilized their forces to battle over its fate. Several efforts to weaken it have come close to success but have fallen short. Like the species it seeks to protect, the law itself may be endangered.

This chapter begins with a closer look at one of these controversies— the conflict between shrimpers and sea turtles. That conflict nearly derailed the reauthorization effort in 1988, as an op-ed I wrote at the time recounts. Getting through Congress, however, was not the end of the matter. There remained a threat that sea turtle conservation efforts in the United States would be upended by the World Trade Organization, a threat described in the second reprinted op-ed.

The conflict over wolves and their reintroduction in the Northern Rockies is the subject of the third article. It tells the little-known story of how a lawsuit filed by environmental organizations that supported wolf conservation backfired and nearly ended the reintroduction effort—an effort that was to become one of the most dramatic successes of the Endangered Species Act. It is an illustration of the unpredictable outcomes that can sometimes result from well-intended but counterproductive litigation. Wolves were also at issue in the fourth article, which examines a surprising threat to the future of the Endangered Species Act. Nearly half a century after its enactment, there is a chance that the increasingly conservative Supreme Court may find it unconstitutional, at least as it applies to many of the species it now protects.

Despite all these threats to the act—from an ever-more-partisan Congress, from international trade rules, from a much-changed Supreme Court, and sometimes from its own litigation-prone advocates—the Endangered Species Act has proven remarkably resilient. Amid the controversies and conflicts that have sometimes dominated the headlines, it is easy to overlook what the act has accomplished. This chapter ends with a previously unpublished essay, cowritten with my former colleague David Wilcove in the early 1990s. It asks the reader to imagine what the world would be like had there never been an Endangered Species Act.

A Deep Dive into the Sea Turtle Saga

Every year sea turtles, those gentle giants of the ocean, lumber out of the sea in the middle of the night to lay their eggs in the sands of our South Atlantic and Gulf Coast beaches. They have done so since long before any human ever set foot upon those beaches. Weeks later their eggs hatch, and the tiny hatchlings make a perilous dash to the sea. This ritual has played out since time immemorial. Whether it would long continue, however, was very much in doubt by the late 1970s, because by then all five species that occur in US waters were in such peril that they were given the protection of the Endangered Species Act.

A major problem confronting these creatures was the fact that shrimp fishermen unwittingly caught—and drowned—them in their nets. At the time, the National Marine Fisheries Service estimated that about twelve thousand turtles died this way each year, enough to push those already imperiled creatures even closer to the brink of extinction. An unexpected hero in the effort to prevent that fate was the Ronald Reagan administration, whose Commerce Department had set out years earlier to find a way for shrimpers to catch shrimp without killing sea turtles. Success rewarded the effort. A simple device fastened to the net deflected turtles and other large and unwanted objects away from it without significantly reducing the shrimp catch. Mandating the use of "turtle excluder devices" (TEDs) promised to be as successful in protecting turtles as similar regulations were in protecting porpoises from drowning in tuna nets a decade earlier.

As unlikely as the Reagan administration may have seemed in the role of a savior of endangered see turtles, even more implausible was the fact that Congress seemed determined to block this one quite sensible environmental initiative. Unwilling to submit to regulation of their fishery, convinced that TEDs would diminish their catch of shrimp, and determined to keep fishing—and killing turtles—just as their fathers and grandfathers had done, some shrimpers stirred up a major ruckus that was particularly menacing in coastal Louisiana and Texas. Responding to that ruckus, Gulf Coast politicians vowed to keep the administration's proposed regulations from ever taking effect.

The conflict over sea turtles and the shrimp industry threatened to derail efforts to reauthorize the Endangered Species Act in 1988. With the clock ticking to reauthorize the act before its existing authorization expired, the Senate majority leader, Robert Byrd of West Virginia, would not bring the reauthorization bill to the floor because of the objections of his colleague, Howell Heflin of Alabama. Heflin's only concern was with the sea turtle regulations, which he strongly opposed. In an effort to pressure Byrd to bring the bill to the floor, I wrote the following op-ed in West Virginia's leading newspaper, the *Charleston Gazette*. The *Gazette* accompanied my op-ed with an editorial of its own, strongly endorsing my call for Byrd to act.

Fiddler Should Call Tune in Senate for Rare Animals
Charleston Gazette, June 24, 1988*

Senate Majority Leader Robert C. Byrd, D-W.Va., is renowned for his skill with a country fiddle. Toe-tapping enthusiasm for some down-home music breaks out every time the courtly Democrat picks up his bow.

For the past year and more, the nation's conservationists have been urging the Senate leader to put down his bow and pick up his gavel. Byrd has had it in his power to bring legislation to strengthen the Endangered Species Act to a vote on the Senate floor. He has declined to do so, however, and as a result, opportunities to rescue many imperiled wild creatures have been jeopardized.

The most vivid reminder of the gravity of the perils facing our nation's wildlife came just a year ago, when the last surviving dusky seaside sparrow, a Florida songbird, died in captivity. June 16, 1988, was the first anniversary of the passing of this tiny bird, whose melodious song will be heard no more.

With his fine ear for music, the senator from West Virginia ought to appreciate the loss of a fellow music maker like the dusky seaside sparrow. He also ought to understand what it means to compare endangered species today to the canaries that West Virginia coal miners used to carry into the mines with them. The canaries' deaths warned of danger to the miners themselves; the endangerment of our wildlife today offers a similar warning for our own well-being.

Though the sparrow is gone, there is still hope for other creatures. The bald eagle and peregrine falcon, though still endangered, have been making a steady comeback since the Endangered Species Act was passed. The California condor, North America's largest bird, has a new lease on life now that the first condor has been bred in captivity. More than 80 other imperiled US birds can improve their prospects for survival if the Senate approves the legislation before it.

The irony in all this is that little controversy attends the legislation pending in the Senate. The Committee on Environment and Public Works approved it unanimously last year and nearly half the members of the Senate are co-sponsors of it, including many Democrats and Republicans. A similar bill passed the House last December by a vote of 399 to 16. Alabama's Howell Heflin, however, has objected to floor consideration of the measure because he is unhappy with recent regulations that seek to reduce the carnage of endangered sea turtles caused by shrimp fishermen in his state.

As majority leader, Sen. Byrd has the authority to call the Senate's tune, not Sen. Heflin. He ought to use that authority and give the Senate the opportunity to decide, if only for the birds.

Soon after the preceding op-ed appeared, a classic Washington, DC, political compromise was struck, allowing Byrd to bring the reauthorization bill to the floor. Congress would direct the National Academy of Sciences, the nation's foremost scientific institution, to study the matter and report back to it on whether the gear restrictions on the shrimpers were justified. Conservation interests were satisfied with this resolution because they had a well-justified confidence that the study would affirm the need for the controversial regulations.

When the academy's report was subsequently issued in 1990, it did indeed offer a ringing endorsement of the need for regulations to reduce the drowning of sea turtles in shrimp nets. In fact, the academy report concluded that the number of turtles being killed by the fishery was even greater than the government had previously estimated. The handwriting was now on the wall: American shrimp fishermen would have to equip their nets with devices that would exclude sea turtles from being caught in them.

Within a few years, the conflict threatened to flare anew. American shrimp fishermen competed in a global market with foreign fishermen who were not required to equip their nets with TEDs. The American fishermen argued that this put them at a competitive disadvantage and that they had lost market share as a result. Congress responded to their concern with legislation allowing the import of wild-caught shrimp only from nations that required their fleets to use the turtle-saving devices. That requirement, however, was challenged as a violation of international trade law, a challenge that the World Trade Organization affirmed in 1998. I wrote the following op-ed for the *Atlanta Constitution*, highlighting the progress that had been made in restoring sea turtle populations in the United States and the need for international efforts to do the same.

US Can't Save World's Sea Turtles on Its Own
Atlanta Constitution, June 10, 1998

This spring, researchers from the University of Georgia's Marine Extension Service were amazed by the number of endangered sea turtles they encountered along the coast. For years, they and other observers have tracked the diminished numbers of these imperiled leviathans during the process of catching them, tagging them and then releasing them. This spring, however, the Georgia vessels had what one federal scientist called a "phenomenal catch," several times higher than two decades earlier.

In South Carolina this year, researchers conducting aerial surveys of the state's coastal waters were similarly startled when they encountered juvenile sea turtles in numbers far greater than they had seen before. Meanwhile, on the short stretch of beach in Mexico where the rarest sea turtles begin their long journey, the numbers of female Kemp's ridley sea turtles crawling ashore to lay their eggs are soaring.

These remarkable events don't appear to be some aberration attributable to El Niño weather patterns. Rather, they are strongly encouraging signs that a decades-old effort to avert the extinction of our biggest and most awe-inspiring turtles is producing solid results.

That conservation effort has been built on three steps:

- Restricting development and other disturbances on key turtle-nesting beaches.
- Encouraging a small army of dedicated volunteers to guard the nests to help greater numbers of the tiny hatchlings make their perilous journey to the sea.
- Requiring shrimp boats to equip their trawls with special devices (called "turtle excluder devices," or TEDs) that prevent turtles from being caught and drowned.

The irony is, however, that just as our nation's long commitment to sea-turtle preservation is beginning to show signs of success, an international body has undermined sea-turtle conservation elsewhere.

A panel of the World Trade Organization concluded in March that the rules of international trade prevent the United States from requiring that wild-caught shrimp be imported only from nations that mandate their shrimp fleets to use TEDs. The United States has had that import restriction since 1989.

By prohibiting the import of shrimp caught without TED-equipped nets, the US government sought to ensure that sea turtles elsewhere could recover, just as they are now doing here. The requirement also meant that US shrimpers, who incur the cost of equipping their nets with the conservation devices, could compete on a level playing field with shrimpers from abroad.

The World Trade Organization's decision effectively says to the United States that it must open its market to shrimp from any nation in the world, including those whose shrimping practices are driving sea-turtle populations ever closer to extinction. The Clinton administration has appealed. When considering that appeal, the World Trade Organization ought to open its eyes to what researchers here have seen: It is within our power to preserve some of the world's most magnificent creatures, but only if we use all the necessary tools and sustain the efforts over decades.

The US appeal of the World Trade Organization's ruling was successful. In 2001 it secured a reversal of that ruling. As a result, American shrimp fishermen could no longer contend that their foreign competitors had an unfair advantage. Gratifyingly, sea turtle numbers in the United States have continued to climb as a result of both the gear restrictions and the improved protection of nesting beaches. In 2019, for example, nearly seven thousand sea turtle nests were counted on South Carolina beaches, the greatest number in nearly four decades of record keeping.

Restoring Wolves to Yellowstone—and How It Nearly Did Not Happen

The hard-won gains for sea turtle conservation are among the most significant accomplishments of the Endangered Species Act. Another is the restoration of wolves to the Yellowstone ecosystem in the Northern Rockies that began in 1995. Ironically, that remarkable achievement was nearly thwarted by a singularly ill-advised lawsuit by a few environmental organizations. The story of how that lawsuit nearly compelled the federal government to remove the very wolves they had just translocated from Canada is told in the following article from a Fish and Wildlife Service publication.

Tenth Circuit Court Upholds Wolf Reintroductions
Endangered Species Update 17, no. 2 (2000)

The United States Court of Appeals for the Tenth Circuit has clarified
the authority of the US Fish and Wildlife Service to establish "experimental populations" of endangered species under Section 10(j) of the
Endangered Species Act. The clarification came in a January 13 decision upholding the actions of the Service in establishing experimental
populations of gray wolves (*Canus lupus*) in the Yellowstone area of
Wyoming and Montana and in central Idaho (*Wyoming Farm Bureau
Federation et al. v. Babbitt*). The court's decision overturns a 1997
district court decision that found the Service's actions unlawful and
ordered the removal of the reintroduced wolves and their offspring.
As a result of the appellate court decision, the wolves can stay and will
continue to receive the protection under which their numbers have
steadily grown to more than 250 animals. The decision also removes
a potential obstacle to the establishment of experimental populations
of a number of other endangered species.

The principal issue in the case was whether the government could
use the authority of Section 10(j) to establish "experimental populations" of wolves in the two areas, given that there was some evidence
that individual, naturally occurring wolves may also occur in those
areas from time to time. "Experimental populations" of endangered
species are subject to less stringent protection than are endangered
species generally. Because of the differing levels of protection afforded experimental and non-experimental populations, Section 10(j)
requires that experimental populations be "wholly separate geograph-
ically from non-experimental populations of the same species." The
Service contended that it had the authority to proceed under Section
10(j) because there was no "population" of wolves in either Yellowstone or central Idaho. In the Service's view, the occasional wolf that
may occur there from time to time did not constitute a population.
Instead, a population required the presence of at least two successfully
breeding pairs.

Two sets of interests disagreed. One was composed of the American Farm Bureau Federation and several of its state affiliates. They
alleged that the presence of occasional wolves in central Idaho and
Yellowstone meant that the government had acted unlawfully in
reintroducing wolves there under Section 10(j). The remedy, they

argued, was to declare the reintroduction unlawful and to remove the wolves.

Four groups represented by Earthjustice Legal Defense Fund, including the National Audubon Society and three small local groups, also challenged Interior's action. The Earthjustice groups alleged that there were naturally occurring wolves in central Idaho and that the government's action in establishing an experimental population of wolves there stripped native wolves of the greater protection to which they were entitled. Because the government could not treat these as part of an experimental population under Section 10(j), they sought an order declaring the government's action unlawful, but allowing the naturally occurring wolves to receive the full protection of endangered species.

The two cases were eventually consolidated. Two groups that had devoted significant resources to the wolf reintroduction effort, Defenders of Wildlife and the National Wildlife Federation, intervened in support of the Service's position. However, the district court agreed with the Farm Bureau and Earthjustice premise that Section 10(j) could not be utilized wherever any naturally occurring individual wolves might be. Moreover, it ruled that the appropriate remedy was to remove the unlawfully introduced wolves. It stayed that order, however, pending an appeal.

The National Audubon Society reconsidered and reversed its position shortly after the district court decision. Represented by new counsel, it filed a motion seeking permission to realign itself with the government's position and to join the briefs of the Service and a number of other environmental organizations that supported the Service's position. By virtue of switching its position, Audubon enjoys the rather unusual distinction of being the only party to prevail in both the district court and court of appeals. The remaining Earthjustice clients pressed ahead with the position they had taken below.

The court of appeals decision unanimously disposed of the various arguments against the Service's action. The court held that the restrictive interpretation advocated by the Farm Bureau and the Earthjustice group "could actually undermine the Department's ability to address biological reality ... and thus handicap its ability to effectuate species recovery." In so ruling, the court has removed a cloud of uncertainty that has hung over possible reintroduction efforts, including one being considered in New Mexico for the northern aplomado falcon

(*Falco femoralis septentrionalis*). This, the rarest of North America's falcons, has not recently bred in New Mexico, but occasional individuals are sighted in the state. The Tenth Circuit decision thus makes it very likely that a reintroduction of falcons there can proceed under Section 10(j). The court decision also likely removes a potential obstacle to the use of Section 10(j) to reintroduce grizzly bears (*Ursus arctos*) to the Selway-Bitterroot area of Idaho.

Expanded use of Section 10(j) may hasten the recovery of these and other species. Although the provision has been used sparingly, and some experimental reintroduction efforts have failed, species for which experimental populations have been established are generally doing much better than others. In its most recent (1996) report to Congress, the Service concluded that fewer than ten percent of the then-listed species were improving in status. Of the species for which experimental populations have been established, however, more than 70 percent are improving.

Is the Endangered Species Act Unconstitutional?

Despite the success of the Endangered Species Act in reducing the drowning of sea turtles, restoring wolves to the Northern Rockies, and furthering the recovery of many other species, the prospect of congressional action weakening it has loomed over the act for the past three decades. There is another sword of Damocles over the act that has gotten much less attention but is no less serious. It is the possibility that the increasingly conservative Supreme Court may find the act to be unconstitutional insofar as it restricts the taking of species that occur in only one state (as a great many do) and that are not the objects of significant interstate commerce.

For most of the past century, the Supreme Court has embraced a broad interpretation of that part of the Constitution giving Congress the authority to regulate interstate commerce. As a result, the federal government has been able to regulate a broad array of activities that would otherwise lie within the authority of the states. The first indication that the court might be willing to embrace a more restrictive interpretation of federal authority came in 1995 in *United States v. Lopez*. The case had nothing to do with the Endangered Species Act—at least on the surface. Beneath that surface, however, lurked a hidden danger.

At issue in the *Lopez* case was a federal law making it a crime to possess a gun in a school zone. The Supreme Court had to decide whether that law was within the scope of the authority given to Congress in the Constitution's interstate commerce clause. Reasoning that the law had no significant effect on interstate commerce, the court declared it unconstitutional. Since then the composition of the court has shifted further to the right, raising the question of what other federal laws might be at risk under the logic of the *Lopez* ruling. Could the Endangered Species Act be in the crosshairs?

The appellate courts in several federal judicial circuits have considered claims that Congress exceeded its constitutional authority in various ways under the act. Although every one of these courts has thus far rejected those claims, it is worrisome that each court has given a different rationale for its decision. Should an appellate court rule against the act, the resulting split in the circuits could set the stage for a Supreme Court resolution of the issue. Given the current composition of the court, the outcome of such a case is very much uncertain.

The article that follows examined this issue in the context of a 2000 decision of the Fourth Circuit Court of Appeals upholding the constitutionality of the act insofar as it restricted the taking of red wolves that had been reintroduced to North Carolina. My conclusion then was that the decision "probably removes the threat that the ESA will be dealt a major constitutional setback for the foreseeable future." Today we are well beyond what was the foreseeable future when I wrote those words in 2001. With the addition of Justices Brett Kavanaugh, Neil Gorsuch, and Amy Coney Barrett to the Supreme Court since then, I could no longer reach that reassuring conclusion.

Major Endangered Species Act Developments in 2000
Environmental Law Reporter 31, no. 3 (March 2001)*

Unlikely as it may seem, the constitutionality of certain of the ESA's core restrictions is still being questioned nearly three decades after its enactment. The US Supreme Court's willingness to re-examine the scope of federal authority under the US Constitution's Commerce

Clause since *United States v. Lopez*[1] has put the ESA in the crosshairs for the following reasons: (1) most endangered species occur only within a single state, (2) relatively few endangered species have commercial value that makes them the object of interstate commerce, and (3) most, if not all, of the activities that the ESA prohibits, especially those that run afoul of the prohibition against "taking" protected animals, could be characterized as essentially local, and many of those activities are not economic in character.

The DC Circuit faced the first of the Commerce Clause challenges to the ESA in 1997. In *National Ass'n of Home Builders v. Babbitt*,[2] the DC Circuit considered whether the ESA's prohibition against taking the Delhi Sands flower-loving fly, an endangered insect that is found only in California and that has itself never been the object of interstate commerce (apart from a handful of instances involving specialist collectors), exceeded the constitutional authority of the federal government. Although the court upheld the law against this challenge, it split two to one, and the two judges who ruled in support of the law were unable to agree upon a rationale for doing so.

A similar challenge, involving restrictions against the killing of reintroduced red wolves in North Carolina, was pending before the Fourth Circuit Court of Appeals earlier this year when the Supreme Court issued its decision in *United States v. Morrison*.[3] *Morrison* struck down provisions of the Federal Violence Against Women Act on the *Lopez* theory that they exceeded federal authority under the Commerce Clause. Gender-based violence, in the Court's view, was simply noneconomic in character and therefore unlike the sorts of activities whose regulation had been upheld in earlier Supreme Court cases.

The question for the Fourth Circuit in *Gibbs v. Babbitt*,[4] therefore, was whether the taking of red wolves was an "economic activity" as that term was used in *Lopez* and *Morrison*. In the view of the majority it was, and the opinion stating that view is a powerful and persuasive defense of endangered species protection from Commerce Clause challenge. Interestingly, the opinion was written by Chief Judge Wilkinson, who had joined the Fourth Circuit majority decision in the ruling that the Supreme Court affirmed in its *Morrison* decision. The author of that earlier Fourth Circuit decision, Judge Luttig, vigorously dissented from Wilkinson's red wolf ruling.

Chief Judge Wilkinson's conclusion that prohibiting the killing of red wolves on privately owned land substantially affects interstate commerce rested upon several bases. First, he pointed out that the motivation to kill wolves was largely to protect economic assets.[5] Second, without red wolves, there would be no red wolf-related tourism or scientific research, nor would there be the possibility of future trade in wolf pelts.[6] Third, he held that although the killing of an individual wolf might be of negligible consequence for commerce, the proper inquiry was on the aggregate impact of such activities.[7] Finally, though farmers might kill red wolves for economic reasons, the wolf may confer benefits on commerce by controlling species that destroy crops.[8] In what may be the most significant sentence in the opinion, Wilkinson asserted that "Congress is entitled to make the judgment that conservation is potentially valuable, even if that value cannot be presently ascertained."[9]

In a concluding rebuttal to Judge Luttig's dissent, Chief Judge Wilkinson offered a warning that perhaps the Supreme Court would have been well advised to read before its recent venture into electoral politics.

> Reversing the presumption in favor of constitutionality plunges our dissenting brother into the thick of political controversy.... Both sides in this political stand-off have their legitimate points to make.... Why the judicial branch should place its thumb on either side of this old political scale is simply beyond our comprehension.... An indiscriminate willingness to constitutionalize recurrent political controversies will weaken democratic authority and spell no end of trouble for the courts.[10]

The *Gibbs* decision, both because of its thorough and careful reasoning and because it came from the circuit perhaps most likely to use the Commerce Clause to circumscribe federal authority, probably removes the threat that the ESA will be dealt a major constitutional setback for the foreseeable future. Nonetheless, predicting what the next step in the *Lopez* and *Morrison* jurisprudence will be is speculative at best, particularly since both Chief Judge Wilkinson and Judge Luttig appear on many lists of potential appointees to the Supreme Court by President George W. Bush.

When Congressman John Dingell Jr. retired in 2015 after nearly sixty years in the House of Representatives, the House lost not only its institutional memory of the Endangered Species Act but also the act's most fearsome advocate. In the House today there is only one member who served when the act was passed in 1973—Alaska's Don Young (about whom much is said in chapter 9). Indeed, as of this writing in early 2020, only 11 of the 435 members of the House were serving when the act was last reauthorized in 1988 (one of those is the current Speaker of the House, Nancy Pelosi). Only four of today's senators were serving then. It is, therefore, understandable that many of those now serving in Congress may be unaware of what the act has accomplished and unaware of what the world would be like had there never been an Endangered Species Act.

In the early 1990s, my then-colleague David Wilcove, now a celebrated professor at Princeton University, and I wrote an essay in which we imagined what the world would have been like without the Endangered Species Act. David's idea for the essay was inspired by the Jimmy Stewart Christmas movie, *It's a Wonderful Life*. Just as Stewart's character, George Bailey, restores his spirits by reflecting on all the good things that would not have happened had he not lived, so too in this essay do David and I recount many of the dramatic conservation accomplishments that would not have occurred had there not been an Endangered Species Act. The essay was never published, but I kept it among my files because I thought it taught a useful lesson, one that remains true decades later.

It's a Wonderful Life—Thanks to the Endangered Species Act

–David Wilcove and Michael J. Bean

There is panic in several Wyoming towns tonight. Fifty masked bandits have swept in and are terrorizing the residents. And believe it or not, the federal government put them there. Fortunately, these are prairie dog towns and the bandits are black-footed ferrets. In the biggest comeback since Lazarus, the once nearly extinct ferret is on the road to an amazing recovery. So is the California condor, which will soon soar again over the mountains of Southern California, as it has since the days of the mastodons and saber-toothed tigers. The condor, like the ferret, has been rescued from the brink of extinction.

Ferrets and condors returning to the wild, peregrine falcons in Manhattan, red wolves in North Carolina—could it be that the Endangered Species Act is working? This conclusion will come as a surprise to many, including those who view it as an obstacle to progress and others who complain that it isn't accomplishing much. The facts tell a different story: the Endangered Species Act is saving some of our most imperiled species without shutting down the engines of economic growth. It's a message most people need to hear before the chorus of naysayers drowns out the good news.

The best way to appreciate the act is to imagine what life would be like without it. What would be different today if Congress had never passed the Endangered Species Act in 1973? The ferret, condor, and red wolf would surely be gone by now, leaving only a handful of stuffed specimens as reminders. Joining them would be the whooping crane, manatee, and Schaus' swallowtail butterfly. To see a bald eagle might require a trip to Alaska, the populations now rebuilding in the lower forty-eight states having been wiped out by pesticides and habitat disturbance. Residents of California would not be able to watch southern sea otters loafing in the kelp beds or admire brown pelicans diving for fish. And visitors to Yellowstone National Park would have no chance of glimpsing a mother grizzly bear and her cubs as they amble across a meadow. Like the bald eagle, grizzlies would be gone from all states but Alaska.

More than thirty national wildlife refuges would not exist. These were established primarily to protect endangered species, and each year thousands of Americans visit them to hike, fish, hunt, watch birds, and enjoy nature. Scientists eager to learn how new species evolve would pursue their studies without the palila, akepa, and other Hawaiian honeycreepers—even though the Hawaiian honeycreepers rival Darwin's famous finches in their scientific importance. Researchers studying how animals adapt to hot, arid climates (a skill we might want to know more about in the greenhouse future) could not look to the desert pupfish, Stevens kangaroo rat, or Coachella Valley fringe-toed lizard for answers, unless pickled or stuffed ones suffice. To be fair, biology would not come to a screeching halt without the Endangered Species Act, but it wouldn't be the same.

Nor has the economy come to a screeching halt with the Endangered

Species Act, notwithstanding the frequent protestations from loggers, shrimpers, ranchers, and developers. In a recent eight-year period the Fish and Wildlife Service reviewed nearly fifty thousand federal permits and projects to see if they would adversely affect endangered species. More than 99 percent received a "green light" to go forward, and most of the remainder could be modified to avoid undue impacts on endangered species. In Palm Springs, Las Vegas, and Austin, the act has facilitated comprehensive development plans that will benefit endangered species and permit development. Easy? No. Possible? An emphatic yes.

Fair-weather friends of the act are quick to point out that most endangered species are not recovering and many are vanishing even before getting on the list. They're right, but the problem lies not with the act but with its implementation. Saving endangered species isn't necessarily cheap, but the act has operated on a yearly budget of thirty to forty million dollars. That's about the cost of a few miles of interstate highway near urban areas.

Congress will soon begin considering the act's future. Opponents, buoyed by their recent success in undermining wetlands protection, are turning their attention to it. Events such as the release of the black-footed ferret are a good time to contemplate what's at stake. The Endangered Species Act is a good law, one that industry can live with and ferrets, condors, grizzlies, and hundreds of other species can't live without.

9

The Endangered Species Act's Most Unexpected Ally

By the early 1990s, the bipartisan support that the Endangered Species Act once enjoyed had all but vanished. The early conflict over the Tennessee Valley Authority's Tellico Dam and the endangered snail darter was followed by even more wrenching regional conflicts that pitted shrimp fishermen against imperiled sea turtles, logging interests against the northern spotted owl, and land development interests against rare songbirds in Texas and Southern California. These dramatic clashes contributed to a broad realignment of political support for environmental issues in general, a realignment in which Republican support was increasingly hard to find for environmental laws and programs that had once had significant bipartisan backing.

Thus it was that most wildlife conservationists feared the worst when, two years after the 1992 election of Democratic president Bill Clinton, Republicans won control of both the House of Representatives and the Senate for the first time in nearly half a century. This stunning achievement was credited to a firebrand congressman from Georgia, Newt Gingrich, who was rewarded by his colleagues by being named Speaker of the House. Gingrich is said to have "pioneered a style of partisan combat . . . that poisoned America's political culture and plunged Washington into permanent dysfunction."[1] That is a weighty charge, and it may well be true. Yet, when the Endangered Species Act faced its gravest threat since its enactment, it was Gingrich who protected it and kept it intact. The story of how that improbable result came about is told in the following article published in the Environmental Law Institute's magazine.

Chapter 9

The Gingrich That Saved the ESA
Environmental Forum, January/February 1999*

When the elections of 1994 swept the Republican Party into control of Congress, the prospect for a rollback of major environmental laws seemed almost certain. Among the most likely targets was the Endangered Species Act. Jurisdiction over that contentious statute lay with the newly constituted House Resources Committee. Just days before the 104th Congress was to begin, the Committee's gruff Alaskan Chairman, Don Young, gave an incendiary interview to BNA's *Daily Environment Report* in which he made no secret of his loathing of environmentalists and his distaste for the ESA. He declared that revision of the ESA was his top priority, a job he vowed to complete within six months. That Young never accomplished his top priority is well known. Much less well known is the successful behind-the-scenes effort to save the ESA in which the new Speaker of the House, Newt Gingrich, played a central role. What follows is the improbable story of how Gingrich helped save the ESA . . . for the time being.

Though the House of Representatives in 1973 had approved the ESA by a vote of 390-12, by the beginning of the 1990s congressional opinion was sharply split over what ought to be done with the nation's most important conservation law. The former consensus in favor of strongly protecting endangered species had been shattered by a series of tumultuous conflicts: timber interests in the Pacific Northwest were reeling from cutbacks in logging on federal forests attributed to the northern spotted owl; real estate interests in southern California were in rebellion because of the sudden need to accommodate the California gnatcatcher; shrimpers in the Gulf and south Atlantic blockaded harbors to protest regulations designed to reduce the drowning of sea turtles in their nets; a series of lesser conflicts boiled elsewhere. What had been a mom-and-apple-pie issue was suddenly a political hot potato. As a result, the 102nd Congress, which was to have reauthorized the ESA by September 1992, never took it up.

In the 103rd Congress, the last one in Democratic control, Massachusetts Democrat Gerry Studds championed the ESA's reauthorization with a bill strongly backed by the environmental community. Studds was chairman of the former House Committee on Merchant

Marine and Fisheries, which then had jurisdiction of the ESA. With the chairman as its chief sponsor, the Democrats solidly in control of the House, Bill Clinton and Al Gore newly settled in the White House, and Bruce Babbitt at the helm in the Interior Department, the Studds bill ought to have enjoyed smooth sailing. It didn't. Indeed, it was another Democrat (at least then he was still a Democrat), Billy Tauzin of Louisiana, who introduced a rival bill around which the "wise use movement" and many regulated interests rallied. Tauzin's bill stayed virtually neck and neck with that of Studds in the race to line up cosponsors.

Because of the many ESA controversies and the nearly equal division of support between the rival bills, Studds was reluctant to bring his bill to the House floor, and the environmental community, sensing the same dangers, never pressed him to do so. Instead, it pursued a more modest goal of enlisting more cosponsors for the Studds bill than Tauzin was able to garner for his, hoping to set the stage for an increasingly overdue reauthorization in the next Congress. Each week, environmental lobbyists met to review the latest cosponsor lists. The most puzzling moment came in November 1993, when Georgia Representative Newt Gingrich became the 85th cosponsor (and the 11th Republican cosponsor) of the Studds bill. Who, the environmentalists asked, had been responsible for that? Shoulders shrugged. No one had been assigned the job of seeking Gingrich's support. Could the new list be a mistake? Was it a joke? No one knew.

The 1994 elections, which with the change in majority to the Republicans brought about earthshaking changes in key House leadership posts, devastated the ranks of the former Studds cosponsors. Replacing Studds as chairman of the committee with ESA jurisdiction was Don Young. Young was not extending any olive branches. In his BNA interview, Young called environmentalists a "self-centered bunch, the waffle-stomping, Harvard-graduating, intellectual bunch of idiots." Less than a week later, the *Anchorage Daily News* quoted him calling environmentalists "the most despicable group I've ever dealt with." On the ESA, Young liked to point out that he was the only member of his committee who had voted for the ESA in 1973, but that "we had envisioned trying to protect, you know, pigeons and things like that. We never thought about mussels and ferns and flowers and all these . . . subspecies of squirrels and birds."

Looking at the new Republican hierarchy, it was hard to find anyone likely to restrain Young. It certainly would not be Tom Delay, the new Republican whip. This former bug exterminator had railed against the ESA during the House debate on the regulations requiring shrimpers to modify their nets to avoid drowning sea turtles. It most assuredly would not be Dick Armey, the new majority leader. Armey was an advisor to, and frequent mouthpiece for, the deceptively named National Wilderness Institute, an organization whose only apparent purpose was to publish regular screeds against the ESA. That left only Newt Gingrich, self-described revolutionary, instigator of the "Contract with America," inflammatory orator, darling of the Republican conservatives, demon in the eyes of the Democrats—and animal lover.

Yes, Newt Gingrich was an animal lover. At least that is what his mother told Connie Chung. That maternal assessment gained credibility when the *Washington Post* published a two-part series on the new House Speaker on December 18 and 19, 1994. In 214 column-inches of text, one tiny nugget of information leapt off the page for some of us in the conservation community. It was an account of how, as a ten-year-old boy, Gingrich had waged a virtual crusade to persuade state and city leaders to build a zoo in Harrisburg, Pennsylvania. According to the *Post* account, a local newspaper had written of "an 'unusually bright lad' who met with officials about his plans to organize '300 or more promoters' to provide $100 a month 'to finance a zoo.' He asked the city and state to 'dedicate a piece of land where a zoo might be established, with moat.'" The Post also reported that the youthful Gingrich's "first career goal was to be a paleontologist."

There is a simple fact that anyone who had a deep childhood fascination with animals understands that few others can appreciate: no matter how many other interests one acquires as an adult, one never loses an interest in animals. Ten-year-old boys can be passionate about baseball, airplanes, or science fiction, yet completely lose interest in those topics as adults. But a ten-year-old boy with a passion for animals is hooked for life. Harvard biologist Edward O. Wilson, whom National Zoo Director Michael Robinson once called "the Homer of biology," coined a term for this phenomenon: biophilia.

To those of us who were concerned about endangered species (and the fate of the Endangered Species Act), the possibility that the new Speaker was a biophile raised a glimmer of hope. If it could be arranged, would E. O. Wilson be willing to come to Washington to talk to Gingrich about biodiversity, about conservation, about the

Endangered Species Act? When the question was put to him, Wilson was intrigued and quite willing. In fact, he remembered that Gingrich had tried to pay him a visit when the congressman was in Cambridge a year earlier, but Wilson had not had time to meet him. Also willing was Thomas Eisner of Cornell University, whose explorations into the chemistry of nature and its possible human uses opened up a whole new dimension in the debate about conserving biological diversity. And so too was Harvard's Stephen Jay Gould, who, as the nation's best known paleontologist, was likely to interest the fossil-collecting Gingrich.

With Wilson, Eisner, and Gould all committed to a meeting that had not yet even been raised with anyone in the Gingrich camp, the question then became how to contact Gingrich, who was then in constant demand by all sorts of people. The way to Gingrich, it turned out, was through a zoo. Terry Maple, director of the highly acclaimed Atlanta Zoo, was said to be close to Gingrich. The Environmental Defense Fund's David Wilcove contacted Syd Butler, with whom he had worked when they were colleagues at The Wilderness Society. As the new executive director of the American Zoo and Aquarium Association, which represents most of the nation's zoos, Butler knew Maple and agreed to ask his help in arranging a meeting between Gingrich and the scientists. Butler suggested bringing in Bill Conway as well. As longtime head of the New York Zoological Society, Conway was perhaps the best known and most widely respected figure in the zoo world.

Maple confirmed that Gingrich's interest in animals and zoos was not only real, but rather extraordinary. The Speaker, he related, had been a generous benefactor to the Atlanta Zoo, long before he could command hefty speaker fees or book royalties. Maple was so effusive in his praise of Gingrich that one almost wondered whether he was part of the Gingrich publicity machine. And yet, Maple was rock solid on the issue of conservation, a passionate believer in the importance of conserving biodiversity. He thought Gingrich would relish the chance to talk to some of the nation's most eminent conservationists and agreed to help arrange it.

Although Maple had no doubt of where the Speaker's heart lay, the scientists who had been recruited to meet with him were more skeptical. They had agreed to take part more out of curiosity about this firebrand suddenly thrust into national prominence than out of conviction that the meeting would serve any real purpose. And, truth be told, we all feared they would be meeting with a slick, boorish blowhard who would go through the timeless Washington ritual of listening distractedly for a few minutes, then escort them to the door so that he could return to the dirty business of the revolution. Nonetheless, at a noisy Thai restaurant the night before the scheduled meeting, they tried to script the pitch they would make to Gingrich.

The next morning, March 3, 1995, Wilcove and I paced nervously in the hallway outside the room where Wilson, Eisner, Gould, Conway, and Maple were meeting with Gingrich. The meeting had begun at 8am, and it was already 9:20. Whatever was happening, the scientists clearly had not been given the brush off. Suddenly, the door opened and the scientists emerged with a story that they themselves could hardly believe.

Gingrich had shown an impressive knowledge of biodiversity and the history of conservation. Conway in particular was struck that Gingrich had talked at length about William Hornaday, who had been one of the pillars of the New York Zoological Society in the early decades of this century. Either Gingrich had a staff extraordinarily capable of ferreting out obscure information to impress his guests, or he actually knew and cared a good deal about conservation. Eisner remarked that although he could not quite believe that he was saying it, Gingrich appeared to be a biophile. The Cornell ecologist had emphasized to Gingrich the potential discoveries yet to be made in nature by bringing with him a small vial containing an endangered Florida mint plant, in which Eisner had discovered an extraordinarily potent natural insect repellent. Gingrich was intrigued by it and asked to keep the vial. Gould, the most skeptical of the bunch, thought Gingrich was probably sincere, but doubted that he could control the forces he had unleashed. Little was said specifically about the ESA, but there would be time for that later, for Gingrich wanted the group to meet again soon over dinner.

Meanwhile, Don Young was going full speed in his effort to dismantle the ESA. Jurisdiction over the ESA would normally have been lodged in a subcommittee headed by New Jersey Representative Jim Saxton. Saxton, however, was a moderate and did not share Young's views of the ESA. Young therefore created a special "Endangered Species Task Force" within the Resources Committee, and gave it jurisdiction over the ESA. Young stacked the Republican side of the Task Force with a virtual "who's who" of known ESA antagonists. There was Idaho's Helen Chenoweth, who, noting that a "species goes out of existence every twenty seconds," reasoned that "surely a new species must come into existence every twenty seconds"; Wyoming's Barbara Cubin, who once said that "the federal government doesn't have a right to own any lands, except for post offices and armed services bases"; California's John Doolittle, who when confronted with scientific studies backing the threat to the ozone layer, responded that he was "not going to get involved in peer-review mumbo-jumbo"; California's George Radanovich; Oregon's Linda Smith; and others. To chair this august group, Young selected another ally, second term congressman and California farmer Richard Pombo. The Task Force held a series of raucous field hearings that were more like pep rallies for the wise use movement than congressional oversight hearings. The witness lists were heavily stacked with ESA opponents, and the efforts to silence the law's supporters were often heavy handed. Gingrich almost certainly read about the latter when on April 2 the *Atlanta Constitution and Journal* leveled an editorial blast at the Task Force for abruptly canceling a hearing at which Gingrich's friend Terry Maple was to testify.

On the evening of May 10, in the Speaker's ornate private dining room in the Capitol, the follow-up meeting that Gingrich had suggested was about to begin. Gould was absent, and a few new faces were part of the group awaiting the Speaker's arrival. When a beaming, ebullient Gingrich burst into the room, he had at his side an unexpected, and decidedly unhappy looking guest, Richard Pombo. Pombo must have been dragooned into the meeting, for a black cloud hung ominously over his visage, and it only grew darker as the evening wore on. Having effectively shut out most of the conservation science community from his Task Force's hearings, Pombo was now face-to-face with the nation's most learned advocates of conserving biodiversity, and the Speaker was treating them like soulmates.

Dinner that evening lasted more than two hours. The conversation ranged broadly, encompassing the ESA, tax reform to encourage conservation, and the highly contentious National Biological Survey. On that last subject, Gingrich insisted that it was critically important that the nation acquire more scientific information on biodiversity, suggesting that the NBS be folded into the Smithsonian Institution and be given an expanded mission to include a global inventory of species.

Pombo quietly brooded most of the evening. When he did speak, he was alternately pained and defiant. He protested that the environmental community was more interested in labeling his ideas as right wing than in fairly considering them. He boasted, however, that it really did not matter what anyone else thought because "I can get any bill I want past the House." He grumbled about fairy shrimp and other endangered creatures that, he contended, were unnecessarily interfering with the lives of his constituents. If Gingrich thought that exposing Pombo to some of the best minds in biology would be a transformative experience, he was surely disappointed. Gingrich, the historian, animal lover, and devotee of grand ideas, who appeared to enjoy nothing so much as surrounding himself with great thinkers, must have noted the irony: on one side of his dinner table sat E. O. Wilson, the Homer of biology; opposite Wilson sat the Homer Simpson of biology.

When dinner ended, Pombo hastily departed. Gingrich invited the other guests upstairs to his suite of offices. He wanted to show them the huge model of a *Tyrannosaurus rex* head that adorned his outer office, a loan from the Smithsonian Institution. He also wanted to tell them something in private. His message was simple. He would not let a bad ESA bill come to the House floor, and he would rely upon them to gauge the value of any bill that might be offered. As they walked down the stairs from his office, they passed Dick Armey, unaware of who the scientists were or of what they had just been told.

Two weeks later, Pombo's Endangered Species Task Force was wrapping up its business with the last of its hearings, the only one held in Washington. There came a last minute request to testify at the Washington hearing that Pombo could not refuse. It came from Gingrich himself. Even more remarkable than the sight of the Speaker of the House testifying at a hearing on the ESA was what he had to say. "There are enormous interests that we have as human beings in maintaining biological diversity," Gingrich declared. "This is not just about large vertebrates. This is also about the fungi and the various things that produce the medicine of the future." To Pombo, it must have seemed that he was reliving the bad dream that was the dinner party of a few nights earlier. Only this time, the necessity of preserving fungi was not being proclaimed by a bunch of ivory tower scientists, but by his very own party leader. Where, Pombo must have wondered, is this revolution going?

For those who had cheered when Young vowed to overhaul the ESA in the first six months of the new Congress, Gingrich's words sounded like a betrayal. Moreover, after the dinner meeting attended by Pombo, word leaked out that Gingrich was conniving with the other side. Thomas E. Woods of the conservative Ludwig von Mises Institute wrote in the *Christian Science Monitor* on August 1, 1995, that "the most fervent environmentalist among the Republican leadership turns out to be Newt Gingrich himself," who, Woods sinisterly noted, "has held informal meetings with prominent pro-green scientists for months now, including Thomas Eisner and Marxist paleontologist Steven [*sic*] Jay Gould." Robert J. Smith of the Competitive Enterprise Institute whined in *Human Events* that Gingrich had met repeatedly with supporters of the ESA, while "many of the leading free-market environmentalists in Washington, DC, have tried for over a year to get even a 15-minute meeting with Gingrich . . . to no avail." Conservative columnist Alston Chase took exception to Gingrich's meeting with Harvard's Wilson, asking why "did the speaker turn to the People's Republic of Cambridge to find an expert on ecology?" Perhaps it was because Wilson had won virtually every scientific award and accolade a biologist can win.

Suddenly, not only were conservative interest groups turning up the heat on Gingrich, but so were his Republican House colleagues. At yet another meeting with the scientists in late June, Gingrich told of attending a recent heated meeting with Ralph Regula and about 40 western members, most of them freshmen, concerning funding for the National Biological Survey. Gingrich described the meeting as "somewhere between hysteria and rage," and added "they really jarred me and I don't often get jarred." A revolution was brewing within the revolution.

Gingrich's surprise testimony had thrown a monkey wrench into the plans of Young and Pombo. Young's six-month deadline came and went without any overhaul of the ESA and without even a bill having been introduced. Though Young was off schedule, he was still on target. On September 7, 1995, he and Pombo introduced their bill. It effectively neutered every provision of the existing law. Young and Pombo had given their "wise use" constituency everything it wanted, but they had offered Gingrich nothing. In a series of letters to Gingrich, the scientists pointed out the obvious.

Though more balanced than Pombo's Task Force, Young's Resources Committee was heavily tilted in his favor. He could either offer compromises to win over more moderate Republican members and perhaps some Democrats, or he could simply push his bill through the Committee over their objections. He chose the latter, but may have had a last-minute pang of doubt. As the committee assembled for its pro forma "markup" of their bill on October 12, Young was reportedly overheard asking Pombo if he understood that Gingrich would never let them bring the bill to the floor. They went ahead anyway and secured the committee's approval by a margin of 27 to 17. Now, only Newt Gingrich stood in the way of full House consideration of a bill that made conservationists cringe. Would he keep the promise he had made to the scientists, or would the Jacobin wing of his revolution force him to abandon it? Two days after the committee markup, Maple and Butler met with Gingrich in Atlanta. Gingrich reassured them that the group of scientists had not been on "a fool's errand." Later that month, Gingrich and Eisner met at the Atlanta airport, where Gingrich said of the Young and Pombo effort, "they sure got it wrong, didn't they?"

In the heady first hundred days of the 104th Congress, Gingrich had successfully pushed item after item from his "Contract with America" through the House. Now, however, things were bogging down, his troops were restless, and increasingly their arrows were aimed at him. The one place he could find refuge and solace was at the zoo. Just about every time Gingrich went to a major city for a speech or other event, he made it a point to visit the local zoo—in Chicago, Utica, San Diego, Los Angeles, and elsewhere. He would call Maple for help in arranging a visit. Maple finally explained that Gingrich was now a sufficiently important public figure that he no longer needed Maple's introduction to get a tour.

Gingrich's zoo visits were not just photo-ops. At Chicago's Brookfield Zoo, he spent the better part of a day touring the zoo in the company of George Rabb, the director and a major figure in international endangered species conservation. Rabb later joined a meeting in Gingrich's Georgia office in January 1996. Gingrich, sporting a tie adorned with giraffes and elephants, began that meeting by recounting his visit to the Brookfield Zoo. He and Rabb laughed when recalling the discomfort of Gingrich's bodyguard when he accompanied the Speaker into the cage of an aardvark that took an interest in Gingrich's sneakers. Gingrich also talked animatedly about being inside a cage with a hairy-nosed wombat.

Gingrich's enthusiasm for animals led to a series of ill-fated television appearances in the company of various wild animals from the Columbus, Ohio, zoo, whose director, Jack Hannah, became a Gingrich buddy. The appearances backfired, with both liberal and conservative commentators savaging them as witless publicity stunts.

In the *New York Times*, Frank Rich accused Gingrich of using "defenseless animals . . . as an election year smokescreen to camouflage his party's environmental record." Conservative commentator Tony Snow said that Gingrich appeared to have "turned desperate, like the widow who fights off loneliness by taking in 97 cats." Both of them were at least partly right, but neither of them understood that when in the company of animals Gingrich was, once again, the ten-year-old boy in Harrisburg.

Though Young and Pombo's bill had cleared the committee in October, month after month passed without any effort to bring it to the floor. Meanwhile, the environmental movement had rallied public opinion against the excesses of the 104th Congress. Hill watchers knew that the closer fall elections came, the less likely any highly contentious environmental bill would be brought to the floor for a vote. By now, the Republican revolution was sputtering, and its shock troops would soon turn on their leader, who understood as they never did that their agenda was likely to backfire and hand the Democrats a potent weapon in the upcoming election.

In April 1996, Gingrich repeated publicly what at least a few had known for nearly a year. In an interview with Greenwire, Gingrich was asked, "is it accurate to say that you don't intend for it [the Young-Pombo bill] ever to get to the floor?" Gingrich answered, "yeah, and I don't think the committee expects it to." In June, Gingrich delivered the same message to the annual "Fly-in-for-Freedom" gathering of "wise use" interests; only for this audience he attributed his unwillingness to move the bill to a lack of votes on the House floor. Choosing his words carefully, Pombo acknowledged that there were not enough votes "for the speaker to feel comfortable pushing it on the floor."

For the Fly-In folks, this was too much; they knew now that the fly in the ointment was Gingrich. According to the *Washington Times*, a meeting between the Fly-In crowd and members of Congress who were part of the Western States Caucus "quickly deteriorated into a squabble" with "tempers flaring" over Gingrich. At one point, Utah Republican James Hansen "stormed out of the room." Later, Oregon Representative Wes Cooley "blurted out what no one else had been willing to say: 'Let's cut the bullcrap. The main problem is Newt Gingrich.'"

Conservative interest groups went into fever pitch. David Ridenour, vice president of the National Center for Public Policy Analysis, issued a press release denouncing Gingrich as "the single greatest threat to needed reform of environmental laws." Gingrich, Ridenour asserted, "ought to be the environmental movement's poster boy—not its villain." Don Young expressed his chagrin openly. "What I should have done is repealed the whole act. If I had done what Doc [Hastings, a Republican freshman Congressman from Washington] told me, I would have repealed the whole thing. Right quick. Before anybody realized what had happened."

But it was too late. The Young-Pombo bill never came to the House floor. Gingrich had kept his word. Aware of the futility of trying again in the face of Gingrich's opposition, Young and Pombo never even introduced an ESA reauthorization bill in the 105th Congress. Let the Senate deal with it first, they reasoned. The Endangered Species Task Force that Pombo had headed in the 104th Congress was never reconstituted in the 105th.

Gingrich, the historian, is now himself part of history. Some will doubtless credit him with at least a share of responsibility for balancing the federal budget, reforming the welfare system, and a host of other significant changes; others will remember him as the architect of a "Contract with America" that threatened to undermine a host of social and environmental gains. At least a footnote in history, however, ought to record as well his singular role in saving the Endangered Species Act from what had once seemed an almost certain dismembering.

10

The Inconvenient Truth of Unintended Consequences

Although Newt Gingrich's unexpected help thwarted congressional efforts to weaken the Endangered Species Act, it was becoming increasingly clear to me that there was a problem with the act that could not be ignored. That problem was illustrated by the example of a fast-talking Texas businessman named H. Ross Perot. Most people remember Perot as the most successful third-party candidate for president in modern American history. The 19 percent of the vote he received in the 1992 election came mostly at the expense of President George H. W. Bush and likely resulted in his defeat by his challenger, Bill Clinton. I remember Perot as the guy whose company reportedly ran its bulldozers around the clock to clear as much habitat as possible before the listing of a Texas songbird as an endangered species made such clearing potentially illegal. On the plus side, however, Perot's effort to outrun and outsmart the agency charged with implementing the Endangered Species Act prompted me to think seriously about how to make the act more effective in conserving rare species on privately owned land, where many such species predominantly occur.

Perot's business empire included commercially valuable land in the Texas Hill Country near Austin. In the late 1980s the US Fish and Wildlife Service was considering adding a songbird—the golden-cheeked warbler—to the list of endangered species because of the steady loss of its breeding habitat. Uncertain of the restrictions that might result from the bird's eventual listing, Perot's company concluded that the safest bet was to crank up the bulldozers full throttle and destroy any habitat the bird might be using before the service could complete the procedures necessary to put it on the list. As a result, a lot of habitat was lost and the challenge of recovering the bird made more difficult.

Perot's actions got attention because he was, after all, Ross Perot. They were hardly unique, however. Other landowners, blessed by relative anonymity, have done much the same. One who garnered nearly as much attention was a gentleman named Ben Cone. A member of a prominent North Carolina family, Cone owned an eleven-thousand-acre tract of pine forest in the eastern part of the state. Red-cockaded woodpeckers, an endangered species that depends on older pine trees, occupied about one thousand acres of Cone's property. Their presence limited—but did not necessarily prohibit—Cone's ability to harvest trees on the affected acreage. Fearing that the rare birds would "infest" other parts of his property, Cone announced that he would begin cutting the still-unoccupied areas while he could. In doing so, Cone was only doing what forestry consultants throughout the Southeast had recommended that many other landowners do: cut their trees before they got old enough that woodpeckers might start living in them. Similar panic cutting had occurred in the Pacific Northwest, where forest landowners feared that if they did not cut their trees quickly, northern spotted owls would move in along with a bundle of federal regulations.

With examples like these in mind, I gave a presentation in late 1994 as part of a service-sponsored seminar on "Rediscovering the Land Ethic." A few months later I repeated that presentation at a conference put on by the Institute of Ecosystem Studies. In it I discussed the challenges of "ecosystem management" and in particular the problem of unintended consequences of the Endangered Species Act. What I had to say on that topic would be quoted more often than perhaps anything else I had ever said about the Endangered Species Act, but the people doing the quoting were the act's longtime critics.

A Policy Perspective on Biodiversity Protection and Ecosystem Management

The Ecological Basis of Conservation: Heterogeneity, Ecosystems, and Biodiversity, edited by S. Pickett et al., 1997*

Secretary of Labor Robert Reich gave a speech this past fall on the subject of "competitiveness." Here is part of what he said: "What do we mean by 'competitiveness' anyway? Rarely has a term of public discourse gone so directly from obscurity to meaninglessness without

* Reprinted by permission from Springer Nature: Chapman & Hall, *The Ecological Basis of Conservation: Heterogeneity, Ecosystems, and Biodiversity* by S. T. A. Pickett, R. S. Ostfeld, M. Shachak, and G. E. Likens, editors, ©1997.

any intervening period of coherence."[1] Much the same, I fear, can be said about "ecosystem management."

Just as everyone embraces the notion that our country must be "competitive," so too everyone—or nearly everyone—now thinks that our natural resources must be managed using an "ecosystem approach." Unfortunately, not everyone shares a very clear idea of just what that means. This conference intended to provide some clarity to that idea. The challenge is more than just that of assembling a cook book of "how-to" steps for practical managers. There is a deeper problem, as evidenced by the invitation each of us received to the conference. The letter of invitation noted that "the ongoing change in conservation policy, from the focus on single species and individual land parcels to functioning communities, ecosystems, and landscapes, is taking place in the near absence of a firm foundation in ecological theory." That statement ought to give us all considerable pause. More recently, I took part in a gathering of timber industry biologists and environmentalists where the view of at least some was that although they could not clearly define ecosystem management, they knew it when they saw it—rather like Supreme Court Justice Potter Stewart once said of pornography.

Despite the uncertainties being voiced by some, I am pleased to report that at least a few people have a clear fix on what ecosystem management means. Take Ike Sugg of the Competitive Enterprise Institute, for example. According to Sugg,[2]

> this so-called "ecosystem approach" will be the effective end of the right to private property in rural America. . . . In short, the ecosys-tem approach is nothing more than a pretext for shattering what few fragile limits remain on government's ability to regulate land use. . . . Defenders of property rights be forewarned, ecosystem management is the new rhetoric for regulating everything.

If that sounds a little alarmist, keep in mind that the same issue of the Competitive Enterprise Institute's newsletter in which Sugg's state-ment appeared also carried a story reporting that "Organic farming looms as the largest current threat to both humanity and wildlife."[3]

Another who has figured out what ecosystem management means is Alexander Cockburn, a columnist who leans nearly as far to the left as Sugg leans to the right. According to a column Cockburn wrote for *The Washington Post*, "as now being employed by Babbitt and by looters of the public domain, an ecosystem approach is just a piece of conceptual flim-flam disguising dismemberment of existing environmental protections."[4]

These are, of course, quite diametrically opposite views, from two government outsiders. What is the inside view? I found fascinating the definition given by Assistant Interior Secretary George Frampton in a recent published interview. Here is what he said:

> Ecosystem management is going to be the hot phrase of the 1990s. I'm not sure the Bush administration ever knew what it meant. . . . What we mean by ecosystem management is good science, looking at a range of species in communities and trying to plan for some optimization of resources. Not just one resource at a time.[5]

I think what Frampton said could be paraphrased as follows: "the management of all the various renewable resources of the [land] so that they are utilized in the combination that will best meet the needs of the American people." And that, sadly, comes straight from the definition of "multiple use" in the Multiple-Use Sustained-Yield Act of 1960. Perhaps everyone can now relax: ecosystem management is nothing more than the familiar old multiple-use management in new rhetorical garb.

I cannot resolve this debate, or even contribute much of value to it. Neither will lawmakers, whose grasp of what the new terminology really means in terms of on-the-ground decisions about resource management will be superficial at best. With consensus elusive among managers and ecological theorists about what ecosystem management is or should be, don't expect the increasingly polarized US Congress to provide meaningful guidance. Don't even expect it to show much interest. Consider what Wayne Gilchrist, a Republican Congressman from Maryland, was quoted in the press recently as saying about the new Congress's attitude toward environmental issues. Gilchrist declared: "I have never seen so many people afraid of information in my life [or] so extravagantly funded by interest groups that stand to make a lot of money from misinformation."[6]

This Congress, quite clearly, is not going to blaze any new policy trails in the area of ecosystem management. The task, therefore, is to put some flesh on the bones of this new concept through the development of policy within existing legal authorities. I will try to illustrate what I mean by reference to the Endangered Species Act and one of the species that it has long sought to conserve.

The Endangered Species Act never uses the term "biodiversity" and uses the word "ecosystem" only once. The act's statement of purposes begins with the declaration that "[t]he purposes of this Act are to provide a means whereby the ecosystems upon which endangered species and threatened species depend may be conserved." Given that this is the first stated purpose of the act, one might reasonably expect that the operative provisions of the act would specify how that purpose is to be achieved. They don't, at least not explicitly and directly. No mention of conserving ecosystems appears in the provisions of the act governing the development of recovery plans for listed species, the delegation of conservation authority to the states, the detailed duties of federal agencies, or the general prohibitions applicable to both public and private parties. The task thus falls to managers and policy makers within the Fish and Wildlife Service to design the strategies that achieve the act's purposes without the benefit of detailed congressional guidance.

When Congress enacted the Endangered Species Act of 1973, it "grandfathered" onto the endangered list about 200 species that had been designated as endangered under predecessor legislation. Among these was the red-cockaded woodpecker, which was listed as an endangered species in 1970. The woodpecker once occurred throughout the pine forests of the Southeast. Although it could be found in a number of different forest types, the type with which it was most closely associated and within which it was most abundant, was the longleaf pine forest type of the Southeastern coastal plain.

The original range of the longleaf pine stretches from extreme southern Virginia to east Texas and may have included some 60 million acres.[7] It supported a variety of species long since gone. For example, "[p]ractically all southern records of the historic and prehistoric bison are within the longleaf pine range," including droves of bison observed by the early American explorer Mark Catesby.[8] By 1955, 80 percent of the original longleaf pine acreage had been lost; only 12.2 million acres remained. By 1985, two thirds of that was gone—only 3.8 million acres remained; 94 percent of the original acreage was gone. Between 1975 and 1985, despite the Endangered Species Act, nearly a million acres of longleaf pine forest—some 20 percent of the total remaining in 1975—was lost throughout the Southeast. Since 1985, the loss of longleaf pine forest has continued apace.

Not surprisingly, just as the ecosystem on which it principally depends shrank, the red-cockaded woodpecker also declined. In the 1980s the number of red-cockaded woodpeckers on private land in the Southeast declined by an estimated 20 percent. On public land, the trend was also downward, but less dramatic.

Two conclusions seem inescapable from these figures. First, the red-cockaded woodpecker, despite nearly a quarter century of protection as an endangered species, is much closer to the brink of extinction today than it was when protection was first bestowed on it. Second, the ecosystem on which it principally depends has not been conserved, but has steadily and dramatically declined.

Let me add to those fairly obvious conclusions three more controversial conclusions of my own. The first is that the strategies pursued to conserve the woodpecker have contributed to the decline of its ecosystem, at least on private land; second, that the policies that have guided those strategies have implicitly abandoned what many regard as one of the central tenets of ecosystem management; and third, that the conservation of the woodpecker and its supporting ecosystem can yet be achieved through new but untried approaches that the Endangered Species Act allows.

On the first point, most of the ecosystem on which the red-cockaded woodpecker depends is found on private land. Thus, any effective strategy to conserve any more than isolated fragments of the ecosystem must seek to preserve the bird and its ecosystem on private land. In fact, however, there is increasing evidence that at least some private landowners are actively managing their land to avoid potential endangered species problems—that is, restrictions on land use stemming from the act's prohibition of "taking" endangered species—by avoiding endangered species. Because the woodpecker principally uses older trees for nesting and foraging, some landowners are harvesting their trees before they reach sufficient age to be attractive to woodpeckers. Because the woodpecker prefers open forest conditions with minimal hardwood understory—a condition maintained historically by regular and recurrent fires—landowners can eliminate or avoid endangered species complications by refraining from understory management. Because the woodpecker prefers longleaf pine over other species, landowners can reduce their likelihood of having woodpeckers by planting other species.

It is important to acknowledge that actions like these are not necessarily the result of malice toward the woodpecker or the environment. Rather, they can be rational decisions motivated by a desire to avoid potentially significant economic constraints. In short, they are nothing more than the predictable responses to the familiar "perverse incentives" that sometimes accompany regulatory programs.

That is point 1: the strategies pursued to date to conserve the red-cockaded woodpecker on private land have contributed to the decline of its ecosystem. Point 2 is that one of the central tenets of ecosystem management has been essentially abandoned in those strategies. Specifically, the one thing that nearly everyone writing about ecosystem management agrees on is that it implies looking beyond the property boundary to some larger watershed, ecosystem, or landscape unit, and that it seeks to influence management decisions within that broader unit. By contrast, the recovery plan for the red-cockaded woodpecker essentially writes off the larger, private landscape. With only a single exception, the areas where recovery is to be pursued are major federal land ownings. More recently, the Fish and Wildlife Service has encouraged the development of habitat conservation plans under which private landowners with existing breeding birds can make the progeny of those birds available for relocation onto public land for a period of years, after which the birds and their habitat on the private land can be eliminated.

These strategies may secure the survival of the red-cockaded woodpecker for many more decades. They will not, however, promote the restoration and maintenance of the ecosystem on which it depends, except on widely scattered federal holdings where recovery efforts are to be focused. Are there recovery strategies that could do so? I believe there are, and that they include significant opportunities on private lands.

What are they? First, from my conversations with landowners in North Carolina, I believe there are some private landowners with land that, if properly managed, could provide suitable habitat to support red-cockaded woodpeckers. In most instances, this is forest land that once supported red-cockaded woodpeckers, but no longer does because it has not been actively managed for some time, and the resulting encroachment of the hardwood understory precludes its current use by that species. A "hold harmless" agreement with such landowners would be sufficient to cause some landowners to undertake the needed management measures voluntarily. Under such an agreement, in return for carrying out the management actions that will create the habitat conditions the woodpecker requires, the government simply gives assurances that future incompatible land use decisions will not be regarded as violations of the act. The mechanism for providing such assurances exists, I believe, in the provisions relating to incidental taking under both Sections 7 and 10 of the act.

In short, creative regulatory relief will be a sufficient incentive for some private landowners to begin the sort of management that will benefit both the woodpecker and its ecosystem. For other landowners, stronger economic incentives may be needed. How can they be provided? Unfortunately, the automatic response is often to think solely in terms of tax relief or government payments. These certainly can be important incentives, but the likelihood of securing either in the current fiscal and political climate is probably not great.

Other, more innovative approaches are probably needed as well. Such ideas might include mitigation banking, transferable development rights, and even major investments in forest preservation and management by utilities seeking credit for offsetting increased emissions of carbon dioxide. For individual private landowners, the revenue stream from sources such as these, when added to revenue from the sale of timber and pine straw, may make longleaf pine restoration and management an economically attractive alternative. Suddenly, halting the decades long decline of longleaf pine forest acreage can begin to look less like a pipe dream and more like a potential reality.

The lesson in this, I believe, is that one of the beneficial effects of the recent interest in ecosystem management—whatever it is—is that it has encouraged all of us to think in ways that break down some of the traditional molds and barriers. It has encouraged us to recognize the shortcomings of past ways of business and think more broadly about possibilities. We need to extend this way of thinking and this willingness to reexamine old approaches. Just as ecosystems don't stop at the property line, opportunities to conserve them do not lie solely in the province of traditional resource management policies. By creatively aligning conservation interests with the economic impulses that drive private behavior, some of the goals that have seemed beyond our grasp may be brought within it.

The line in the above that the Endangered Species Act's critics loved—and quoted widely—was the one about how landowner actions like those of Perot and Cone were "not necessarily the result of malice toward the woodpecker or the environment" but were instead "nothing more than the predictable responses to the familiar 'perverse incentives' that sometimes accompany regulatory programs." To the critics, this sounded like an affirmation of their view that the act was an irretrievable failure. It wasn't. Rather, it was a call for creative new approaches to the act's implementation, a task to which I would devote much of the remainder of my career. The chapters that follow elucidate the development of some of these new approaches and highlight both the work that has been done and much that remains to be done.

11

Looking to Aldo Leopold for Solutions

In the far southeastern corner of Iowa, the Mississippi River connects two small towns, each with a colorful history, less than twenty miles apart. One, Fort Madison, is my hometown. The other, Burlington, is the hometown of Aldo Leopold, whose prolific writings continue to influence conservation thinking many decades after his death. Fort Madison claims the distinction of having been "the first permanent US military fortification on the upper Mississippi,"[1] although one has to take the word "permanent" with a grain of salt. In 1813, the fort was abandoned and burned by its US Army occupants while retreating from attack by Indians allied with the Sauk warrior Black Hawk. Burlington has the distinction of having been characterized by Mark Twain in his 1883 work, *Life on the Mississippi*, as a "very sober town" because of the pendency then of a bill to "prohibit the manufacture, exportation, importation, purchase, sale, borrowing, lending, stealing, drinking, smelling, or possession, by conquest, inheritance, intent, accident, or otherwise, in the state of Iowa of each and every deleterious beverage known to the human race except water."[2] Four years later, Leopold was born there.

For me, the river and its environs offered endless opportunities to explore, enjoy, and develop a passion for nature. In a time when children were pretty much free to roam about without constant parental supervision or rigid schedules, the outdoors was my playground. My experiences there shaped my interests, my worldview, and ultimately my choice of careers. Leopold's experiences on and around the river had a similar lasting impact on him. Ultimately, Leopold became a towering figure in conservation during the first half of the twentieth century. He has remained an iconic figure in American conservation due to his gifts as a writer and his prodigious output of thoughtful essays. Leopold died in 1948, a little more than a year before I was born in Fort Madison.

Leopold was one of several Iowans who had a major impact on conservation. The first noteworthy piece of national wildlife conservation legislation, the Lacey Act, bears the name of its principal author, Iowa congressman John Lacey. Jay N. "Ding" Darling, though born in Michigan, lived much of his youth in Sioux City, Iowa. He became a forceful advocate for conservation through his political cartoons in the *Des Moines Register*, for which he was twice awarded a Pulitzer Prize. A national wildlife refuge in Florida is named for him. It is Leopold, however, who has had the most profound impact on the generations of conservationists who followed him. In my wrestling with the question of how to make the Endangered Species Act more effective on private lands, and how in particular to reduce its unintended consequences there, I found that Leopold offered many useful lessons. The following essay was my effort to capture those lessons.

Lessons from Leopold in Assessing the ESA
Endangered Species Bulletin 24, no. 6 (November–December 1999)

Some 63 years ago, Aldo Leopold called the need to conserve threatened forms of wildlife "the crux of conservation policy." Nearly four decades later, Congress made the first serious national effort to address this challenge. With enactment of the Endangered Species Act of 1973 (ESA), Congress undertook to stem the loss of the nation's most imperiled plant and animal life.

We now have more than a quarter century's experience with which to evaluate the law's impact. In doing so, it is useful to keep in mind that Leopold carried with him a notebook in which he jotted down quotations that he found noteworthy. One came from Robert Louis Stevenson: "to hold the same views at 40 as we held at 20 is to have been stupefied for a score of years." With the benefit of more than a score of years of experience under the ESA, it is time to re-examine it.

Leopold is an appropriate guide for this task because a good argument can be made that the success or failure of the ESA will be determined by how well it works on private land. First, very few endangered species have all of their habitats on federal land. Many have none of their habitat there, and many more have a substantial portion of their habitats on non-federal (and mostly private) land. Second, outside of the West, federal land comprises less than a tenth of the land area of most states, and even in parts of the West, such as California, many of the concentrations of endangered species are on private rather than federal land. As Leopold noted, "[t]he only progress that counts is that on the actual landscape of the back forty," and most of the back forty is in private ownership.

One could change all this simply by acquiring all the habitat needed for each species. The magnitude of that challenge, however, is revealed by the recent agreement to spend several hundred million dollars to acquire a very tiny fraction of the existing habitat of the threatened marbled murrelet. In the 1930s public land acquisition for conservation purposes began in a big way. Leopold hailed the fact that "[f]or the first time in history we are buying land on a scale commensurate with the size of the problem." At the same time, however, he warned that land acquisition alone was not a sufficient conservation strategy. He worried that "bigger buying . . . is serving as an escape mechanism—it masks our failure to solve the harder problem. The geographic cards are stacked against its ultimate success. In the long run it is exactly as effective as buying half an umbrella."

The "harder problem" to which Leopold referred was the problem of ensuring proper management of land not in public ownership. Failure to solve that problem leaves wildlife resources huddled under Leopold's metaphorical half an umbrella. If private lands are not managed compatibly with the needs of species found on public lands, then those public lands will, at best, become islands of protected habitat, too small in many instances to support viable populations of imperiled species, too far removed from each other to enable dispersal and genetic interchange, too few in number to guard against the vagaries of demographic chance and natural disaster, and too exposed to threats from outside their boundaries from pollution, exotic species, water depletion, and other factors.

Leopold recognized two approaches to conservation on private land: one attempts to deter undesirable practices through prohibition and regulation; the other encourages desirable practices through incentives. The administrators of the ESA have thus far relied upon the tool of regulation; they are only now beginning to explore the tool of incentives. Strict regulation will continue to be needed, particularly in urbanizing landscapes, where development threatens permanent losses of habitats and the rare species they support.

Habitat conservation plans have been used most often, and probably have their most useful potential, in these urbanizing landscapes. When landowners are developers, intent on converting raw land into suburban subdivision, the conservation trade-offs are stark. Land either remains unconverted and retains some or all of its habitat value for endangered species, or it is converted and typically loses all of its habitat value for such species. In this context, habitat conservation plans are a mechanism to win from deep-pocketed development interests the dedication of at least some land to conservation purposes, and the funding to manage those lands appropriately, in exchange for sacrificing other lands to development. It is admittedly a Faustian bargain, but the alternative of just saying no to all future development in endangered species hotspots like southern California, Florida, and much of the Sunbelt, is wishful thinking.

The stark all-or-nothing choices facing conservation in the urbanizing landscape are different from the choices in the "working landscape" of farms, ranches, and forest lands. Here, the choices are not between land uses with no habitat value and other uses with ample habitat value. Rather, they are between means of farming, ranching, and forestry that provide relatively more habitat value for imperiled wildlife and those that provide relatively less. The challenge is to make it in the interest of those landowners to make the environmentally preferable choice.

Unfortunately, it is in this working landscape that the ESA's results have been most disappointing. Rather than enlisting working landscape landowners as allies in the effort to conserve imperiled species, the ESA has made them wary of involvement. Landowners who might restore habitats, control exotics, manage to achieve desired successional stages, or allow rare species to be reintroduced to their land have been reluctant to do these things for fear that such good deeds will only be rewarded by the imposition of land use restrictions once rare species respond by occupying their land. Thus, while the ESA's prohibitions aim to prevent the destruction of the habitats that support endangered species today, those same prohibitions have sometimes deterred landowners from creating the habitats that will be needed to support those species tomorrow.

Leopold recognized that economic self-interest would not often cause landowners to conserve threatened species. Indeed, this fact is exactly what set threatened species apart from game species in Leopold's mind. He observed that "[m]ost species of shootable non-migratory game have at least a fighting chance of being saved . . . [because] powerful motives of local self-interest are at work in their behalf." But the same cannot be said "of those species of wilderness game which do not adapt themselves to economic land-use, or of migratory birds which are owned in common, or of non-game forms classed as predators, or of rare plant associations which must compete with economic plants and livestock, or in general of all wild native forms which fly at large or have only an aesthetic and scientific value to man." Leopold astutely observed that "[t]he private owner who today undertakes to conserve beauty on his land, does so in defiance of all man-made economic forces from taxes down—or up." He referred to the landowners on whose land rare species occurred as "the 'suppressed minorities' of conservation." Calling such landowners "custodian[s] of a public interest," he forecast "that conservation will ultimately boil down to rewarding the private landowner who conserves the public interest."

Leopold's belief that rewarding private landowners who can serve the public interest is the key to successful conservation reflected an evolution in his thinking. A decade earlier, he put more hope in the promise of regulation. Then he wrote that "to protect the public interest, certain resources must remain in public ownership, and ultimately the use of all resources will have to be put under public regulation, regardless of ownership." By 1934, he was willing to compress the history of conservation and America into two sentences: "We tried to get conservation by buying land, by subsidizing desirable changes and land use, and by passive restrictive laws. The last method largely failed; the other two have produced some small sample of success."

A similar compressed history of the ESA might be written at this point. By buying land, we have achieved some small samples of success in protecting endangered species. Through restrictive regulation, we have largely failed to improve the status of rare species, though we have prevented the status of some from deteriorating as much as they otherwise might have done. We have yet to make a serious effort at subsidizing desirable changes in land used for the benefit of endangered species. That is the most urgent task that lies ahead.

By the time this essay was written, I had already fastened on one idea to enlist private landowners into becoming the allies of rare species conservation that Leopold taught they had to be. Working closely with three extraordinary Environmental Defense Fund colleagues—David Wilcove, an ecologist and gifted writer; Melinda Taylor, a talented environmental lawyer; and Robert Bonnie, who had a graduate degree in forestry from Duke University and a true passion for the longleaf pine ecosystem of the Southeast—together we came up with an embarrassingly simple idea, which we called a "safe harbor agreement." Trimmed of all its details, the idea was to let good deeds go unpunished. Why that was necessary under the Endangered Species Act and how it could be accomplished were addressed at length in the following article.

Overcoming Unintended Consequences of Endangered Species Regulation
Idaho Law Review, 2002[*]

I. Lessons from a Butterfly

When the US Fish and Wildlife Service, prompted by litigation, recently designated critical habitat for the threatened bay checkerspot butterfly (*Euphydryas editha bayensis*), one of the areas it included was Stanford University's Jasper Ridge Biological Preserve. Jasper Ridge once hosted large numbers of this showy subspecies of the widespread Edith's checkerspot butterfly, but now it has none. Regrettably, the designation of the preserve as critical habitat for the butterfly will do nothing to bring about the return of this now imperiled subspecies to the site, nor would it have prevented the disappearance of the bay checkerspot from Jasper Ridge had it been done years earlier. Even more unfortunately, the designation of critical habitat will probably make the return of the bay checkerspot to Jasper Ridge even less likely to happen than if the site had not been so designated. Why that is so reveals an important lesson about the conservation of rare species on privately owned land, which this paper shall endeavor to impart.

The bay checkerspot butterfly is probably the most extensively studied butterfly in all of the United States, even more so than the more familiar and widespread monarch butterfly. Jasper Ridge is no small part of the explanation for this fact. It was there that Stanford Professor Paul Ehrlich began censusing bay checkerspot butterfly populations more than forty years ago. Over the course of the past four decades, Ehrlich and legions of Stanford graduate students have carried out countless research projects, resulting in literally dozens of published scientific articles focused on the butterfly. Among those students was Dr. Dennis Murphy, who, along with Ehrlich and their colleague Bruce Wilcox, petitioned the US Fish and Wildlife Service to protect the subspecies under the Endangered Species Act (ESA) in 1980, an action the Service took seven years later.

When the bay checkerspot butterfly was added to the threatened

[*] Reprinted by permission from *Idaho Law Review*.

species list in 1987, the Stanford researchers believed it was relatively secure at the Jasper Ridge Preserve. Only a decade later, however, the butterfly was gone from the site. For the first time since Ehrlich's studies began, none were seen on the Preserve in 1996. The following year only six butterflies were sighted, which Murphy believes were likely the result of a few caterpillars having undergone multiple-year diapause. In Murphy's words, they apparently constituted "the very last gasp of a doomed population," for no others have been seen there since then.

At the same time that the bay checkerspot was disappearing from Jasper Ridge, it was declining rapidly or had already vanished at other protected sites as well, including at a preserve in southeastern San Jose, California. There, the cause was fairly obvious: the butterfly's larval host plant, the dwarf plantain (*Plantago erecta*) had been nearly overrun by introduced annual grasses following the cessation of grazing on the site. Why this happened was a bit of a mystery, given that the San Jose site (like nearly all the sites where the butterfly and its host plant occur) was characterized by nutrient poor serpentine soils and non-native grasses that typically have little luck invading such areas. Stuart Weiss, a postdoctoral fellow at Stanford, seems to have solved the mystery and identified the culprit: air pollution. Auto exhaust in Silicon Valley was dumping some ten to twenty kilograms of nitrogen per hectare each year on the San Jose site. The added nitrogen made it possible for introduced grasses to take over serpentine sites where there would normally be insufficient nutrients for them to gain a foothold. So long as cattle were present, they kept the introduced grasses from taking over, but once the cattle were removed, the invasive grasses exploded.

Although the Jasper Ridge Preserve, which is subject to prevailing offshore Pacific breezes, has significantly less atmospheric nitrogen deposited on it, Murphy thinks that the same problem of non-native grasses increasing after the cessation of grazing virtually guaranteed the butterfly's eventual disappearance from Jasper Ridge. Also important, in both cases, are the losses of suitable habitats outside the protected areas. As development has eliminated many former habitats and isolated remaining populations, the ability of the butterfly to recolonize a given site from nearby sites has declined because many of those once nearby sites no longer exist. Whereas formerly butterflies might temporarily disappear from a site and then be replenished by immigrants from nearby sites, now they have virtually no chance of getting to sites like Jasper Ridge unless people deliberately introduce them.

The fact that four years had passed since the last bay checkerspot butterfly was seen at Jasper Ridge did not keep the Fish and Wildlife Service from designating it as critical habitat on April 30, 2001. Although acknowledging that the butterfly "may now be extirpated" there, the Service nevertheless asserted that it was "confident that a stable population of the subspecies can be restored to Jasper Ridge because the area is protected and managed as a biological preserve by Stanford University and suitable habitat continues to be present." Conspicuously missing from this confident assertion is any indication that the Service had actually asked the landowner, Stanford University, whether it would be willing to cooperate in efforts to restore the butterfly to the site. Had the Service been familiar with a bit of prior history on that topic, it might have been more cautious in expressing its optimism.

In 1996, following the discovery that bay checkerspot butterflies were no longer at Jasper Ridge, Murphy was eager to attempt to restore them. Elsewhere, the Service had just approved its first "safe harbor" program, under which private landowners could agree to carry out positive actions to benefit endangered species without incurring new or added land use restrictions on their property. Murphy thought the safe harbor idea would overcome the only possible objection that Stanford administrators could have to restoring an endangered species to Jasper Ridge—the possibility that its presence could be a problem in the highly unlikely event that the university wanted to use the property for some purpose other than biological research in the future. With Ehrlich's backing, Murphy moved the proposal through the Stanford bureaucracy toward the top. On the way, he met an unexpected obstacle, Condoleezza Rice, who was then Provost of the university and who is now President George W. Bush's National Security Advisor. Murphy's proposal had the misfortune of bad timing. It was the summer of 1996, and President Clinton's reelection campaign was in full swing. The peripatetic Interior Secretary, Bruce Babbitt, was vigorously trumpeting the President's environmental policies all around the country. The opportunity to announce an agreement with Stanford University to restore an endangered species on Stanford property would have given Secretary Babbitt yet another campaign photo opportunity in the politically important state of California. And that, according to Murphy, was something Rice was not about to countenance. She refused to approve the plan.

The opportunity to reintroduce the bay checkerspot to Jasper Ridge in 1996 pursuant to a safe harbor agreement may have been the last, best chance to restore the species to that site. Now, according to Murphy, "without some combination of grazing, fire and heroic mechanical treatments, there is no future for the bay checkerspot butterfly on Jasper Ridge." The designation of critical habitat cannot compel those heroic measures, nor is it likely to elicit them on a voluntary basis. If anything, it makes them less likely. To the extent that the university wants to keep open all options for the future use of Jasper Ridge Biological Preserve, it will need to be reassured that it can do so while restoring a threatened species to currently unoccupied critical habitat. The job of selling reintroduction to university administrators has been made much more difficult by the critical habitat designation.

II. The Inadequacy of Doing No Harm

The story of the bay checkerspot butterfly and Jasper Ridge Biological Preserve is, in microcosm, that of a great many other endangered species and the privately owned lands that once supported them and could again be made to support them. Without measures that Murphy calls "heroic" but that are in fact often quite mundane, there is no future for many of these species on such lands (or, indeed, on lands that still support them today). Thus, the question for conservationists is how to elicit the management activities essential to perpetuating the conditions these species need.

Lest anyone think that the bay checkerspot, in its dependence on active management of its habitat, is a unique case, one only has to consider the nature of the threats facing many endangered or threatened species. One of the most important of these threats is the disruption of natural disturbance regimes such as periodic fire. In the Southeast, a host of endangered species, including the Florida scrub jay, red-cockaded woodpecker, gopher tortoise, sand skink, and dozens of others, are naturally adapted to habitat conditions produced by frequent, lightning-caused fires. However, over the past century, a network of roads, agricultural fields, and other anthropogenic features have created artificial fire breaks in a landscape where lightning-caused fires once burned freely across extensive areas. Thus, even without active fire suppression efforts, wildfires can no longer operate on the scale they did historically. Add fire suppression to the mix, and the ecological results become even more profound. In Florida scrub communities (the natural communities richest in endangered species in the state), fire suppression has allowed scrub to grow to unnatural heights, thus further reducing the likelihood of a burn except during extreme drought. The result is that Florida scrub jays and other scrub-associated rare species continue to decline, even on sites protected from development. Absent fire, or management that mimics the effects of fire, those species will eventually disappear altogether from such sites. The same is true of many other rare species associated with fire-dependent communities, such as the Kirtland's warbler in Michigan, several rare insects and plants in California's coastal terrace natural communities, and the Karner blue butterfly in the Northeast and Great Lake states. Even the Plymouth red-bellied turtle of Cape Cod has suffered from the absence of fire, which has allowed pines to encroach upon previously sunny pond shores, creating unfavorable conditions for nesting.

Disruption of natural disturbance regimes is just one of the important factors threatening the future of many rare species. Another is competition from, or predation by, non-native, introduced species. To give but one example, in California, native (and threatened) California red-legged frogs have disappeared from many sites shortly after non-native bullfrogs became established in such sites. Thus, without active bullfrog control measures, red-legged frogs are unlikely to persist in sites where they now occur or to be successfully established in sites where otherwise appropriate habitat conditions are restored. Habitat restoration itself may require aggressive efforts to control invasive weedy plants and reestablish the mix of native riparian plants that provide habitat conditions conducive to the red-legged frog, least Bell's vireo, southwestern willow flycatcher, and other rare species.

Sometimes, even native species may need to be controlled in order to make it possible for imperiled species to recover. Two imperiled song birds, the least Bell's vireo of California, and the black-capped vireo of Texas, have experienced dramatic local increases in nesting success as a result of aggressive control efforts aimed at the brown-headed cowbird, a native nest parasite that has increased dramatically its range and numbers as a result of broad land use patterns throughout the country. Without such aggressive control efforts, prospects for recovery for either of these species are dubious at best. Indeed, the draft recovery plan for the least Bell's vireo calls for establishing a perpetual endowment for controlling brown-headed cowbirds and/or exotic plants.

In other cases, recovery efforts may be constrained, even when suitable habitat is abundant, by the limited availability of reintroduction sites. Take, for example, the northern aplomado falcon, which was entirely extirpated from the United States by the middle of the twentieth century. A highly successful captive breeding program produced many birds for reintroduction, but the scarcity of publicly owned lands in south Texas severely constrained reintroduction opportunities. Without the consent of private landowners, reintroduction could not be accomplished on their land, and the option of continuously flooding public sites with newly released birds was unworkable. As pairs established territories around release sites, further releases at those sites became impossible.

All of the above examples are given to illustrate one simple point: to improve the current condition of many endangered or threatened species, it is insufficient simply to prohibit harmful activities. Rather, in a great many cases, it will be necessary to carry out active management measures intended to confer a positive benefit on the species of concern, such as habitat manipulation, exotic species control, or simply allowing access for purposes of reintroduction. Further, for many rare species, publicly owned lands and lands owned by conservation organizations such as The Nature Conservancy, are simply too few, too small, and too poorly distributed to ensure recovery. Thus, other lands, including lands whose principal purpose is not conservation, must necessarily play a part in the recovery efforts aimed at threatened and endangered species.

III. Realigning Incentives

The problem, however, is that many of the owners of those other lands have no incentive to do the things that would make their lands a better place for imperiled species. This is not a new observation. Aldo Leopold noted more than sixty-five years ago that the essential difference between threatened species and game species was that for the latter, "powerful motives of local self-interest are at work in their behalf." In contrast, Leopold argued, threatened species are threatened precisely because no one's self-interest is served by managing for them. Two-thirds of a century later, that fact remains unchanged. Indeed, in one respect, the situation has worsened. In Leopold's time, although self-interest offered no motive to conserve threatened species, self-interest rarely provided a reason for landowners to consider managing their land so as to preclude such species from utilizing it. Today, as one of the unintended consequences of the ESA, it does. Consider this advice from a chapter entitled "Practical Tips for Developers" in the National Association of Home Builder's publication, Developer's Guide to Endangered Species Regulation:

> Unfortunately, the highest level of assurance that a property owner will not face an ESA issue is to maintain the property in a condition such that protected species cannot occupy the property. Agricultural farming, denuding of property, and managing vegetation in ways that prevent the presence of such species are often employed in areas where ESA conflicts are known to occur. This is referred to as the "scorched earth" technique. . . . The scorched earth management practice is highly controversial, and its legality may vary depending upon the state or local governing laws. But developers should be aware of it as a means employed in several areas of the country to avoid ESA conflicts.

The scorched earth technique has a superficially more benign counterpart: simple unwillingness to do the mundane management activities that could create or enhance habitat for rare species (for example, prescribed burning, planting of native vegetation, bullfrog and cowbird control, etc.). From the perspective of an imperiled species, the result is pretty much the same: less available habitat and lower quality of that which is available. At least two explanations exist for the unwillingness of many landowners to undertake these management measures: (1) the fear that the "reward" for creating good habitat that endangered species may later occupy will be new restrictions on human use of that habitat, and (2) the fact that management measures always entail cost, and sometimes quite substantial cost. Safe harbor agreements can satisfactorily address the first. As for the second, a significant initiative to provide financial assistance to landowners willing to manage for the good of rare species is essential.

Underlying safe harbor agreements is the seemingly novel idea that at least some good deeds should go unpunished. The basic structure of such agreements is quite simple: a landowner commits to do something beneficial for an endangered or threatened species—something that he has no legal obligation to do—and the government in turn provides that landowner with an assurance that his voluntarily undertaken beneficial action will not cause any increase in the legal restrictions on the use of his land under the ESA. In the simplest situation, a landowner whose current use of his land is unrestricted under the ESA—because no listed species or suitable habitat occurs on it—agrees to restore habitat for that species. If success rewards his effort and the listed species then uses the property, its presence will not impose restrictions on the landowner's use of the land. Such agreements become somewhat more complicated if endangered species are already present on the land because the restrictions on land use that already present species impose need to be clearly expressed in some appropriate manner as "baseline" restrictions. Where such baseline restrictions exist, the assurance provided to the landowner by a safe harbor agreement is that he or she will not be subjected to additional restrictions under the ESA, even though the species in question may become more numerous or widespread on the property.

Safe harbor agreements have a solid legal footing in the ESA. They can be (and have been) authorized under at least two different provisions of the law, and could be under a third as well. The first safe harbor agreements were done pursuant to section 10(a)(1)(B), which authorizes the taking of listed species incidental to any "otherwise lawful activity." This is the same provision of the Act under which "habitat conservation plans" (HCPs) are done. When done under this authority, safe harbor agreements can be regarded as a subset of HCPs. They differ from typical HCPs in the following respect. In a typical HCP, the landowner has immediate plans to do something harmful to a listed species (for example, replace some part of its habitat with a shopping center), and must prepare an HCP to mitigate for the proposed harmful activity. In a safe harbor agreement, the landowner's only immediate plan is to do something beneficial to a listed species (for example, create habitat for it where currently there is none). He may or may not eventually want to do something in the future that will necessitate a permit (for example, build a shopping center on the habitat he has created), but if he does, the permit issued in conjunction with his safe harbor agreement gives him that future authorization. Put differently, a typical HCP authorizes the immediate incidental taking of a listed species that is currently present on a property; a safe harbor agreement authorizes the future incidental taking of a species that is not now present and that would not be present in the future but for the beneficial action voluntarily undertaken by the landowner. Thus, the conceptual "leap" from HCP to safe harbor agreement was a very modest one.

Because safe harbor agreements are a somewhat novel use of the HCP provisions of the Act, certain of those provisions, designed with projects having on balance a negative environmental impact in mind, were awkward to apply to projects having on balance a positive environmental impact. In particular, the requirements of section 10(a)(2)(B)(ii) that any authorized incidental taking be minimized and mitigated proved conceptually challenging. The voluntarily undertaken beneficial activities, without which the later incidental taking could not even be possible, might be viewed as the mitigation for that later taking, though doing so distorts the true nature of the agreement. Alternatively, qualifying the future right of incidental taking, such as by requiring prior notice to the government and an opportunity for the government to try to rescue and relocate any affected animals, satisfies the statutory requirement, but may often be of little practical value to the species.

For reasons such as these, the Fish and Wildlife and National Marine Fisheries Services now encourage safe harbor agreements to be done under the authority of section 10(a)(1)(A), which authorizes any otherwise prohibited action "to enhance the propagation or survival" of a listed species. Historically, this provision has been used almost exclusively in connection with captive breeding efforts. However, the language of the provision is by no means limited to that context, and the opportunity the Services took to consider how best to authorize safe harbor agreements helped them realize the much broader potential reach of this authority. Optically, safe harbor agreements appear to fit well with the language of section 10(a)(1)(A). They are clearly done for the purpose of enhancing the survival of a listed species. Further, the statutory requirements applicable to permits under this authority are straightforward and simple, as they should be with respect to any voluntary agreement with landowners. Those requirements are that the permit was applied for in good faith, will not operate to the disadvantage of the species, and is consistent with the purposes and policies of the Act.

Safe harbor agreements could also be authorized under section 7. In the parlance of section 7 implementation, an agreement between

a private party and one of the Services is a "federal action," thus
bringing it within the scope of section 7. Future incidental take by
the landowner, after carrying out the beneficial actions required
by the agreement, could be authorized by means of an "incidental
take statement" included in the biological opinion applicable to that
federal action. This mechanism has the virtue of simplicity, avoiding
the need for a separate permit and the associated notice and comment
requirements. This approach is clearly available when there is at least
some federal funding of the landowner's beneficial management
practices, such as through the Partners for Fish and Wildlife Program.

Safe harbor agreements offer a means not only for the Services
to enlist private landowners in voluntary conservation efforts, but
for private conservation organizations to do so as well. To date, at
least five national conservation organizations have used safe harbor
agreements to further their conservation agendas. The first to do so
was The Peregrine Fund, which for years sought permission from
south Texas landowners to release captive-reared northern aplomado
falcons (*Falcon femoralis septentrionalis*) on their land. Most landowners refused, citing fear of the regulatory consequences as their
principal objection. After the safe harbor idea emerged, The Peregrine
Fund went back to many of the same landowners, asking them to
reconsider in light of the assurances that a safe harbor agreement
could offer. The offer of those assurances was all it took to unlock
the ranch gate. Within four years of initiating its safe harbor efforts,
1.5 million acres of Texas ranchland had been voluntarily opened to
falcon reintroduction efforts, and the wild population of birds had
increased to thirty pairs.

Elsewhere, The Nature Conservancy and Environmental Defense
have each secured permits to administer safe harbor programs. The
Conservancy's effort aims to encourage compatible forest management for the benefit of the endangered red-cockaded woodpecker
(*Picoedes borealis*) on lands around its Piney Grove Preserve in southeastern Virginia. The preserve currently contains virtually the entire
population of this species in that state, yet the preserve itself is too
small to support a woodpecker population large enough to be viable
over the long term. Safe harbor agreements with neighboring landowners made it possible to increase the total area of habitat suitable
for this species. Similarly, in Texas, a safe harbor program adminis-
tered by Environmental Defense seeks to restore and enhance habitat
for the black-capped vireo (*Vireo atricapillus*) or golden-cheeked

warbler (*Dendroica chrysoparia*), primarily on ranches adjacent or near to public land areas supporting significant populations of these species.

Two other environmental groups have also made recent use of safe harbor agreements. The Turner Endangered Species Fund, the conservation arm of media magnate Ted Turner, has recently proposed to enter into a safe harbor agreement for a Turner-owned property in northern Florida. In Hawaii, Ducks Unlimited has utilized a safe harbor agreement to help carry out a wetland restoration project benefiting two endangered water birds in that state, the Hawaiian duck (*Anas wyvilliana*) and the Hawaiian goose (*Nesochen sandvicensis*). What these and other groups recognize is that if conservation of endangered species can be made no longer threatening to private landowners, many of these landowners will be willing to take part.

The benefits of safe harbor agreements should not be oversold, however, as some sort of Panglossian solution to the problem of endangered species. Safe harbor agreements are one needed tool in the wildlife conservationist's toolbox, but unless that toolbox is filled with a great many other tools, the conservation effort will surely fail. The conservation benefits secured by safe harbor agreements are, by definition, impermanent. They can disappear as soon as the landowner exercises his right to return his property to its baseline conditions. Impermanent benefits, however, are not illusory benefits. For as long as the voluntarily created improvements are in place, rare species can enjoy more habitat, greater connectivity of habitat, reduced risk of extinction due to catastrophic events, increased likelihood of successful reproduction, and myriad other potential benefits. Safe harbor agreements offer a means of securing conservation improvements on land owned by those for whom the tax benefits of donating a conservation easement are inadequate and for whom funds to purchase such easements are insufficient. In short, safe harbor agreements offer a means of buying time until more permanent conservation strategies can be put in place, and for many species, time is rapidly running out.

Less tangible, but no less important, safe harbor agreements offer a means of regaining the trust and goodwill of private landowners. That is important not for pollyannaish reasons, but for the eminently practical reason that the nation's farmers, ranchers, and forest landowners own much of the remaining habitat for many endangered or threatened species, as well as much of the land on which suitable habitat could be restored. The stringent regulatory requirements of the ESA may be the only way of salvaging something for conservation out of the onslaught of development pressure that is turning natural habitat into cities and suburbs. Those same requirements, however, are ill-fitted to the working landscape of farms, ranches, and forests. Other approaches are clearly needed, and those that can be aligned with broader landowner interests clearly warrant use.

As noted earlier, however, even the most highly motivated landowner ultimately faces the sobering fact that the management measures needed to improve the lot of most endangered species are expensive, sometimes very expensive. In the absence of any source of financial incentives, safe harbor agreements can only operate where landowners are willing to absorb the cost themselves, or in those relatively few situations where there is a serendipitous congruence between management measures needed by rare species and management measures that enhance income. That fact severely circumscribes the universe of safe harbor agreements. It also forcefully argues for a serious effort to create positive incentives for landowners to undertake the management activities on which the recovery of many species will depend.

12

Turning Rare Species into Assets

Despite their popularity with landowners, and despite their success in furthering the recovery of red-cockaded woodpeckers and other imperiled species, safe harbor agreements fall well short of "rewarding the private landowner who conserves the public interest" in rare species conservation, which Leopold saw as a necessity for success in that endeavor. Through such agreements, landowners may no longer perceive endangered species as liabilities, but something more is needed to turn these species into assets. For some rare species, that "something more" has taken the form of a practice variously known as mitigation banking or conservation banking.

To understand conservation banking (the name by which I will refer to it), one must first understand the concept of environmental mitigation. Under the Endangered Species Act and many other environmental laws, to gain the approval of governmental regulatory agencies, a party proposing a project that is expected to detrimentally affect endangered species (or wetlands, or other nominally protected resources) must agree to fund or carry out measures that will offset, at least in part, if not altogether, the expected detrimental effects of the project for which approval is sought. Those offsetting measures are generally referred to as compensatory mitigation, or simply mitigation.

Historically, mitigation measures were typically designed and implemented contemporaneously with, or even after, the implementation of the project for which they were to compensate. When mitigation measures failed, as they sometimes did, the result was that the development project's detrimental impacts on protected resources went unmitigated. For this and other reasons, environmental practitioners and government regulators began to recognize the potential benefits of implementing mitigation measures in anticipation of future projects for which such measures would compensate. Credit for these mitigation measures could be held in reserve—"banked"—for future use to compensate for impacts caused by the credit holder's own development projects or by those of others. The ability to sell credits to third parties makes it possible for a landowner to generate revenue by restoring or enhancing protected resources on his or her land. In short, through conservation banking, endangered species or other protected resources could become assets for private landowners.

Conservation banking has flourished as a way to accomplish the wetlands protection goals of the Clean Water Act, which requires that projects that will discharge dredged or fill material into waters of the United States (including wetlands) secure a permit from the US Army Corps of Engineers. It was slower to catch on under the Endangered Species Act, but by the late 1990s a number of banks had been established under that law as well. The article that follows, coauthored by Marybeth Bauer and Jessica Fox,[1] describes some of the conceptual issues and early experience with conservation banking for endangered species. It begins, however, with a personal anecdote about my encounter with an endangered species mitigation project while collecting fossils.

Landowners Bank on Conservation: The US Fish and Wildlife Service's Guidance on Conservation Banking

–Marybeth Bauer, Jessica Fox, and Michael J. Bean

Environmental Law Reporter, August 2004[*]

Swept Away: A Cautionary Tale Regarding Endangered Species Mitigation

For many years, fossil enthusiasts have searched for Miocene fossils on a secluded beach south of Chesapeake Beach, Maryland. About a decade ago, without warning or explanation, a formidable chain link fence appeared on the beach, anchored at one end to the nearly vertical cliffs behind the beach, and extending at the other end about 30 feet into the Chesapeake Bay. No sign warned against trespassing, and since the water is shallow there, most fossil hunters simply waded around the fence to get to the more productive areas on the other side. A year later, the fence was even less of an obstacle. Enterprising beachgoers had scraped out a small passage between the cliff face and the landward end of the fence through which a person could squeeze.

The bayside end of the fence was sagging, having been battered by storms the previous winter. More storms the next winter pretty much leveled the fence. Soon, not a trace of it remained. Most visitors then never knew why the short-lived fence had been erected. Most visitors today are unaware it ever existed.

The mystery of why the fence suddenly appeared is revealed in—of all places—the US Fish and Wildlife Service's (FWS') endangered species *Consultation Handbook*.[2] The handbook gives extensive guidance to the FWS staff regarding implementation of §7 of the Endangered Species Act (ESA).[3] Section 7 is the provision of the Act that requires federal agencies to consult with the FWS to ensure that the actions they authorize or carry out do not jeopardize the continued existence of endangered species. The handbook illustrates its detailed guidance with numerous documents showing how to implement various stages of the consultation process. Among those illustrative documents is a letter dated July 11, 1993, that discusses the mysterious fence.

The letter addressed plans for a boardwalk along the bayfront from the center of town to a point just short of the fossil hunters' beach. The boardwalk, by facilitating access, was sure to increase public use of the beach. That concerned the FWS, since the beach was not only a good place to find the fossilized remains of long-extinct sharks and whales, but also one of the few remaining places to find the not-quite-extinct Puritan tiger beetle, an endangered species. The solution to this dilemma, the FWS believed, was to condition the approval of the boardwalk (which required a permit from the US Army Corps of Engineers) on the erection of a fence that would deter public access to the part of the beach most valuable to the endangered beetles. In short, the fence was a strategy to mitigate the impact to the beetle of the increased public use that the boardwalk was certain to cause.

There is more than small irony in the inclusion of this letter in the handbook. Its purpose there is to illustrate how FWS employees should draft a letter to a sister agency concerning a particular aspect of the §7 consultation process. As a letter, it is indeed a model of clarity, brevity, and impeccable grammar. However, beyond the four corners of the letter lies a more important and dismaying story. The story of the short-lived fence is, in microcosm, an illustration of much that is wrong with endangered species mitigation.

Mitigation measures have often been inadequately conceived, poorly executed (the fence was built in the wrong place, though given the lack of signage and maintenance, its placement hardly mattered), and infrequently monitored. As a result, they have sometimes utterly failed to achieve their intended purposes. Scarce resources have too often been expended on well-intended mitigation efforts that ultimately failed to produce any real conservation benefit. Instead of being made whole through compensatory mitigation measures, rare species ended up worse off.

This is a matter of no small consequence. If the ESA is to succeed, then mitigation must succeed, since mitigation is a pervasive aspect of the law's implementation. Widespread public perceptions to the contrary, the ESA prohibits very little. Instead, it allows a wide range of activities that detrimentally affect listed species, subject only to mitigation requirements intended to minimize or compensate for those detrimental impacts. For example, private land development or logging of private forest land that harms an endangered wildlife species is unlawful without an FWS permit authorizing the "incidental taking" of the listed species.[4] Such a permit, in turn, requires a habitat conservation plan (HCP)[5] that, among other things, must "minimize and mitigate the impacts"[6] of the authorized activity on the listed species. In effect, HCPs, which in the past decade have become the primary means through which private economic activity is reconciled with the requirements of the ESA, are simply mitigation plans.[7] For federal actions subject to the consultation requirements of §7, there is no explicit mitigation requirement set forth in the statute. Nonetheless, it is common for federal agencies to design a proposed project with mitigatory features, e.g., the fence on the beach, to ensure that the project will not run afoul of the substantive requirements of the law.

Given the importance of mitigation to the success of the ESA, the question must be asked: how can mitigation be better accomplished? One promising new approach is conservation banking.[8]

The basic idea of banking as a mitigation strategy is simple: in anticipation of future mitigation requirements, someone, e.g., an individual landowner or state highway department, invests in conservation activities at a bank site, e.g., acquiring high quality habitat or restoring degraded habitat for a particular species. The FWS accepts such an investment as compensatory mitigation for future activities detrimentally affecting the species or habitat type conserved on the bank site.

Conservation banking has a number of potential advantages over traditional approaches to mitigation. By completing necessary mitigation prior to project impacts, banking ensures that the mitigation is done, and done properly. Further, in theory, banking allows mitigation on a larger scale, providing advance mitigation at a single large site for multiple future projects that would otherwise be mitigated at several smaller sites. In addition, banking creates the opportunity for some landowners to turn endangered species on their property, or restorable habitat for such species, into assets. That turns on its head the conventional wisdom of many landowners that endangered species are a liability to be avoided because of the land use restrictions that can accompany them. Finally, since the number of credits that some banks earn is a function of how successfully species or habitats are restored, bankers have a compelling economic incentive to do the best restoration job possible.

Despite these potential benefits, conservation banking for endangered species is still in its infancy. It may be about to undergo a growth spurt, however, as a result of formal banking guidance recently issued by the FWS. Before turning to that guidance, a brief look at one recent bank illustrates the potential of this new conservation tool to benefit endangered species and landowners alike.

The Hickory Pass Ranch Conservation Bank

The endangered golden-cheeked warbler couldn't ask for a more suitable home than the privately owned 3,000-acre Hickory Pass Ranch in the Texas Hill country. And conservationists couldn't ask for a more suitable parcel of land to be managed as habitat for the migratory songbird, a 5-inch-long yellow-cheeked and black-bodied spectacle of our natural heritage that sings *bzzzz layzee dayee*, ending on a high note. The golden-cheeked warbler nests only in central Texas woodlands with mature Ashe juniper mixed with oaks, elms, and other hardwoods. This type of woodland is widespread on the Hickory Pass Ranch, which houses a large population of golden-cheeked warblers. But Ashe juniper woodlands have been rapidly disappearing in central Texas due to land clearing for urban development and other human purposes. Accordingly, active management of the ranch to maintain its high quality habitat for the golden-cheeked warbler is important to the recovery of the species.

To proponents of the warbler, the time-honored conservation strategy of land acquisition might have seemed a promising way to ensure the perpetual management of the ranch for the benefit of the species. The Hickory Pass Ranch lies within the proposed acquisition area for the Balcones Canyonlands National Wildlife Refuge, which is managed to conserve nesting habitat for the golden-cheeked warbler. Acquisition of the ranch by the refuge would have guaranteed its management for this purpose.

However, for reasons that commonly thwart this conservation strategy, land acquisition was not an option. Funds for refuge acquisition were insufficient and the ranch owners had no wish to sell. To its owners, the ranch represents not only a conservation opportunity but also a family legacy, the setting for stories made and told across generations. Hickory Pass Ranch is a family ranch and the owners intended to keep it in the family for their three daughters and future generations. Given this intention, the goal of ensuring active management of the ranch to maintain warbler habitat needed to be reconciled with the ranch's continued private ownership and operation.

In this respect, the golden-cheeked warbler is not alone. Most of the nation's threatened and endangered species require some form of active management of private land to further their recovery—for example, controlling invasive species, replicating natural disturbance regimes through prescribed fire, or maintaining suitable hydrological characteristics in wetland habitat. Seventy-three percent of the land in the contiguous United States is privately owned, and most of our nation's threatened and endangered species have most of their habitats on nonfederal land (most of which is privately owned). Accordingly, recovering our nation's threatened and endangered species requires enlisting private landowners as partners in conservation.

However, there are powerful disincentives against the willingness of private landowners to manage their land for the benefit of listed species. First, active management typically requires considerable time, expense, and/or technical expertise. For example, controlling invasive species on just 100 acres of wetland habitat could cost as much as three new Ford Rangers—a sum that would make a sizeable dent in a mortgage.

Second, by making the land inviting to an endangered species, active management could invite substantial burden for a landowner in the form of regulatory restrictions on land use. Under the ESA, activities that harm an endangered species by modifying its habitat are prohibited without a permit.[9] Consequently, if a landowner restores habitat that becomes occupied by an endangered species, a permit may be necessary for such prevalent and profitable activities as mining, logging, and grazing. The permit process is often lengthy, laborious, and uncertain. Moreover, if the permit is denied, the landowner may be forced to forgo revenue from the use of the land. These burdens of active management confirm Aldo Leopold's warning, made 70 years ago in his famous essay entitled *Conservation Economics*,[10] to be wary of "the time-honored supposition that conservation is profitable."

The lesson from Leopold's insight is that the challenge of making conservation *possible* on private lands can be won by making conservation *profitable* for the economic and other goals of private landowners. For the owners of the Hickory Pass Ranch, creating a conservation bank on their property for the benefit of the golden-cheeked warbler has done just that. The Hickory Pass Ranch Conservation Bank ensures that the golden-cheeked warbler remains an economic asset to the owners rather than a potential regulatory liability, preserves the ranch as a family legacy, and sustains the owners' ranching way of life.

Under their agreement with the FWS, the ranch owners placed an initial parcel of 500 acres of high quality warbler habitat under a permanent conservation easement with the option to increase the bank to cover their entire 3,000 acres of habitat. Among other conservation assurances, the owners pledged to manage the initial parcel for the permanent conservation of habitat important to the golden-cheeked warbler; limit grazing density to maintain hardwood seedlings that will eventually replace canopy trees; and restrict building sites to designated areas at least 50 feet from heavy canopy warbler habitat. In return, the FWS pledged to award the owners one "conservation credit" for every acre of land placed under conservation easement. The owners can sell these credits to parties who are required by law to compensate for their adverse impact on the golden-cheeked warbler elsewhere.

The allure of conservation banking is multifold. It supplies private property owners with an economically viable land management alternative, allows the FWS to secure the conservation of contiguous, high quality habitat, and provides those in need of mitigation with additional mitigation options. In the case of the Hickory Pass Ranch Conservation Bank, the golden-cheeked warbler is assured a contiguous parcel of high quality habitat over the long term, and the owners expect sufficient economic gain (with credits currently priced at $5,000 each) to continue managing the land as a family ranch without selling parcels to developers.

Conservation banking can restack the "economic cards" in favor of conservation on private land by turning listed species into economic assets (rather than regulatory liabilities). For some parcels, use as mitigation may have a higher value than other alternative land uses. Moreover, this relatively new conservation tool creates a rich variety of other incentives for private landowners to become active conservation partners, including the possibility of earning a public reputation as a conservation ally, preserving a way of life that comes with working the land, enjoying the aesthetic qualities of the bank site and the recreational opportunities that are compatible with its purpose, or using the site for educational purposes. Conservation bankers can also use banks to meet their own expected future mitigation needs. For example, the Chiquita Canyon Conservation Bank in southern California was destined to be a luxury golf course when the Transportation Corridor Agency (TCA) purchased a conservation easement on the nearly 1,200-acre site protecting coastal sage scrub habitat important for the California gnatcatcher. Although the primary motive for establishing this bank was to generate mitigation credits that can be applied toward future highway projects, the TCA now enjoys additional benefits including improved public relations. They host annual educational tours of the site during which they exhibit their voluntary habitat improvement activities that will not only benefit the gnatcatcher, but also increase the number of other rare species in the area. For the TCA, establishing a conservation bank and protecting an ecologically important area was a good business decision.

Basics of Banking

Endangered species conservation banking is conceptually similar to wetlands mitigation banking under the Clean Water Act (CWA).[11] The first conservation bank was developed in 1995, the same year that federal interagency guidance on wetland mitigation banking was published. The wetland and conservation banking guidance documents treat many of the same issues, but not always in the same way. Differences in program goals (no net loss of wetlands; recovery of endangered species) and characteristics of the resources at issue (relative permanence of wetlands; relative transience of some endangered species habitats) warrant different policy outcomes.

From its beginning in California less than a decade ago, conservation banking has steadily grown in popularity. Concurrently with the establishment of the first US bank in 1995—the Carlsbad Highlands Bank in San Diego County, which provides coastal sage scrub habitat for the California gnatcatcher—California released an *Official Policy on Conservation Banks*.[12] California, like most states, has its own endangered species legislation,[13] which can be more restrictive than the federal law and apply to more species. Though initially established pursuant to that state policy, most California banks have subsequently been allowed to sell credits to fulfill federally imposed mitigation requirements as well. Since 1995, the number of banks in California has grown to around 50. Beyond California, recent conservation bankers include a forest products company in Georgia, a private rancher in Arizona, and the Mobile Area Water and Sewer Commission in Alabama. Banks have been established for species as diverse as the Pima pineapple cactus, golden-cheeked warbler, and vernal pool fairy shrimp. At least one state, Hawaii,[14] has an endangered species law that specifically authorizes "habitat banking."

Conservation banks are properties managed to provide permanent conservation benefits to listed species for the purpose of compensating for adverse impacts to those species elsewhere. The FWS awards bank owners "credits" in proportion to their conservation accomplishments. Owners may use credits to mitigate for their future development projects or sell them to third parties for profit. The price of credits is typically set by the owner and is influenced by the cost to manage the bank and market demand.

By selling credits earned at one bank to many land developers, banks aggregate the mitigation activities of numerous development projects into one site. Consolidation has advantages over more traditional project-by-project forms of mitigation, which often result in a piecemeal approach to conservation that has little conservation benefit and fails to advance regional environmental goals.

Like financial banks, conservation banks have a currency. The currency of a conservation bank is the unit of measure according to which: (1) the number of credits awarded to the bank quantifies the natural resource values conserved at the bank site; and (2) the number of credits developers must purchase from the bank quantifies the adverse impacts of their activities. Banks commonly use a currency of acres of habitat. For example, the owners of Hickory Pass Ranch receive one credit for every acre of the ranch placed under conservation easement, and require developers to purchase one credit for every acre of golden-cheeked warbler habitat adversely impacted.

Of course, not all acres of protected habitat represent the same conservation value to listed species. For example, sites vary in habitat quality, contribution to regional conservation goals, and distance from other protected areas. The Hickory Pass Ranch has high conservation value to the golden-cheeked warbler because it contains high quality habitat that links discontinuous refuge lands. Likewise, adverse impacts vary with regard to their degree of permanence, the number of individuals taken or disturbed, and the quality of habitat affected. An appropriate crediting and debiting system must reflect such differences. The standard way of accounting for these differences is to apply "compensation ratios" when determining the number of credits awarded to a bank and the number of credits required for purchase to mitigate for adverse impacts. For example, when a development activity degrades especially high quality habitat, a compensation ratio of three credits to mitigate for every acre of impacted habitat might be appropriate. On the other hand, if a bank is established in a particularly important ecological area, a ratio of one credit to one-tenth of an acre has been applied, as in the case of the Wright Preservation Bank for the Sebastopol meadowfoam, Burke's goldfields, and California tiger salamander.

From the foregoing discussion, it should be clear that conservation banking is a more complicated endeavor than trading schemes for pollutants such as sulfur dioxide or carbon dioxide (CO_2). One ton of CO_2 emitted to the atmosphere is much more fungible than an acre of habitat for a particular endangered species. The location of an acre in relation to other protected sites, developed areas, roads, and other surrounding land uses can profoundly affect the ecological value of that acre to the species that uses it. Determining the value of specific acres may often need to occur on a project-by-project basis. Thus, conservation banking will almost certainly entail a degree of intervention on the part of the FWS or others that is much greater than what characterizes pollution-trading schemes. The need for intervention suggests that the role of banking in endangered species conservation efforts will always be rather limited, though for some species it may be substantial.

Analogous to the customer base of financial banks, conservation banks have "service areas." The "service area" of a bank is the geographic area (such as a watershed or county) within which the bank's credits can be used to compensate for adverse impacts to the species covered by the bank. In other words, as the FWS' guidance explains: "[I]f proposed projects fall within a specific conservation bank's service area, then the proponents of those projects may offset their impacts, with the FWS' approval, by purchasing the appropriate number of conservation credits from that bank."[15]

Despite the growing popularity of conservation banking, banks outside California have been established on an ad hoc basis without the benefit of official guidance—until now. In May 2003, the FWS released guidance for the establishment, use, and operation of conservation banks to satisfy mitigation requirements under the ESA.[16]

Conclusion

By providing greater procedural and substantive clarity to conservation banking, the guidance may increase the use of this new tool. Because some recently approved banks do not appear to conform to the guidance, however, it may raise the bar to such efforts. Properly done, conservation banking offers the potential to improve endangered species conservation, and furnish important incentives for at least some landowners to participate in conservation efforts. It is not a panacea, nor is likely to be perfect, but it does not have to be. If it can accomplish enduring mitigation more successfully than the approach that produced a short-lived fence on a secluded Chesapeake Bay beach, it will be a useful addition to the endangered species conservation toolbox.

Interest in endangered species conservation banking eventually led to an intriguing but challenging question. Would it be possible—and desirable from a conservation perspective—to allow adverse impacts to one endangered species to be offset by mitigation measures benefiting another species? To many in the conservation community that is likely to be seen as a heretical idea. But in 2008, Jonathan Remy Nash made a strong conceptual case for doing just that in an article for the *Environmental Law Reporter*. The article that follows was my comment on Nash's idea. In it, I describe a host of practical obstacles to the idea while acknowledging that the goal of recovering endangered species might be accomplished more quickly and for more species were those obstacles to be overcome.

Comment on "Trading Species: A New Direction for
Habitat Trading Programs"
Environmental Law Reporter, August 2008˙

In the air and water pollution control arenas, the trading of pollution allowances has been embraced as a flexible and cost-effective way of achieving prescribed pollution reduction goals. Its advantages over prescribed technology requirements or across-the-board reduction requirements are manifest. The marketability of allowances creates an incentive for excess reductions by those who can achieve them cheaply, as well as a less costly means of achieving compliance with mandated goals by those who would otherwise face formidable compliance costs. The Clean Air Act's cap-and-trade system that has proven so successful in reducing emissions of acid rain precursors is now the presumptive best approach for reducing the threat of climate destabilization.

With the success of trading approaches in tackling air and water pollution challenges, it is necessary to consider whether a similar approach might be useful in tackling the problem of endangered species. In his article, "Trading Species: A New Direction for Habitat Trading Programs," Jonathan Remy Nash considers what, if anything, learned from the experiences with pollution allowance trading might be usefully applied to create an effective trading program for endangered species.[17] His answer, not surprisingly, is essentially "not much."

Trading programs assume the existence of a fungible or nearly fungible thing being traded. For climate purposes a ton of carbon emitted into the atmosphere in Peoria, Illinois, is equivalent to a ton of carbon emitted into the atmosphere anywhere else in the world. The location of the emission source (or sink) does not matter. For acid rain precursors and other air pollutants, however, the location of the emission may well matter. And for water pollutants, the location of the emission source is very likely to matter. As Nash explains, there are potential ways to adjust trading values for these site-specific considerations, though at the cost of increased administrative complexity, reduced market size, or both. These challenges, however, pale in comparison to the challenges of achieving fungibility of trading units for any market involving endangered species.

For example, the value of an acre of habitat for a particular endangered species will likely depend upon a myriad of variables. Is it isolated from other similar habitat, or is it embedded in a larger contiguous block of habitat? What are the land uses (and protection status) of the lands immediately around it? What is its shape? Is it likely to be relatively self-sustaining without active management, or will active management be essential to maintaining its value? Is it actually occupied by the species of concern, or is it not? If not, how likely is it that the species will occupy it in the future? Is it of exceptional quality or simply marginal? If marginal, can its quality be enhanced, and if so, at what cost? The answers to all of these questions (and many others) necessarily affect the value of any given acre for any particular endangered species. A trading program that is based upon acres of habitat as the unit of exchange, and that does not take these factors into account, will simply result in acres of low economic value being conserved and acres of high economic value being lost, without any necessary benefit to the species.

Even without the above challenges, there is a further reason that robust markets for endangered species are unlikely to develop. Most endangered species have very limited geographic distribution. In the history of the Endangered Species Act (ESA), there has been only one endangered species, the recently delisted bald eagle, that had an essentially national distribution. Virtually no endangered species occur in more than a dozen states, and roughly one-half occur only in a single state. A significant number occur in only one or a few localities within a single state. The smaller the distribution of the species, the smaller the universe of potential buyers and sellers of its habitat (or credits or other measures of impact.) Thus, even if fungible trading units could be developed for an endangered species, the markets for those trading units would almost always be extremely thin.

It should be noted that the fungibility dilemma exists whether or not there is a trading market. Every time the US Fish and Wildlife Service (FWS) or the National Oceanic and Atmospheric Administration (NOAA) Fisheries approves a project detrimentally affecting an endangered species or its habitat, conditioned upon an offsetting or compensatory measure, it is making a comparison between the magnitude of the detrimental impact and the magnitude of the offsetting impact. If that comparison is based on some consistently applied principles, those same principles could be applied to achieve equivalencies of traded actions in a market setting. Of course, the possibility also exists that current mitigation decisions are not based on consistently applied principles, but on purely ad hoc determinations for each new project. The frequent failure of the FWS and NOAA Fisheries to clearly articulate the basis upon which their mitigation decisions are made leaves this matter unresolved.

Nash explores one effort to develop generalized principles that could underlie an endangered species' habitat trading effort. It is worth noting that this effort, called the "habitat transaction method," was proposed in an article published in 1994.[18] At first, it had little impact. A year later, on the other hand, the FWS approved its first—and much simpler—endangered species conservation bank. When a bank was established for a species, credits could be used to mitigate development impacts elsewhere upon that species.[19] In the ensuing decade, the FWS has approved a few dozen other conservation banks, virtually all of them along the same model. In 2003, it published national policy guidance on endangered species conservation banking.[20] That policy guidance, like the banks the FWS had previously approved, assumes that detrimental impacts to an endangered or threatened species will be offset by compensatory measures for that same species at an approved bank site, and that both can be measured by acres affected. Publication of policy guidance, though it has clarified somewhat the rules and procedures applicable to conservation banks, has not catalyzed significant new investment in them. The inherently limited nature of the markets for credits from such banks is the most likely explanation.

To overcome this and other problems, Nash proposes a system of "constrained permit trading" in which an initial allocation of development permits is made that leaves all affected species (not just endangered species) at or above "minimum viable" levels. Those initially allocated development permits could then be traded, provided the trades continue to leave all species at or above viable levels. Unclear from Professor Nash's description is the scale at which species viability is assessed. A species could be rendered unviable in a particular local community by a development project there, while still remaining fully viable at the county level, state level, or national level. Maintaining the viability of all species at the local level may be a worthy environmental goal, but it would present a dramatic expansion of regulatory control beyond what the ESA currently imposes. If the national scale is the appropriate scale at which to assess viability,

Nash's proposed approach may differ very little from current practice, inasmuch as the only species likely to be rendered unviable by local development projects are those that are currently protected by the ESA.

There is a further problem with Nash's proposal, which is that it appears to sanction developments that make all endangered species worse off, without any being made better off, so long as those made worse off are not made so much worse off that they cross a threshold of unacceptability. The goal of the ESA, however, is to make already endangered species better off, not simply to limit how much worse off they can be made. Is there a trading system that could better advance this goal? Taking a cue from Nash's title, could "trading species" better advance this goal?

To address that question, let us imagine a hypothetical world in which there are only two endangered species. Let us also imagine that in this world we have so refined the tool of population viability analysis that we are reasonably confident that we know the likelihood of survival of these species under present circumstances and under a variety of possible new circumstances. Species A has a 60% probability of surviving for another century. Species B has only a 30% probability of surviving for the same period. The habitat upon which species A depends is found mostly on land with high commercial value; species B, on the other hand, is found mostly on land of low commercial value.

A landowner proposes to develop land occupied by species A. If he does so, the development will reduce that species' probability of survival to 50%. To mitigate this impact, a variety of rather expensive measures can be undertaken, but these will only boost the survival probability up to 55% (a legally acceptable outcome at present, if the mitigation is the maximum practicable and if the reduced survival probability does not jeopardize the species' continued existence). If the government approves this arrangement, the final result will be that in our world of only two endangered species, the probabilities that each will survive will have declined from 60 and 30% to 55 and 30%.

Because of the disparity in land values where the two species occur, an even smaller mitigation investment, if directed to species B, could double its probability of survival from 30 to 60%. If the government permitted the landowner to mitigate in this manner, the final result would be that the probabilities that the two species will survive will change from 60 and 30% to 50 and 60%. Viewed from the perspective of an overall effort to avert the loss of species diversity, this is clearly a better result than if (as at present) mitigation is required to be directed only at the species affected by the development. Indeed, it is even a better result than simply prohibiting the development, which would leave the probabilities of survival frozen at 60 and 30%. From the landowner's point of view, it is a better result as well, since it reduces the cost of mitigation.

This hypothetical suggests the potential desirability of a policy under which a developer whose activities will damage the habitat of a listed species would be allowed to compensate for those damages by helping another listed species such that its probability of survival is increased by more than the original species was harmed. The species that loses habitat becomes a "donor species"; the one whose habitat is protected or restored as compensation for the harm done to the donor species becomes a "recipient species." The common currency of these interactions could be the *percentage change* in survival probabilities for the affected species, as determined by population viability analysis.

What objections might be made to this idea? The immediate objection, of course, is that we lack the ability to conduct such population viability analyses. This is undeniably true. However, it is equally true that the government today routinely approves development actions that detrimentally affect listed species, and imposes mitigation obligations, in the face of the same lack of ability to rigorously assess the impact of either on the affected species.

A second objection is that allowing negative impacts to one species to be offset by compensatory measures for another species puts the former species at increased risk of extinction. Unfortunately, that happens today even without any compensating benefits to another listed species. Federal agencies are routinely permitted to carry out detrimental actions so long as they do not cross the threshold of causing "jeopardy" to a listed species, and private interests are required to mitigate for the impact of their actions on listed species only "to the maximum extent practicable." Nothing suggested here contemplates removing the "jeopardy" floor.

A third objection is that the species protected by the ESA actually include a diverse mix of species, subspecies, "distinct population segments" (such as individual salmon runs), and perhaps someday soon, further categories. Trading across these very units would seem to put lesser taxa (such as distinct population segments) on an equal footing with full species. It would also put highly endemic species on an equal footing with more wide-ranging "keystone" or "umbrella" species. And finally, it would put species from taxonomically prolific groupings, e.g., tiger beetles, on an equal footing with a species from taxonomically limited groupings, e.g., canids. All of these are true, and deserving of attention. It should be noted, however, that the law currently makes no distinction among these various categories and extends to all of them the same legal protection (with the single exception that the law treats plants less protectively than it treats animals).

One can readily imagine still other objections, but there is no need to examine them further here. The very idea of trading species is admittedly a fantasy, given the limits on our actual knowledge of the status of most endangered species and of the likely impacts of various development activities on them. It also cannot be squared with long-standing practice under the ESA, which requires that impacts to any listed species be mitigated by offsetting actions to benefit that same species. Still, two considerations ought to permit one to indulge this fantasy for a while. The first is that the very same knowledge limitations have not prevented the government from approving major development projects in return for mitigation commitments of dubious efficacy. The second is that the goal of recovering endangered species might actually be accomplished more quickly and for more species by allowing the sort of flexibility explored here.

Conclusion

Although conservation banking and safe harbor agreements are now commonly used in the implementation of the Endangered Species Act, one will not find a reference to either of these conservation tools in the text of that law. Rather, they are innovations that owe their origins to the willingness of the US Fish and Wildlife Service to use the broad, general language of the statute as the authority to fashion creative new conservation approaches—approaches that were almost certainly not foreseen when the act was passed. Rather than being the rigid, inflexible law that its critics often accuse it of being, the Endangered Species Act has shown itself capable of creative and flexible administration.

That creativity and flexibility will be sorely needed if the Endangered Species Act is to succeed in preventing the impoverishment of the nation's biodiversity. Neither mitigation banking nor safe harbor agreements are a panacea against the tide of extinction. Rather, they are tools in the conservationist's toolbox, highly useful in some circumstances but of no utility in others. The challenge confronting conservationists is to have as many different tools in that toolbox as possible and to be using them all while constantly testing and employing new tools. In particular, tools that incentivize and reward actions—by private landowners and others—that further the recovery of already endangered species, or that keep other species from becoming endangered offer hope that we can leave to our descendants an undiminished inheritance of wealth and abundance in the natural world.

Epilogue

April 22, 2020. Earth Day at fifty. An Earth Day unlike any that preceded it. Americans were urged, wisely and appropriately, to stay at home, to venture outside only for the most essential purposes, to wear masks, and to minimize their contact with other people—even their friends and neighbors. We are among the most sociable of animals, a fact that makes "social distancing" feel so foreign and so strange. There was an odd sort of silence to the spring of 2020, one in which birdsong could be heard, but the usual noise from traffic and from the daily bustle of human activity was strangely missing. At some point, hopefully not long after the next Earth Day, we will be able to resume living our lives in a manner we consider "normal," to reconnect with neighbors and with nature. What should we do with our newly restored freedom? High on the list, I suggest, is to take a walk in the woods with a child.

It has been my good fortune to have had a career dedicated to the protection of the natural world and the wild creatures we share it with. As that career now nears its end, I have considered how my interest in and passion for nature originated and stuck with me over the decades. That interest and passion was rooted, I strongly believe, in the experiences I had as a child; in a grandmother who supplied me with fascinating insects from her garden; in the days I spent exploring the creek and woods behind my Iowa home; in slogging through the sloughs and backwaters of the Mississippi River in search of crayfish, frogs, toads, turtles, and most especially snakes; and in collecting geodes and fossils from the limestone outcroppings on the Illinois side of that great river. If the generations that follow are to develop a similar interest in and passion for nature, they must have the opportunity to experience it firsthand. That realization prompts my simple suggestion for what to do on Earth Day or soon thereafter.

In 1982, US arms negotiator Paul Nitze and his Soviet counterpart, Yuli Kvitsinsky, took a celebrated walk in the woods near the Swiss-French border. They emerged with a proposal for arms reductions that was intended to lift the decades-long fear of nuclear war from the world's people. As the apprehension of armed conflict between the superpowers has since receded, worries about growing environmental problems have increasingly taken their place. For those seeking not only solutions to these problems but perhaps also a fitting way to celebrate future Earth Days, do what Nitze and Kvitsinsky did: take a walk in the woods.

Count Leo Tolstoy may have overstated it a bit when he wrote that "everything bad in the heart of a man should, it seems, disappear in contact with nature—that direct expression of the beautiful and the good."[1] Nevertheless, contact with nature is certainly capable of transforming our values, if only by inculcating in us a very strong commitment to protecting the environment. Unfortunately, contact with nature is something that most of us in today's urbanized society have very little of, a fact that may well inhibit our ability to solve environmental problems. The resolve to tackle those problems is far less likely to come from an abstract intellectual understanding of their importance than from the value-transforming experience of enjoying personally the wonders of nature.

So, on the next Earth Day, or on any other day for that matter, leave the highway and the sidewalk behind and enter the woods. Take off your running shoes, remove your earbuds, and pause long enough to listen to the music of nature itself. In the trees overhead, colorful songbirds just returned from the distant tropics will give ample reason to be thankful that our spring has not yet been silenced. In the lakes and ponds, the chorus of frogs and toads will fill the air with their own peculiar love songs. On the forest floor, a profusion of vibrant wildflowers will paint a picture prettier than any to be found on canvas.

It isn't necessary to know the names of any of these, for, as Walt Whitman cautioned, one must not "be too precise or scientific about birds and trees and flowers."[2] Rachel Carson, herself a scientist, knew just what Whitman meant. In her eloquent essay about introducing children to nature she said that "it is not half so important to *know* as to *feel*."[3] When feeling is aroused, the thirst for knowledge will follow.

The environmental problems that this book addresses—especially the problem of species endangerment to which I have devoted my career—were not created overnight and they will not be solved tomorrow. In all likelihood, the task of solving them will fall to our children and to theirs. For a few days or weeks around most Earth Days, schoolchildren everywhere have collected cans and bottles for recycling, planted trees, or engaged in similar worthy projects. Important as these endeavors are, however, it will be very hard indeed to sustain a child's interest unless that child has a real interest in the environment itself. There is no better place to instill that interest than in nature. So, on future Earth Days or whenever possible, take your child, or a friend's child, and go for a walk in the woods.

Notes

Introduction

1. All quotations from Herman Melville are from chapter 105 of his 1851 classic, *Moby-Dick*. Chapter 105 is titled "Does the Whale's Magnitude Diminish?—Will He Perish?"

2. For a discussion of the prospects for significant polar ice melting, see the notice listing the polar bear as a threatened species, 73 Fed. Reg. 28,211 (May 15, 2008).

3. Thomas Jefferson, *Notes on the State of Virginia* (New York: Harper and Row, 1964), 66.

Chapter 1

1. 426 U.S. 128 (1976).

2. Transcript of oral argument before the court, *Tennessee Valley Authority v. Hill*, April 18, 1978, p. 43, www.supremecourt.gov/pdfs/transcripts/1977/76-1701_04-18-1978.pdf.

3. *Tennessee Valley Authority v. Hill*, 437 U.S. 153, 184 (1978).

4. *New Jersey v. New York*, et al., 283 U.S. 336 (1931).

Chapter 2

1. Richard Rhodes, *John James Audubon: The Making of an American* (New York: Alfred A. Knopf, 2004), 417.

2. Smithsonian Institution Archives, www.siarchives.si.edu/history/general-history.

3. Robert H. Connery, *Governmental Problems in Wild Life Conservation* (New York: Columbia University Press, 1935), 14 (hereafter "Connery").

4. 161 U.S. 519 (1896).

5. Quoted in Connery, 117.

6. Connery, 121.

7. Act of June 30, 1886, 24 Stat. 100, 101.

8. Letter from Theodore Roosevelt to C. Hart Merriam, December 9, 1897, Theodore Roosevelt Papers, Library of Congress Manuscript Division, https://www.theodorerooseveltcenter.org/Research/Digital-Library/Record?libID=o160492.

9. Connery, 97.

10. 46 Cong. Rec. 4871 (April 30, 1900).

11. C. William Beebe, *The Bird: Its Form and Function* (New York: Henry Holt, 1906), 18.

12. 46 Cong. Rec. 4871 (April 30, 1900).

13. Act of March 4, 1913, ch. 145, 37 Stat. 828, 847 (repealed 1918).

14. Connery, 37.

15. 252 U.S. 416 (1920).

16. 252 U.S. 416, 434–35.

17. William T. Hornaday, *Thirty Years War for Wild Life* (Stamford, CT: Permanent Wild Life Protection Fund, 1931), 140 (hereafter "Hornaday").

18. Hornaday, 138.

19. Connery, 89.

20. 278 U.S. 96 (1928).

21. 16 U.S.C. §1333(a).

22. 426 U.S. 528 (1976).

23. Pub. L. No. 89-669, §2(a), 80 Stat. 926 (repealed 1973).

24. Pub. L. No. 91-135, §3(a), 83 Stat. 275 (repealed 1973).

25. Pub. L. No. 91-135, §3(a), 83 Stat. 275 (repealed 1973).

26. Hearings on Endangered Species before the Subcommittee on Fisheries and Wildlife Conservation and Environment, 93d Cong., 1st Sess. 292–93 (1973) (statement of Louis S. Clapper on behalf of the National Wildlife Federation).

27. Statement of President Richard M. Nixon, upon signing the Endangered Species Act, San Clemente, CA (December 28, 1973), reprinted in Senate Committee on Environment and Public Works, *A Legislative History of the Endangered Species Act, as Amended in 1976, 1977, 1978, 1979, and 1980*, at 487 (1982).

28. 441 U.S. 322 (1979).

29. Connery, 114.

Chapter 3

1. Charles Darwin, *The Origin of Species by Means of Natural Selection* (Chicago: University of Chicago Press, 1952), 243.

Chapter 5

1. Graham G. Dodds, *Take Up Your Pen: Unilateral Presidential Directives in American Politics* (Philadelphia: University of Pennsylvania Press, 2013), 148.

2. Aldo Leopold, *The Sand County Almanac and Sketches Here and There* (New York: Oxford University Press, 1949), xvii.

3. Quoted in Laurence J. Peter, ed., *Peter's Quotations: Ideas for Our Time* (New York: William Morrow, 1977), 448.

4. Aldo Leopold, *A Sand County Almanac with Other Essays on Conservation from Round River* (New York: Oxford University Press, 1966), 196.

5. *Literary Essays by Theodore Roosevelt*, Vol. 12 in *The Works of Theodore Roosevelt* (New York: Charles Scribner's Sons, 1926), 425.

6. References to the US Fish and Wildlife Service's Refuge Manual (1982) appear in text by chapter number, followed by "RM" and then the relevant section number. Thus, 2 RM 1.4 is section 1.4 of chapter 2 of the Refuge Manual.

7. Edward O. Wilson, *Biophilia* (Cambridge, MA: Harvard University Press, 1984), 84.

Chapter 6

1. L. Lebreton, B. Slat, B. Ferrari, B. Sainte-Rose, J. Aitken, R. Marthouse, S. Hajbaen, et al., "Evidence That the Great Pacific Garbage Patch Is Rapidly Accumulating Plastic," *Nature* 8 (2018), https://www.nature.com/articles/s41598-018-22939-w.

2. David S. Wilcove, David Rothstein, Jason Dubow, Ali Phillips, and Elizabeth Losos, "Quantifying Threats to Imperiled Species in the United States," *Bioscience* 48, no. 8 (August 1998): 607–15.

3. John Kamensky, "A Brief History: National Partnership for Reinventing Government," January 1999, https://govinfo.library.unt.edu/npr/whoweare/history2.html.

4. Richard M. Engeman, Aaron B. Shiels, and Craig S. Clark, "Objectives and Integrated Approaches for the Control of Brown Tree Snakes: An Updated Overview," *Journal of Environmental Management* 219 (2018), https://digitalcommons.unl.edu/icwdm_usdanwrc/2130.

Chapter 7

1. Edward O. Wilson, "The Little Things That Run the World (the Importance and Conservation of Invertebrates)," *Conservation Biology* 1, no. 4 (1987): 344.

2. Natalie Angier, "Paths of Discovery, Lighted by a Bug Man's Insights," *New York Times*, April 5, 2011.

Chapter 8

1. 514 U.S. 549 (1995).

2. 130 F.3d 1041, 28 ELR 20403 (D.C. Cir. 1997).

3. 529 U.S. 598 (2000).

4. 214 F.3d 483, 30 ELR 20602 (4th Cir. 2000).

5. See 214 F.3d at 492, 30 ELR at 20605.

6. See 214 F.3d at 492–95, 30 ELR at 20605–06.

7. See 214 F.3d at 493, 30 ELR at 20605.

8. See 214 F.3d at 495, 30 ELR at 20606.

9. 214 F.3d at 496, 30 ELR at 20606.

10. 214 F.3d at 505, 30 ELR at 20610.

Chapter 9

1. McKay Coppins, "The Man Who Broke Politics," *The Atlantic*, November 2018, https://www.theatlantic.com/magazine/archive/2018/11/newt-gingrich-says-youre-welcome/570832/.

Chapter 10

1. Quoted in Robert Reich, "Redefining 'Competitiveness,'" *Washington Post*, September 24, 1994, p. D1.

2. Ike Sugg, "Property Wrongs," CEI Update, Competitive Enterprise Institute, November 1993, p. 6.

3. Quoted in Ronald Bailey, "Saving the Planet with Pesticides," CEI Update, Competitive Enterprise Institute, November 1993, p. 3.

4. Alexander Cockburn, "Ulterior Secretary: Babbitt Makes Me Miss Jim Watt," *Washington Post*, August 29, 1993, p. C1.

5. Quoted in Forum Profile, *Environmental Forum*, November/December 1993, p. 28.

6. Quoted in *Greenwire: The Environmental News Daily* 5, no. 2 (1995).

7. Thomas C. Croker, Jr., 1990. "Longleaf Pine-Myths and Facts," In *Proceedings of the Symposium on the Management of Longleaf Pine*, April 4–6, 1989, Long Beach, MS, Gen. Tech. Rep. SO-75, edited by R. M. Farrar Jr. (New Orleans: US Department of Agriculture, Forest Service, Southern Forest Experimental Station, 1990), 2–10.

8. J. L. Landers, N. A. Byrd, and R. Komarek, "A Holistic Approach to Managing Longleaf Pine Communities," in Farrar, *Proceedings*, 137.

Chapter 11

1. "History of Fort Madison," City of Fort Madison, Iowa, www.fortmadison-ia .com.

2. Samuel L. Clemens, *The Complete Works of Mark Twain: Life on the Mississippi* (New York: Harper and Brothers, 1917), 466.

Chapter 12

1. Marybeth is now associate director of the STEM Success Communities program at the University of Michigan. In that role she empowers the next generation of conservationists by providing academic and career support to diverse students pursuing degrees in conservation-related and other science fields. Jessica has become a widely published and highly regarded expert on environmental markets. She is a senior technical executive at the Electric Power Research Institute.

2. USFWS and National Marine Fisheries Service (NMFS), *Consultation Handbook*, March 1998, https://media.fisheries.noaa.gov/dam-migration/esa_section7_ handbook_1998_opr5.pdf.

3. 16 U.S.C. §1536.

4. 16 U.S.C. §1536(b); 50 C.F.R. §402.14(i). See also Bennett v. Spear, 520 U.S. 154, 170, 27 ELR 20824 (1997) (describing a "permit authorizing the action agency to 'take' the endangered or threatened species as long as it respects the [FWS'] 'terms and conditions'").

5. See 16 U.S.C. §1539(a)(2)(B)(i–v).

6. 16 U.S.C. §1539(a)(2)(B)(ii).

7. See USFWS and NMFS, *Habitat Conservation Planning Handbook*, 1996, 3–19 (describing typical mitigation actions). See also Michael J. Bean, "Major Endangered

Species Act Developments in 2000," 31 ELR 10283 (March 2001).

8. See Michael J. Bean and Lynn E. Dwyer, "Mitigation Banking as an Endangered Species Conservation Tool," 30 ELR 10537 (July 2000).

9. See Babbitt v. Sweet Home Chapter of Communities for a Great Or., 515 U.S. 687, 25 ELR 21194 (1995).

10. Aldo Leopold, "Conservation Economics" (1934), in *The River of the Mother of God and Other Essays by Aldo Leopold*, edited by Susan L. Flader and Baird Callicott (Madison: University of Wisconsin Press, 1991), 193.

11. See 60 Fed. Reg. 58605 (November 28, 1995) (wetland mitigation banking policy).

12. California Environmental Protection Agency, *Official Policy on Conservation Banks*, April 7, 1995. See Bean and Dwyer, "Mitigation Banking," 10544.

13. See Bean and Dwyer, "Mitigation Banking," 10544 (citing several statutes, including Cal. Fish & Game Code §§2050–2116 [California ESA]).

14. Haw. Rev. Stat. §195D-21.

15. USFWS, "Guidance for the Establishment, Use, and Operation of Conservation Banks," May 2, 2003, p. 8, https://www.fws.gov/endangered/esa-library/pdf/Conservation_Banking_Guidance.pdf.

16. USFWS, "Guidance," p. 8.

17. Jonathan Remy Nash, "Trading Species: A New Direction for Habitat Trading Programs," 38 ELR (*Environmental Law and Policy Annual Review*) 10539 (August 2008) (a longer version of this article was originally published in *Columbia Journal of Environmental Law* 1 [2007]: 32).

18. Todd G. Olson et al., "The Habitat Transaction Method: A Proposal for Creating Tradeable Credits in Endangered Species Habitat," in *Building Economic Incentives into the Endangered Species Act: A Special Report from Defenders of Wildlife* 27, edited by Hank Fischer and Wendy E. Hudson, 1994.

19. See Bean and Dwyer, "Mitigation Banking," 10537 (discussing the emergence and current state of endangered species mitigation banks).

20. USFWS, "Guidance," 1–7.

Epilogue

1. Quoted in Nicholas A. Robinson, "Soviet Environmental Protection: The Challenge for Legal Studies," *Pace Environmental Law Review* 7, no. 1 (1989): 117, 123, http://digitalcommons.pace.edu/lawfaculty/383/.

2. Walt Whitman, *Complete Prose Works: Specimen Days and Collect November Boughs and Good Bye My Fancy* (Boston: Small, Maynard, 1898), 175.

3. Rachel Carson, *The Sense of Wonder* (New York: Harper and Row, 1956), 45.

Index